Preface

This is a book designed for people who have the responsibility to ensure that a network is protected from purposeful or inadvertant mischief. It is not, however, a technical handbook on the inner workings of security systems. Rather, it is conceptual and problem solving in character. You will find, for example, suggestions on when and where to use encryption techniques. You will not find encryption algorithms described in sufficient detail to write a program. There is other literature available (some of which is cited in this book) that will provide the level of detail useful for programming needs.

While I hope that the chapters flow easily from one to another, it is not necessary to read them in the sequence provided. In order to have the vocabulary used in later chapters, however, it will be useful to read Chapters 1, 2, and 3 first, for they will orient you to the important security issues of the last decade of the twentieth century and will, in addition, define some terms and concepts necessary for understanding security issues. Chapters 4 through 9 can probably be read and understood (after reading Chapters 1 through 3) in any sequence, or can be read as needed. Most people probably do not read a book such as this from cover to cover. For that reason, there is some redundancy built in, particularly with respect to the definitions of a few technical terms. This feature will not interfere with your reading, even if you are one of those few who will read it from cover to cover, but will make its use easier for those who like to read books in a more random fashion.

Throughout the book I did assume that you will have a basic understanding of networks and computers and I do not provide yet another introduction to these topics. There are numerous books available, including several of my own, that can bring you "up to speed" should that be necessary. If you manage a network, if you manage an organizational environment that has a network manager reporting to you, or if you simply wish to be better informed, for whatever the reason, regarding network security, then this book will hopefully prove helpful.

The sources I have used in writing this book are cited in endnotes. Many of the interpretations have come from my experiences as a manager of large computer organizations and, more recently, from my consulting activities. I thank those who have been willing to discuss security issues with me, my wife Beverly, who has read bits and pieces of the manuscript, and Dr. Greg Stone, who read the manuscript with care and insight for John Wiley and Sons. I am, of course, responsible for errors of omission or commission.

Thomas Wm. Madron
Somerset, NJ

Contents

CHAPTER 1

Managing Network Security

What does it mean to have *security*? The answer to this question is neither simple nor straightforward. It involves some kind of an estimate of the ratio of the benefits derived from a protected system to the costs of achieving that protection. That security ratio is not a "law of nature" and will vary from company to company and organization to organization. Because secure information flow is the reason for a concern about network security, the broader issue has to do with the overall concept of *information security*. This chapter provides a security perspective, addresses the problem of defining security, and presents an answer to the question, "Why information security?"

Since the inception of computer networks, security has been a topic often discussed. While most discussion of network security had been limited to the data processing community, the subject sometimes surfaced in the public press. By 1983, however, the issue of computer network security had become the topic of a popular motion picture (*War Games*), and the problem received widespread comment in the popular press. More recently, popular novelists have featured network security as important issues in their plot lines. Tom Clancy, for example, in *The Sum of All Fears,* tells the fictional story of potential security threats to the National Security Agency (NSA) and the Central Intelligence Agency (CIA).

After his principle character, Jack Ryan, summarizes some of the problems with network security threats, for his fictional boss, CIA Director Cabot, Ryan explains the fundamental dilemma with network security in a few lines:

> "Expensive," Cabot noted seriously. "With our budget problems..."

> "Not half as expensive as a systematic compromise of our message traffic is. Director, there is *nothing* as vital as secure communications links. Without that, it doesn't matter what else we have...."[1]

In another recent novel, by Jeffrey Klein, the protagonist, Eli Franklin, a fictional reporter for *Newsweek,* finds a fictional network security consultant for the U.S. military, who summarizes some of the access issues facing the military. Then, with the help of "Zack the Hack," he acquires information on how to access the Pentagon computers, posing as a computer technician. Eli then proceeds to break into some of the Pentagon's financial records in order to gain information for a story.[2] Whether military and national security systems can be compromised so easily is, of course, open to question. That they are targets is not in doubt.

The Defense Information Systems Agency's (DISA; formerly, the Defense Communications Agency fDCAg) Milnet is suffering from security breaches, and the number had escalated to several incidents a day by 1989. By way of contrast, only a year earlier security breaches in the Defense Data Network (DDN) totalled just a couple of incidents per month. DISA officials say the breaches can be traced to ineffective site management, specifically poor administration of system accounts, passwords, and network configuration. Managing the security problem will require a concerted effort by the top leadership and site managers in the Army, Navy, Air Force, and Defense Department agencies that are hooked up to the DDN.[3]

Another example, from the private sector, showing that computer networks are vulnerable and security breeches are costly is a U.S. Justice Department survey taken in 1988 that reported "the average take for today's computer thief is $883,279, compared with only $6,100 for an old-fashioned bank robber."[4] Consequently, as Thomas L. Davidson and Clinton E. White, Jr. have observed, "measures must be taken by the network security system to identify legitimate users for authorized purposes while denying unauthorized access or use of sensitive data."[5]

Two major trends in computing and networking over the past decade or so have contributed mightily to the problems surrounding security: the demands for connectivity, and easy access (user-friendliness) to computing and network resources. A third element entered in the early 1980s, as well: the wide deployment of microcomputers. Successful implementation of a highly connective system tends to thwart some methods of security and control. One of the primary objectives of computer networks (and especially of local area networks) is to provide easy and convenient access to computer systems within an organization, and it is that same ease of use that can sometimes conflict with security needs. The various layers of security are designed to prevent unauthorized access, and herein lies a major issue of security: At what point is the maintenance of security more costly than a security breach? That question must be answered within each individual organization.

Defining Information Security

Protection of information processing is required because information can be compromised through ignorance, inadvertence, accident, or malice. A fundamental objective is to preserve the integrity of information that has been flowing through the system, although other aspects of physical and personnel security are also very important. We need, therefore, to have some common definitions of information security (INFOSEC). The general sense of *computer security* (COMPUSEC) in this context might be stated as the state of certainty that computerized data and program files cannot be accessed, obtained, or modified by unauthorized personnel or the computer or its programs. Security is implemented by restricting the physical area around the computer system to authorized personnel, using special software, and having security built into the operating procedure of the computer. Somewhat more generally, *data security* consists of procedures and actions designed to prevent the unauthorized disclosure, transfer, modification, or destruction, whether accidental or intentional, of data. Today we should substitute the term "information" for "data," simply because network traffic increasingly consists of information that is more broadly defined than data (including images, FAX, video, and so forth).

In order to achieve information security, there must be security mechanisms—operating procedures, hardware and software features, management procedures, and any combinations of these—that are designed to detect and prevent either passive or active threats on any component of an information system. Security is assured through a *security service,* which is an activity or provision of an activity that enhances the security of information systems and an organization's information transfer. In the Open System Interconnection (OSI) Model, the defined services consist of five groups: confidentiality, authentication, integrity, nonrepudiation, and access control.

Over recent years the concern quite rightly has moved in the direction of securing information flows in networks and across communication lines. *Communications security* (COMSEC) is, therefore, the protection resulting from the application of cryptosecurity, transmission security, and emission security measures to telecommunications[6] and from the application of physical security measures to communications security information.

These measures are taken to deny unauthorized persons information of value that might be derived from the possession and study of such telecommunications and are collectively known as COM-SEC.

Each time we become more detailed in the definition of security, a new set of definitions is required. In order to make sense of the four points of the previous paragraph, it is necessary to understand the following:

1. Cryptosecurity—The component of communications security that results from the provision of technically sound cryptosystems and their proper use.

2. Transmission security (TRANSEC)—The component of communications security that results from all measures designed to protect transmissions from interception and exploitation by means other than cryptanalysis. The use of traffic flow security and covert wave forms are examples of TRANSEC.

3. Emission security (EMSEC)—The component of communications security that results from all measures taken to deny unauthorized persons information of value that might be derived from intercept and analysis of compromising emanations from cryptoequipment and telecommunications systems.

4. Physical security—The component of communications security that results from all physical measures necessary to safeguard classified equipment, material, and documents from access thereto or observation thereof by unauthorized persons.

Security systems consist of a combination of software and hardware subsystems. *Communications security equipment,* for example, is equipment designed to provide security to telecommunications by converting information to a form unintelligible to an unauthorized interceptor and by reconverting such information to its original form for authorized recipients, as well as equipment designed specifically to aid in, or as an essential element of, the conversion process. COMSEC equipment is cryptoequipment, cryptoancillary equipment, cryptoproduction equipment, and authentication equipment. The term COMSEC should be limited in its use to National Security Agency (the United States' NSA) approved systems designed to protect *classified* national security information. Parallel systems and services are available, when necessary, to protect the communications privacy of nonclassified public and private systems.

It is apparent that a great deal of contemporary thinking about information security revolves around cryptography and how good the systems are for encrypting information. In fact, part of Clancy's story, referred to above, explicitly deals with the problems of cryptanalysis and the compromise of such systems. This problem is of major importance because encryption is widely thought to be the highest level of security management—hence the continuing search for an unbreakable encryption system. In fact, one of the controversies of recent years has been over the viability of the Data Encryption Standard (DES), promulgated several years ago by the National Bureau of Standards and its successor, the National Institute of Standards and Technology (NIST).

This discussion may be summarized to suggest that information security is the protection of information assets from accidental or intentional but unauthorized disclosure, modification, or destruction or the inability to process that information. *Network security* consists of those measures taken to protect a network from unauthorized access, accidental or willful interference with normal operations, or destruction, including protection of physical facilities, software, and personnel security. Fundamentally, however, effective security measures are a balance of technology and personnel management.

Developing Understandings of Security

Although this is not the medium for a full-scale history of information security, suffice it to say that the problem predates the use of computers and computer networks. Cryptology (the art of creating and breaking ciphers) and cryptography (the branch of cryptology devoted to creating appropriate algorithms) have been around for quite a long time, finding uses over the last couple of centuries, primarily in times of war. It was during World War II, however, that developments in both cryptology and computing took gigantic leaps, although it was not until the 1960s that the concerns and technologies were clearly merged. Prior to the late 1960s the primary concern with computer systems had been their physical security, but during the anti-war protests of the late 1960s and early 1970s the concern shifted to data security.

The shift of concern from physical security to data security was accompanied by two related movements. First, data centers, which during the 1940s and 1950s were structured very much like fishbowls and made available to the public, moved from public display to out-of-the-way locations behind occasionally impregnable walls. Examples of this phenomenon abound. In one data center I managed, when a new computer room was constructed (in this case about 1981), it was moved from a first floor, glassed-in area to a fifth floor double-door, double-locking arrangement, without any windows and resting behind concrete walls. As a further enhancement, off-site backup of data and programs became a customary feature of many data centers. Some data centers handled such conditions well, others did not. At one Latin American university for which I was a consultant in the mid-1970s, the data center director regularly took home backups of data and programs and even some removable disks, in order to protect his data from the periodic invasion of the administration building by students. Similar arrangements occurred all over the world, including in the United States. Formal off-site backups arrangements were often not available or were too expensive to contemplate.

As data itself was recognized as an important investment, the worth of the data became more apparent. One of the apostles of modern computing, Rear Admiral Grace Murray Hopper, during the late 1970s to late 1980s kept making the point that information processors frequently placed emphasis on "processing" information, to the exclusion of understanding the worth of the information itself.[7] The result of these concerns was the implementation of password controls and enhanced physical security. By the late 1970s networking was becoming more widespread, and this spawned such approaches as call-back systems. In this, if dial access was allowed at all, a user would dial into a computer, which would then break the connection and dial the user back to a designated phone number. As we will see in subsequent chapters, technology has now all but obviated the viability of using call-back procedures for security purposes.

By the mid-1980s the issue was clearly one of information security. Yet, conceptually, this notion was still related primarily to computers per se. The 1980s also saw the widespread deployment of information networks that spanned everything from the small office to the entire planet. Although the planetary networks are still under construction in the early 1990s, the fact of their construction is not in doubt. It now appears that, in the 1990s, in order to secure information it will be necessary to secure networks, for computers have become the handmaidens of networks rather than the reverse. Thus, in the 1990s and into the 21st century, in order to secure information we must secure networks. That is the thesis of this book.

Threats to Information Security

There are a variety of reasons given by managers for having or not having implemented appropriate network security measures. Those reasons are often a combination of legitimate concerns, money, zealousness, and fears raised by the networking equivalent of old wives tales. Once the decision has been made to secure a network, it is necessary to identify those problems that actually represent security threats in a specific networking environment. This advice may seem gratuitous, but it is not. For example, according to much of the information in industry literature we might well be led to believe that "worms" and "viruses" are the primary threats with which we should be concerned (see Chapter 7 for an overview of the security threats posed by worms and viruses).[8] Yet the evidence available suggests rather dramatically that such is not the case.[9] The typical threats to information security and estimates of their relative frequencies of occurrence may be seen in Figure 1.1.[10] A security threat should be defined as any action that compromises the security of information owned by an organization.

David Coursey, following the lead of security analyst Tom Ellis, has emphasized the need to look for problems that really exist.[11] Relatively speaking, external threats to information security are small compared to threats from within the organization. "It's gotten a lot of play, and it is exciting to read about people who hack their way into networks and do damage. And while there are some occasions when significant networks have been brought down, my experience in working with clients with a virus problem is indicative of some other more basic problems," Ellis said. "The problem is not that these hackers are so smart they can weasel their way through any system. That's not true at all. Sometimes it's the users or companies that aren't smart enough to know they have to protect themselves." As may clearly be seen in Figure 1.1, most data loss and other problems are caused not by viruses or other external threats, but by human mistakes and failures. After all, only those in positions of trust can betray that trust. Poorly designed systems live up to the work (or lack of it) that went into them and cause problems as a result. Therefore, it is important, as Dorothy Houston, a district security manager with AT&T, based in Warren, NJ, has recommended, that MIS executives look at the vulnerability of information or systems to loss. After the vulnerabilities are defined, it is possible to recommend appropriate solutions.[12]

Although the data in Figure 1.1 are now somewhat dated, it is nevertheless the case that even in a world of worms and viruses "the most consequential and costly loss incurred by organizations each year is the direct result of human errors, accidents, and omissions."[13] Unfortunately, there is no "bullet-proof" method

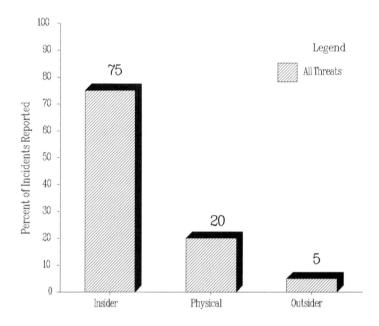

Figure 1.1 Sources of Threats to Information Security.

for averting human accidents, errors, omissions, or stupidity, although appropriate management can reduce the losses from these problems.

Assessing Security Needs

Any organization's most valuable asset is information, but many do not think to protect it. The first step in getting control of a variety of information system problems is a security audit. One list of the steps for an audit, as related by Coursey, has been suggested by Arthur Andersen & Co and AT&T security specialists when they explained how any group can hold a security audit of its own:

1. Decide what security means.
2. Look for problems that really exist.

3. Do not overlook the obvious.
4. Decide how important the information is.
5. Determine the potential loss.
6. Determine the cost to correct the problems.
7. Compare the cost to the loss potential.

Although aspects of security audits will be discussed in somewhat greater detail in Chapter 4, it is helpful to briefly review some of the issues here.

Because information can be compromised, it becomes important in a security audit to understand the controls that are important. Management produces *directive controls* when actions, policies, procedures, directives, or guidelines are issued that cause or encourage a desirable event to occur. Required standards, guidelines, methods, practices, and manual or automated techniques that are designed to result in high-quality, reliable systems are *preventive controls. Detective controls* produce feedback regarding whether the preventive controls have been or are working. When problems occur or have been detected, then *corrective controls,* both manual and automated, provide procedures for correcting errors, irregularities, or omissions. *Recovery controls* provide for the backup and recovery of the system after a failure. While all five of these controls are considerably more complicated than the summary just given, they are extraordinarily important, even in the smallest of organizations, assuming of course that the information being processed is important to the well-being of that organization.[14]

To a large extent, the need for concern regarding security is independent of the size of the network. Ed Foster, among others, has noted the debate over whether to downsize important applications from mainframe computers or minicomputers onto local area networks (LANs) because of data security and access control issues. Many people continue to believe that LANs do not provide enough security. Firms using LANs are reluctant to discuss security breaches, but examples exist of companies that have had their networks tapped by competitors. Many critical applications still reside on mainframes and minicomputers in mid- and large-sized organizations. As a result, a large number of security breaches have involved minicomputers or mainframes. Notwithstanding the vulnerability of mainframes and minis, however, those concerned with industrial espionage fear that LANs can be broken into even more easily. Astute users should be aware, however, that it is possible to transfer applications to a microcomputer environment without opening up a security risk.[15]

In many ways the largest networks, which frequently use public telecommunications networks, are more vulnerable to concerted attacks on network security than are smaller, private networks. Michael Bacon has pointed out that public telecommunications networks, which handle a tremendous amount of traffic, are not secure. The confidentiality of information carried over them is not assured. Neither is their integrity guaranteed. International communications, because they pass through international exchanges, are particularly vulnerable to security breaches. It is also easier to wiretap public communications than private systems. Microwave communications and other technological advances, such as satellites, facsimile, videoconferencing, and cellular radio, are also susceptible to security violations.[16] Yet, important as these concerns are, they tend to ignore the point made earlier that most security threats stem not from external sources but from internal problems.

The Impact of Information Security Measures

A secure network is not necessarily a happy network. There are a variety of costs that must be borne in order to have security. While all these costs will be discussed in greater detail elsewhere, it will be helpful to review the issues briefly at this time. First, network security measures may degrade the performance of the network and the computers attached to it. Second, a secure network is, almost by definition, an unfriendly network. The purpose of protection is to make the network and attached computers *more*, not less, difficult to access. Third, the acquisition of the appropriate security hardware and software will have a financial impact that may be substantial. What an organization's management may be asked to support, therefore, is a system with degraded performance, making use by the end users more painful. On top of these "features," it may have a relatively high cost. Some organizations may conclude that these costs are too much to endure and may actually prefer a system susceptible to security threats. On the other hand, the cost of losing information may also be very high. It should also be added that too often it is thought that the more repressive the protection, the more effective. Fortunately, such a point of view is often incorrect. Protective techniques now becoming available can provide information security in a more unobtrusive fashion than in the past.

Network/Computer Performance

In Chapter 3 we will discuss security in the context of the OSI Reference Model. Suffice it to say here, however, that providing data confidentiality can take place at one or all of six of the seven layers of the OSI Model. One of the major methods for ensuring confidentiality is through the use of encryption. Encryption requires computer power to work, and computing takes time. If all or most of the data associated with most transactions on a system are encrypted, then significant amounts of computer time may be absorbed doing this security function. If there were multiple encryptions—one, for example, at each of six layers of the OSI Model—then large resources are required just to maintain confidentiality and only a single security issue has been addressed. Even when the encryption take place using independent processors, what was once a trivial transaction has now become a time-consuming, resource-consuming computational problem. The net result is that end users would see the results of such a security system as a potentially major decrease in the responsiveness of the central systems. This could result in significant user dissatisfaction.

As might be anticipated, there are differences of opinion as to where in the OSI framework it is best to locate security measures.[17] Because security is a growing concern for managers of corporate networks, those managers want to be sure that confidential documents go through without alteration, eavesdropping, or mishap. It is difficult to put a dollar value on unsecured networks or opportunities missed because of a refusal to use an unsecured network. The military has typically spent heavily to install security measures at OSI Layers 2 and 3. Most corporations do not need nor can they afford such high levels of security; for them, ISO Layer 7, the application layer, makes more sense. Recent developments that have made Layer 7's security possibilities more attractive include the CCITT's passage of X.509, a standard for distributing public encrypting and decrypting keys; new software tools for developing public key security features; growing availability of directory server installations and implementations; and the development of secure applications, such as the Kerberos project from the Massachusetts Institute of Technology.

User Unfriendliness

A network cannot be both secure and user friendly, which means that a network that is open to nontechnical users is difficult to secure. For example, if we password protect access to the network, then password protect the target computer system, then a specific application, and perhaps a particular record or field within a database, a user may have to deal with four or more passwords. If the user ends up using the same password for all protected levels, then the value of password protection is lost. Yet to require multiple passwords is obtrusive from a user perspective. Defenses against computer crime are growing more sophisticated, but so are those people who pose security threats. Organizations that want to reduce the risk of security exposure should not provide services that enhance the ability of an individual from the outside to use the system. Although any system that purports to be secure should acquire the hardware and software necessary to maintain network and computer security, presentations to external users might also avoid naming the organization, identifying the hardware that the system is using, providing an access help screen, or supplying separate prompts for the user name, ID, and password. One secure network simply greets users with the sentence: "Good morning, I am Oscar." The cursor moves to the lower left corner and waits. Users must know what to do next—enter a name, password, ID, or some combination of information. If the wrong response is typed in, the screen clears and the user is told to check the user manual. If a second incorrect response is typed in, the connection is broken.[18] It must be emphasized, however, that the attempt to base a security system on the "secrecy" of procedures is almost certainly doomed to failure.

It is often contended that a network can be either protected or user friendly, but not both. The accuracy of the foregoing statement is, of course, dependent on the protective measures actually taken. If the emphasis is on access control, for example, then protection will necessarily be obtrusive. On the other hand, if the emphasis is on data flow security, then the protective procedures can be made relatively transparent. Moreover, it is often easy to gain access phone numbers. Not only do many appear in *2600*, a hacker monthly newsletter, but they also appear on many electronic bulletin boards. Autodialer programs, also found on bulletin boards, will dial in sequence all the phone numbers in a given area to search for a carrier signal, recording the results for future use. In the attempt to thwart such efforts, many organizations have bought costly but sometimes ineffective dial-back programs and software to fend off these attacks by hackers. Through the use of new telephone services, such as caller identification, it may become possible to put an end to auto-dialing and related tactics. But just as the defenses have grown more sophisticated, so have the attack methods.

Cost

More detailed estimates of cost will be noted in subsequent chapters dealing with specific security products. Host mainframe security software can cost from $52,000 (CA-ACF2) to $69,000

(IBM RACF), plus several thousand dollars a year in maintenance fees. On top of these basic costs, significant personnel time will have to be expended supporting the system. Moreover, all these expenditures secure only the host system without directly addressing the network. Encryption systems running $10,000 or more may be necessary along with a security management system, EDP auditing and auditing management software, and perhaps systems to secure against electronic emanations. By the time all this is completed, it would be easy in an IBM mainframe environment to spend several hundred thousand dollars. Under such conditions a legitimate question to raise is the comparative cost of replacement of machines and data versus the cost of securing the systems in the first place.

Small systems and local area networks (LANs) may be less critical and less expensive to secure, but the same decision sequence is necessary. The cost for security is nontrivial for any system and any network. The consequence of this fact of life is that some balance must be achieved between the cost of security and the potential cost of a nonsecure environment. Some applications will likely require significant security—financial transaction systems, national security systems, and perhaps even university student information systems. But not all systems require the maximum levels of security that we might be able to find on the marketplace.

Getting Serious About Network Security

Network managers maintain that they scrupulously employ every security feature available to them and want more features to be added, according to Peter Stephenson.[19] At the same time, vendors of security software decry the difficulty of selling into the private sector. The discrepancy here has its roots in the major gap between what network management perceives as vital and what corporate management will foot the bill for. An excellent example of this is an agency with which I recently consulted. They did not want departmental LANs attached in any way to their mainframe system because they saw this as somehow compromising their financial systems. They were particularly leery about access from external (dial-access) sources, even though they did allow stand-alone microcomputers to be used as 3378/9 emulators in an IBM 3270 Display System network. Any of those micros could easily be equipped with a modem and software that would allow access from the outside without the operators of the central system being aware of the problem. Their own dial-access lines were protected only by a call-back system (one in which a user dials in, logs in, and then has the connection broken with a call-back to a designated telephone number associated with that user).

With telephone system features such as call forwarding and other techniques, however, call-back systems are very limited in their ability to sustain security.[20] Yet management would not pay for the appropriate security software on the mainframe. Allowing levels of security to be dictated by purely financial considerations is foolhardy. The corporate environment is rife with opportunities for unauthorized access to corporate data. Users neglect proper log-off procedures and share passwords. Security levels are not fully enforced. In most situations, such as the agency I described, some extended system of access control with products such as Computer Associates CA-ACF2 or IBM's RACF (for mainframes) or equivalent LAN access control methods, along with an encryption system and an end-user *authentication system,* would more than adequately secure the network and computing environment. An authentication system, by the way, ensures that a message is genuine, has arrived exactly as it was sent, and came from the stated source. All of these techniques will be discussed at greater length in subsequent chapters.

The point to be made, however, is that corporate managers in organizations large and small must take seriously the various issues relating to security. An appropriate place to start is with a security audit of the network service and the computer facilities of the organization. Such an audit can pinpoint specific sources of potential security breeches for the problems faced by a particular organization. If both qualitative and quantitative risk analysis techniques are also used, it will then be possible to make an estimate of the costs and benefits of improved security measures. We have already noted that security is a combination of technology and management. We have also suggested that for some situations the cost of securing a system may be greater than the replacement cost of information. If we do not seek to understand these issues in our own organizations, however, it will be impossible to come to a rational assessment of the situation.

Concluding Notes

In this chapter I have tried to give an overview of some of the most salient issues surrounding network security. It is important to understand that we are discussing networks of all sizes, not just large ones (or small ones). There are also some ancillary issues that are of importance. We have already noted the problem that security techniques generate with respect to user-friendliness and network performance. There are other issues as well. It is sometimes difficult, for example, to even recognize whether a security breech (or an assumed security breech) was malicious in intent. The result of this problem prompted Mitch Kapor, founder of the Lotus Corporation, to organize the Electronic Frontier Foundation (EFF) in 1990. EFF was created "to help fight serious violations of civil liberties" in the computer/networking industry.[21] Kapor has been criticized for the formation of EFF, since he seems bent on defending people whom some would consider dangerous "hackers."

On the other hand, as Barton Crockett has pointed out, users and experts contend that a provision in a counter-terrorism bill submitted to Congress could substantially erode network security by allowing the U.S. government to decode encrypted communications.[22] The provision advocates that carriers and equipment makers provide the government with the necessary tools to decode communications after legal authorization is obtained. Users and security experts speculate that suppliers would provide decoding capabilities via electronic trapdoors or master keys that could be used to decrypt data, voice, or video communications without a user's consent. Proponents of the provision claim it will assist the government in combating terrorist and criminal organizations that employ complex encryption systems. The provision's opponents believe it will lead to the demise of encryption as an effective security tool.

Clearly the issues surrounding network security are not black and white. There are no "correct" answers to the question of "How much security is enough?" As we look more closely at what network security is, how it impacts organizations and society, and how we can go about securing networks, we will sort out ways of answering some of these questions.

Notes

1. Tom Clancy, *The Sum of All Fears* (New York: G. P. Putnam's Sons, 1991), p. 206.

2. Jeffery Klein, *The Black Hole Affair* (New York: Kensington Publishing Corp., 1991), pp. 49–53.

3. Florence Olsen, "Security Breaches Up Dramatically on Milnet," *Government Computer News*, Vol. 8, No. 25, Dec. 11, 1989, p. 1(2).

4. As reported by J. B. Miles, "Government Makes Network Security a Big Business," *Government Computer News*, Vol. 8, No. 20, Oct. 2, 1989, p. 29.

5. Thomas L. Davidson and Clinton E. White, Jr., "How to Improve Network Security," *Infosystems,* June 1983, p. 110. See also, Madron, *Local Area Networks in Large Organizations*, p. 98.

6. *Telecommunications* is defined as the transfer of data from one place to another over communications lines or channels, or the communication of all forms of information, including voice and video. This is to be compared to *data communications*, defined as the transmission and reception of data, often including operations such as coding, decoding, and valida-

tion. In common discourse it is often difficult not to use these terms as synonyms.

7. See, for example, Thomas Wm. Madron, "Just a Reminder, Data is Priceless," *ComputerWorld*, July 16, 1985. See also Thomas Wm. Madron, *Enterprise Wide Computing* (New York: John Wiley & Sons, 1991), p. 92.

8. See, for example, Dave Powell, "Fighting Network Infection," *Networking Management*, Vol. 7, No. 9, Sept. 1989, p. 38(8).

9. David Coursey, "How to Ensure Network Security," *MIS Week*, Vol. 10, No. 47, Nov. 27, 1989, p. 26(2). See also Carl Jackson, revised, "The Need for Security," *DataPro Reports on Information Security*, Vol. 1 (Delran, NJ: McGraw-Hill, 1991), pp. IS09-100-101 to 129.

10. Jackson, pp. IS09-100-101 to 129.

11. David Coursey, p. 26(2).

12. Ibid.

13. Jackson, p. IS09-100-106.

14. These definitions are taken from Vallabhaneni, pp. 57–58.

15. Ed Foster, "I'd Downsize if I Weren't so Overcome by Feelings of Security," *InfoWorld*, Vol. 13, No. 22, June 3, 1991, p. 36(1).

16. Michael Bacon, "Assessing Public Network Security," *Telecommunications*, Vol. 23, No. 12, Dec, 1989, p. 19(2).

17. Ken Rossen, "Network Security: Just Say 'Know' at Layer 7; Application-Layer Encryption Is the Key to Secure Corporate Communications," *Data Communications*, March 1991, Vol. 20, No. 3, p. 103(3).

18. Harold Joseph Highland, "A Secure Network Must Be an Unfriendly Network," *Government Computer News*, Vol. 7, No. 21, Oct. 10, 1988, p. 91(2).

19. Peter Stephenson, "It's Time to Get Serious About Network Security," *LAN Times*, Vol. 8, No. 9, May 6, 1991, p. 68(1).

20. Call-back systems can sometimes be useful. It is misleading, however, to propose callback systems as a major method for securing networks and/or computers, as in Stephen T. Irwin,

"What Corporate Users Should Know About Data Network Security," *Telecommunications*, Vol. 25, No. 5, May 1991, p. 49(3).

21. Sharon Fisher, "EFF: Attaching the Bill of Rights to Electronic Communication," *Microbytes*, Byte Information Service (BIX), Mon, July 16, 22:41:42, 1990.

22. Barton Crockett, "Provision in Bill Would Let the Gov't Decode Messages," *Network World*, Vol. 8, No. 16, April 22, 1991, p. 2(2).

CHAPTER 2

A Management Model for Network Security

Network and information security is not only a technical function; it also involves personnel security, physical security, backup procedures, recovery procedures, and a number of other related issues. Before we attack the techniques for securing a system, and before we can analyze security risks we face, it is necessary to understand the range of security problems and issues and to designate who, within an organization, has ownership of those problems and issues. The task of this chapter will be to present a "management" model that provides a description of the issues we must face in dealing with network security and information integrity. By "management model" I mean an outline of the significant concepts with which we must deal. In Chapter 3 the Open System Interconnection (OSI) security architecture will be described and will provide a more technical model for information security.

As the issue of network security is confronted, part of the problem facing management is the nature of the "real" threat from the lack of security. It is, of course, very problematic when management refuses the funding for protecting information, computers, and networks in the face of clear evidence of possible problems. On the other hand, it is also clear that there are many myths associated with security issues, and separating myth from reality is not always easy, but it is almost always a management problem. We noted in Chapter 1 a U.S. Justice Department survey taken in 1988 that reported "the average take for today's computer thief is $883,279, compared with only $6,100 for an old-fashioned bank robber."[1] That particular item of information is useful, and perhaps frightening. On the other hand, as Donn B. Parker has pointed out, "there are no valid statistics on the cost of computer crime.... Annual losses have been reported to be $41 billion, $3.5 billion, $3 billion to $5 billion, $555,464,000 (with six digits precision!), and $143 million to 731 million."[2] Such reports may start us thinking about security issues, but they do not constitute the management information necessary to make security decisions for a particular organization. In Chapter 4 we will discuss risk analysis techniques that are appropriate for producing the appropriate management information for a particular company or institution.

Davidson and White suggest thinking of a security system "as a series of concentric circles forming layers of protection around computer data and resources."[3] The outer rings represent the least security, the inner rings the most security. The real difficulty with the concept presented by Davidson and White is that it is too simplistic in light of modern technology. Some similar approach is, however, probably useful in gaining an understanding of the security issue. Rather than concentric circles, we might instead think of security as a series of layers, with the topmost layer representing the tightest security, and the bottom layer the least secure. This approach is depicted in Figure 2.1.

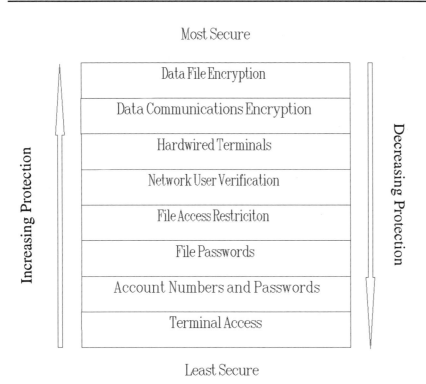

Most Secure

Increasing Protection

Decreasing Protection

| Data File Encryption |
| Data Communications Encryption |
| Hardwired Terminals |
| Network User Verification |
| File Access Restriciton |
| File Passwords |
| Account Numbers and Passwords |
| Terminal Access |

Least Secure

Figure 2.1 Layers of Security.

Computer and Network Abuse

In Figure 2.1 various techniques for information security are suggested, ranging from the least secure to the most secure. It is possible that considering such techniques is something akin to putting the cart before the horse. Another approach is to define a classification system that allows us to know computer and network abuse when we see it, or to help us identify whether it is taking place. As computer technology emerged in the 1940s and 1950s, so too did various forms of abuse. As the technology penetrated sensitive areas, such as military systems, the problem became acute, although it shortly spread to engineering, science, education, and business. It was in 1958 that the first recorded computer abuse occurred, although the first federally prosecuted case did not take place until 1966. By the mid-1970s, therefore, Congress was ready to make some classes of computer use criminal activities.[4]

One way of thinking about computer abuse is through the use of the SRI Computer Abuse Methods Model reprinted in Figure 2.2.[5] Although it oversimplifies the model, Figure 2.2 is depicted as a simple tree structure. In the tree, the numbered leftward branches represent abuses while the rightward branches involve normally acceptable use. The following points should be noted:

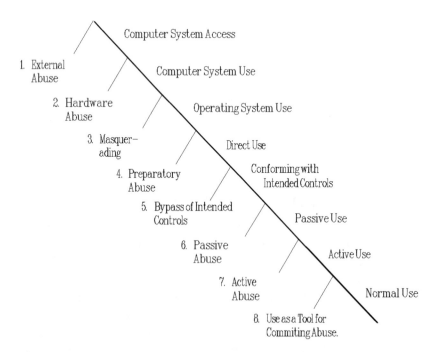

Figure 2.2 Classes of Computer Abuse—SRI Computer Abuse Methods Model.
Source: Donn B. Parker, "Section I: Classifying the Crime," in *Computer Crime Criminal Justice Resource Manual* (Washington, DC: U.S. Dept. of Justice, August 1989).

- External abuse includes those that can take place passively, without access to the target computer systems.
- Hardware abuse usually requires some sort of physical access and active behavior on the part of the source of the threat to the computer systems or network.
- *Masquerading* is the attempt to gain access to a system by posing as an authorized client or host.
- Preparatory abuse is, as the term implies, the preparation for subsequent abuses, such as the planting of a Trojan horse, a virus, or a worm. All of these may in turn show up in subsequent classes.
- The other four classes of abuse involve bypassing of authorization, active abuse, passive abuse, and uses that lead to subsequent abuse.

Basically, every leftward branch in Figure 2.2 suggests a class of threat for which defenses must be found. These are also the classes of threats that must be detected at the earliest possible time. A complicating aspect of this is that the techniques for defense and detection are likely to differ from one branch to the next.

What Is Network Security?

In Chapter 1 we defined information security as the protection of information assets from unauthorized disclosure, modification, or destruction, either accidental or intentional, or the inability to process that information. Network security, you will remember, consists of those measures taken to protect a network from unauthorized access, accidental or willful interference with normal operations, or destruction, including protection of physical facilities, software, and personnel security. Current thinking about security suggests that network security, is a subset of information security. In the United States the formal terminology adopted by the U.S. government uses the term "communications security" (Federal Standard 1037 (FED-STD-1037)), rather than "network security," although these two terms will be used as synonyms in this book. We also noted that effective security measures are a balance of technology and personnel management.

Thus, information security consists of a combination of data security and communications security. Data security is the procedures and actions designed to prevent the unauthorized disclosure, transfer, modification, or destruction, whether accidental or intentional, of data. Communications security (COMSEC) is the protection resulting from the application of *cryptosecurity, transmission security*, and *emission security* measures to telecommunications and from the application of *physical security* measures to communications security information.[6] These measures are taken to deny unauthorized persons information of value that might be derived from the possession and study of such telecommunications and (at the risk of repeating some definitions from Chapter 1) may be defined as follows:

- Cryptosecurity—The component of communications security that results from the provision of technically sound cryptosystems and their proper use.
- Transmission security—The component of communications security that results from all measures designed to protect transmissions from interception and exploitation by means other than cryptanalysis.
- Emission security—The component of communications security that results from all measures taken to deny unauthorized persons information of value that might be derived from intercept and analysis of compromising emanations from cryptoequipment and telecommunications systems.
- Physical security—The component of communications security that results from all physical measures necessary to safeguard classified equipment, material, and documents from access thereto or observation thereof by unauthorized persons.

After having defined the terms information security and network security, it may seem trivial to ask "what is network security?", but the fact is that there is no universal agreement on what constitutes security—or at least appropriate security—in a computing and communications environment. Indeed, in many organizations there is debate over whether security is needed at all or whether the level of security provided is too much or too little. The layers of security addressed in Figure 2.1 relate to only one kind of security: information security. At the very least there are three broad areas of security with which we must be concerned: information security, physical security, and disaster recovery.[7]

A somewhat broader list of concerns would include security issues revolving around the data center, distributed processing, mini- and microcomputer controls, and end-user access. An even more extensive security list might include physical, personnel, data, application software, system software, telecommunications, and operations.[8] S. Rao Vallabhaneni has suggested that in order to implement necessary security it is important to activate five types of controls: directive, preventive, detective, corrective, and recovery.[9] To this list we might also add two more ephemeral and often overlooked controls—legal and ethical.

The rapid and widespread deployment of microcomputers during the 1980s, as much as anything, got the attention of those in industry and government concerned with security. Even as late as 1985 it was common to find a significant amount of confusion concerning what constituted security issues. There was, for example, an attempt to distinguish between terms like *integrity* and *security*. Writing in *Micro Communications* in 1985, M. Durr noted that the increase in the number of microcomputers was intensifying the problem of data integrity.[10] Durr made a distinction between integrity and security by suggesting that "data integrity" referred to errors introduced into data, while "data security" involved protection of the data from outright loss, theft, or malicious change. "Data integrity," in this thinking, referred to unintentional data losses from lost or damaged bits or erroneous manipulation, such as electrical interference on the transmission medium. Error checking protocols can largely overcome (at the cost of degrading throughput) the problem of transmission line interference. The erroneous manipulation of data relates to off-line processing at the micro. People, according to Durr, are the bottom line on data integrity. As will become clear in the discussion on the *OSI Security Architecture,* in Chapter 3, "integrity" is now thought of as a subdivision of "security." Durr was quite correct, however, in identifying *people* as the fundamental source of both the problems relating to information security as well as the opportunities available in solving those problems.

Security in information processing is required because information can be compromised through ignorance, inadvertence, accident, or malice. Note that the fundamental objective is to preserve the information that has been flowing through the system, although other aspects of physical and personnel security are also very important. Because information can be compromised, the controls listed above become important. Management produces *directive controls* when actions, policies, procedures, directives, or guidelines are issued that cause or encourage a desirable event to occur. Required standards, guidelines, methods, practices, and manual or automated techniques that are designed to result in high-quality, reliable systems are *preventive controls. Detective controls* produce feedback regarding whether the preventive controls have or are working. When problems occur or have been detected, then *corrective controls,* both manual and automated, provide procedures for correcting errors, irregularities, or omissions. *Recovery controls* provide for the backup and recovery of the system after a failure. While all five of these controls are considerably more complicated than the summary just given, they are extraordinarily important, even in the smallest of organizations, assuming of course that the information being processed is important to the well-being of that organization.[11]

The five controls just described are those typically addressed by auditors and of concern to computer professionals responsible for the integrity of systems. Such controls are necessary, regardless of whether a failure is the result of accident or malice. The problem of malice can and should also be attacked from other perspectives. Both at the levels of the state and federal governments in the United States, there is serious concern regarding information security. Congress and the legislatures are continuing to pass laws classifying many types of computer fraud, abuse, and theft as crimes. That development is coupled to a growing understanding that the inappropriate use of computers and communication systems reflect ethical failures. From an ethical perspective, robbing someone of information is as much of a theft as robbing a bank. Sabotage of a computer/communications system is no less a moral failure than sabotaging an airplane. Increasingly, such acts are being defined as criminal activity in the law. An example of sabotage is the widely reported case of Robert Morris's "worm" program that "infected" many computers (perhaps as many as 6,000 in 500–700 organizations) on the national Internet in November 1988. Morris was convicted and sentenced in May 1990, the first such conviction under the Federal Computer Fraud and Abuse Act of 1986.[12] Although many computer professionals and others believe that Morris's punishment was far too light to appropriately fit his crime, it was indicative of the growing concern with information system failures due to either malice or stupidity.

Computer/communications security extends far beyond only the use of user identification codes and passwords. It comprises a comprehensive set of rules and practices that help ensure that the information on which our businesses and our society is based will not be compromised. It is easy to see from Figure 2.1 why technical definitions of security are ultimately concerned with encryption techniques, since encryption is the most effective method for securing information. It must also be recognized that security from an auditor's perspective must include procedures that go beyond the technical definitions, since the concern of the auditor it to safeguard the fiscal integrity of the organization to the extent that the fiscal integrity is a function of information processing. Finally, we must also admit that society at large has a stake in information security, since every year the national well-being is more dependent on information flows. Hence, at a societal level we must add law and ethics as elements of a total information security program.

A Manager's Security Model

The "model" of security we will build in this section is not designed to be a formal scientific archetype. There are, of course, more formal approaches. The National Computer Security Center (NCSC) of the U.S. National Security Agency (NSA) has defined several levels of security, each of which involve security models of varying formality.[13] Each of NCSC's levels adds more features and requirements and extends from *D* (nonsecure system) to *A1* (highest security):

D. Nonsecure system.

C. Provides discretionary control. The owner of the data determines who has access to it.
C1. Requires user log-on, but allows a group ID.
C2. Requires individual user log-on with password and an audit mechanism.

B. Provides mandatory control. Access is based on standard DOD clearances.
B1. DOD clearance levels.
B2. Guarantees path between user and the security system. Provides assurances that system can be tested and that clearances cannot be downgraded.
B3. System is characterized by a mathematical model that must be viable.

A. Provides mandatory control. Access is based on standard DOD clearances.
A1. Characterized by a mathematical model that can be proven, and employs a trusted operating system, thus providing the highest security.

This classification scheme is generally consistent with the layers of security suggested in Figure 2.1. The models implied by each increasing level of security are also increasingly formal in character. The objective of this chapter is at once narrower and broader than NCSC's list. It is narrower in that it is not a formal model. It is broader in that it will encompass security issues beyond the technical.

Part of the problem in assessing how to respond to network security needs is in deciding where the network begins and ends. Unfortunately, the common definitions of what constitutes a network do not help much. A communications network may be defined as the total network of devices and transmission media (radio, cables, etc.) necessary to transmit and receive intelligence, or as a series of points connected by communications channels. A computer network is one or more computers linked with users or each other via a communications network, or a system of interconnected computer systems and terminals. A glance at Figure 2.3 will suggest that the foregoing definitions are too hardware oriented. We might suggest, therefore, a modified definition of an *information network* as a series of points connected by communications channels for the purpose of transmitting and receiving intelligence through a consistent protocol stack.

The network depicted in Figure 2.3 is a simplified OSI network consisting of three points: two full "open systems" and a relay. A full open system may be a normal, general-purpose computer or it may be a specialized control device. The key in this model is, however, that the network does not end at a modem between the physical medium and the computer, but at the application layer of the OSI protocol stack. The physical medium may be part of a LAN, a WAN, or a combination of the two. There will be an operating system (OS) for each open system, an OSI protocol stack, and a user program that is supported by both the OS and the OSI protocol stack. In a similar vein, in an IBM SNA network there will be not only the physical medium plus 3270 Display System devices, but also an appropriate front-end processor (FEP) with its software, as well as access method software, such as VTAM, and a teleprocessing (TP) monitor that actually allows a remote user to do something. The hardware plus the SNA protocol suite to the TP monitor is properly part of the network. Mainframe shops are not often organized, following the logic of what has just been described, but the description is accurate.

In OSI all network security services can be handled in Layer 7 (Application), although some security services can be offered at

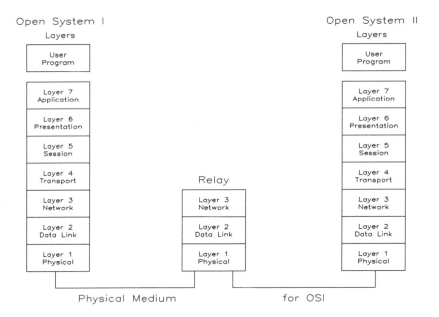

Figure 2.3 OSI Network.

almost all layers of the OSI model. Encryption and decryption of information takes place largely at the Presentation Layer, and the identification and authentication of the intended communication partners take place in the Application Layer, although they can take place in other layers as well.

Behind the network operating system (NOS), characterized by the OSI protocol stack in Figure 2.3, is a computer with its own OS and security system. Thus, even apart from the issues of network security, there is behind the network the need for computer security. Computer security consists of the technological safeguards and managerial procedures that can be applied to computer hardware, programs, data, and facilities to ensure the availability, integrity, and confidentiality of computer-based resources. It also can ensure that intended functions are performed as planned. The various security elements can be depicted as a series of concentric rings, with computer security at the lowest level, followed by data and communications security resulting in information security. This idea is illustrated in Figure 2.4.

From a managerial perspective the relationship among the circles of security illustrated in Figure 2.4 is quite important. The reason for this importance is that, while there are overlapping methods and procedures that can be used for each security level, they do tend to be distinct—at least for computer security on the one hand and data/communications security on the other hand. Even without connecting a computer to an external network, as long as the computer and its use is important to anyone, its integrity must be secured. Similarly, even if we are running something that we can clearly define as a communications network with no responsibility for computers attached to that network, there should still be a concern with communications security. Referring back to Figure 2.3, for example, physical security of the two

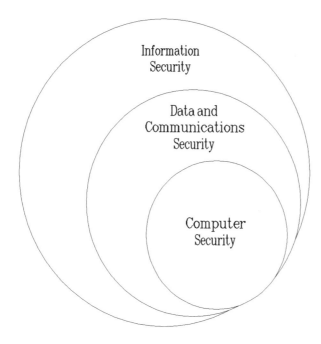

Figure 2.4 Circles of Information Securtiy.

end nodes on which the full OSI protocol stack exists might be the responsibility of two different computer center managers. On the other hand, the physical security of the relay node might be the responsibility of the network manager. Encryption of files residing on the end nodes may be a function of the management of the end node computers, while encryption of data moving from one end node to another will likely be the responsibility of the network management.

A further management issue must be emphasized as well. While programs and data can be secured by using identification numbers, passwords, encryption, and other techniques, at some point systems programmers or other technically competent persons can ultimately gain access to those codes and to the file areas of the users. This fact ultimately raises the issue of privacy for users of the system. It also raises the problem of personnel management. As James Kobielus has pointed out, information and telecommunication system advances have made communication easier, but it also has undermined aspects of privacy.[14] A simple example will suffice. Any CEO of any corporation will have some documents that must be considered *very* private or even critical due to competitive pressures or because of personnel issues. Even if the CEO's files are secure from most employees, it is entirely possible that the organization's systems programmers could look through them, thus jeopardizing their integrity. Unhappily, it is not at all unusual for systems programmers to browse files, and this is clearly a management issue.

One way to protect such files, of course, is to allow end-user encryption of their own files. Unfortunately, this is not a complete solution. Many, perhaps all, of the files of any given employee (including the CEO) in a company will, in fact, be the property of the corporation. If the employee leaves either by choice or involuntarily, the corporation should and may need to have access to those files. If they are encrypted through a method whereby the employee controls the only key, then the corporation may never get access to those files. We may need, therefore, to add another circle to Figure 2.4. This added circle can be seen in Figure 2.5.

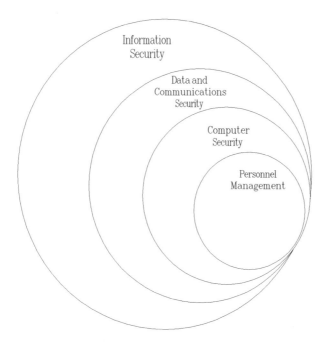

Figure 2.5 Expanded Circles of Security.

What I have tried to suggest in Figure 2.5 is that in order to achieve information security the manager must contend with personnel, computers, data, and communications/networks. The issue of personnel is much broader than only those people in the information management loop, but for the information manager there is the need to be aware of the issues involved. As Kobielus has pointed out, every time people use networks, cellular phones, or credit cards, they are providing others with information about their lives. The issue of privacy is an important one in ongoing public policy debates. Network managers concerned about their roles in guarding privacy should ask their firms to establish internal privacy protection codes. The codes can then be translated into privacy rules. The rules should address a number of issues, including data inventory, network security, remote monitoring and tracking, and ownership of the data. From a technical perspective, it should be understood that cryptographic protection is the *only* method available to protect privacy.

Building Network Security

Now that we have some sense of what network security is, and some of the management issues involved, it is useful to briefly outline how we might go about implementing a security system that matches the needs of a particular organization. Table 2.1 contains a very abbreviated view of the way in which an organization might move from no security to high security. In reality, of course, most organizations do not start with zero security. On the other hand, it is likely that many have next to nothing. For example, a recent client of mine was concerned about security, and various people spent a good bit of personnel time worrying about it. On the other hand they did not want to spend the money to properly secure the system. Internally they allowed only "hardwired terminals" and externally used a dial-back system. The difficulty with these solutions, however, was that internally they did allow personal computers with a 3270 emulator board to be the hardwired terminal. With virtually no technical knowledge at

TABLE 2.1. Steps in Information Security

Stage	Method
Assess security threats	Security audit
	Establish a security policy
Evaluate risks and costs	Qualitative and qauntitative risk analysis
Minimum protection	ID numbers and passwords
Medium protection	Access restrictions (e.g., dial back)
	Data file password protection
	File access restriction
	User authentication and verification
High protection	Data communications encryption
	Data file encryption

all, many people in the organization knew that all they had to do was to equip their office PC with a remote emulator package, such as Carbon Copy, and a modem, and they could dial in from home or elsewhere, use the central system through the emulator in the office PC, and no one would ever know the difference. Dial-back systems for authorized remote access are a dying technology, in that standard telephone services, such as call-forwarding, can completely subvert the intent of dial-back. Newer telephone services, such as Caller ID, can also be used as a more certain method of identifying the source of those seeking access to a system. What this meant to this particular organization is that if there had been a serious security threat there was virtually no security other than user IDs and passwords.

Assuming that a security threat has been identified and that methodologies have been selected, we then need products to secure the system. Stephen T. Irwin has suggested that network access control devices allow network managers to limit access to host computers and reduce the risk of computer crime, which cost many companies millions of dollars a year. Some of the various network control techniques include hand-held password generators, encryption devices, call-back systems, magnetic cards, physical tokens, and host resident-based security software. Network managers need to weigh each of these methods for their advantages, disadvantages, and cost-effectiveness.[15]

heading Vendor Solutions

In response to real or apparent threats to security, vendors have devised a variety of network access control products designed to limit access to host computers. Available security systems fall into at least four major categories. They are:

1. Host resident security software—In a multi-user operating environment, most LAN or host operating systems provide initial user-ID and password access. In point of fact this information is available for accounting purposes as much as for security. Host resident security software will, indeed, provide additional levels of password protection, but it will also limit access to specific disk drives, to particular

directories, and/or to specific files. It may also limit access to specified software, inform operators or systems managers that someone is attempting to access forbidden resources, and provide an audit trail on anyone using such limited-access resources.

2. Encryption devices that encode the data before transmission and decode it upon arrival at its destination—While we have already discussed encryption as a technique, there are many devices available for its implementation. The most secure encryption systems are implemented in hardware although software systems also exist. Encryption systems will be discussed in some detail in Chapter 5.

A variation on general encryption techniques is the use of portable, electronic encryption keys for use with encrypted passwords or as a means of decoding encrypted messages. About the size of a pocket calculator, the portable password generator can be issued to authorized personnel. Each hand-held password generator unique encryption key is tied to the user's personal identification number (PIN). In response to a challenge from the network access control device (after the user enters his or her PIN number), the handheld device—which shares the same encryption algorithm as the access control device—generates a unique password that the user then enters into his or her PC or terminal. If correct, the user is passed through to the host computer.

3. Call-back systems that call back preprogrammed phone numbers—As we have already noted, call-back systems, while quite popular (probably because they are cheap), are likely to be a transitory technology. Through the use of standard telephone system products, such as call forwarding, call-back can be thwarted. Moreover, with the advent of automatic number identification (caller identification) services, dial-back equipment will rapidly become completely obsolete.

4. Physical token or magnetic cards that are actually inserted into the remote computer or terminal and "read"—Token

devices are physical "keys" or magnetic cards that enable users to make one call to the host system. The caller accesses the host computer via a PC or terminal, and then, in order to obtain authentication, inserts a magnetic card or key into a reader or lock on the PC or terminal when asked to do so by the host computer. If correct, the caller is passed directly to the computer. The token system's disadvantage is that if a card or token is lost or stolen a data thief can easily access the network. To maintain security, the lost tokens must be reported to the system administrator quickly, so they can be immediately disabled.

5. Bio-feedback systems—These are more esoteric devices that test voice prints, check fingerprints, measure retinal patterns, and the like, for a person to gain access to a facility or a service.

These systems have advantages and disadvantages that must be weighed carefully by the appropriate manager in light of the security needs of his or her company's network and the price/performance trade-offs of each solution. Most of the systems listed above will be evaluated in the course of this book. Each of these and others have either or both substantial monetary costs or performance costs associated with them. Yet it is also very easy to be seduced into thinking that security is high when it is almost nonexistent. In order to test the effectiveness of existing security systems, some organizations will authorize, and some security consultants will recommend, the use of "tiger team testing."

In a "tiger team" test a real surprise attack against a computer system and/or network is initiated. The validity and utility of such an approach is at best questionable, since it may be dangerous, inefficient, ineffective, and unethical.[16] If successful, a tiger team test may well get the attention of management as nothing else would. On the other hand there are many disadvantages, including a negative impact on employees, systems, and public trust. Moreover, such a test typically tests one or a few vulnerabilities when there may be a large number; the test may be atypical and idiosyncratic; and the probability of failure is relatively high. An alternative is the use of a threat scenario case study method, with the full knowledge and participation of all those who may be affected by a security threat.

Organizing Network Security

Although I will not belabor the issues, there are two points that need to be made concerning organizing for network security. First, an internal information security policy needs to be developed that realistically reflects security threats to a particular organization. Second, an organization needs personnel to handle security. In a large organization this may be a department with several people. In a small organization it may be only part of the job description of a single individual.

An Information Security Policy

As has been noted previously, security needs differ for different organizations. Sooner or later, however, most organizations will have to confront the security issue. In particular, the issue should at least be investigated by virtually every organization that uses computers, networks, and information. If important operational subsystems of the organization—such as payroll, accounts payable, purchasing, communications, computerized control of manufacturing processes, or access control—are dependent on computers and networks, then security must be considered. If there is *any* evidence that any of these subsystems have been compromised in any way, or that profitability is compromised by virtue of security threats to these and other subsystems, then security should be implemented.

Security is not the province of any one department, and a good policy can only come when all the appropriate players are involved. Thus, in order to establish a creditable security policy, a committee should probably be formed that will document the need for both the initial investigation and the subsequent policy development. An appropriate committee might include people from computer and network operations, auditing, finance, legal, security, human resources, and major user areas. In a for-profit corporation the latter might be departments concerned with customer service, accounts payable, and the like. In a university it might be the registrar's office, research administration, and teaching departments heavily dependent on the network. The security committee should be able to identify potential problem areas and perhaps to relate actual breeches of security.

A report coming from the committee might include a description of the problem faced, a demonstration of the potential financial impact of a major security breech, or the extent to which an important information resource might be compromised that would result in serious loss of public trust. An example of the former might be the loss of a specific manufacturing process or a shut-down for a period of time of such a process. An example of the latter might be the compromise of the grade files in a university. The report should also suggest potential security solutions and a security policy statement that will clearly define the goals of a good security system, as well as specifying the ownership of particular systems. Finally, a recommendation should be made for what is essentially an information security department and its location in the organization.

The Information Security Department

As was indicated above, the size of the information security department will vary depending on the specific needs of a particular organization. An information security officer typically has the responsibility to control access to data, passwords, security codes, and network control; disaster recovery; personnel security training; investigate security breeches; and related matters. An information security department may consist of one or more individuals, but the primary officer should be a manager with decision-making responsibilities. He or she should not be a person so far down the chain of command that it is impossible to get anyone's attention, or one who only carries out the decisions of others. The title of the principle security officer might well be something like "Director of Information Security." Support positions might include a security technician, a security system administrator, and possibly a systems programmer and/or network specialist detailed to support the security function.[17]

Concluding Notes

In this chapter I have attempted to raise issues of particular concern to management as network security is considered. Two managerial behaviors often occur when the potential need for security is broached. First, although management never wants to lose information, in most organizations the actual value of that information has never been assessed. Auditors today typically harass Boards of Directors and managers regarding the lack of security for information essential to profitability, but these admonitions are often avoided rather than observed. Thus, the second managerial behavior is often a reticence to do anything about security due to the cost of actually doing something about it. ("If we don't know its worth, we won't spend any money on it" or "we don't know its worth, so it must not be worth very much.")

Another significant problem is that it is frequently the MIS department that pushes security (as it should), although security is actually a subject that should be of concern to all upper management and ultimately to the entire corporate enterprise. After all, if the company cannot be profitable without its information, then it would seem important to protect those data. In not-for-profit organizations it is sometimes thought that work can go on without the computerized information, although in most instances this is a false perception. One of the reasons why MIS departments have a difficult time getting security funded is that those departments always appear to have their hands out and other requests almost always have higher priorities (until, of course, the disaster occurs).

In this chapter, therefore, I have attempted to clarify the nature of abuses, provide a perspective on what network security is all about, and build a manager's model for information security.

Finally, I attempted to provide an overview (since the remainder of the book will build on this) of some of the issues concerning the building of a secure system and on how we might organize ourselves to provide security.

Notes

1. As reported by J. B. Miles, "Government makes network security a big business," *Government Computer News*, Vol. 8, No. 20, Oct. 2, 1989, p. 29.

2. Donn B. Parker, "Seventeen Information Security Myths Debunked," *ISSA Access*, Vol. 3, No. 1, first-quarter 1990, pp. 43–46; also reprinted in *Datapro Reports on Information Security* (Delran, NJ: McGraw-Hill, 1990), pp. IS09-150-101:107.

3. Ibid.

4. The efforts made in the mid-1970s to amend Title 18 of the U.S. Criminal Code results in Article 1030, Chapter 47, making crimes of unauthorized acts in, around, and with computers.

5. Donn B. Parker, "Section I: Classifying the Crime," in *Computer Crime Criminal Justice Resource Manual* (Washington, DC: U.S. Department of Justice National Institute of Justice, August 1989). This document, while in the public domain, is also reprinted in the *Datapro Reports on Information Security* (Delran, NJ: McGraw-Hill, 1990), pp. IS09-200-101ff.

6. These particular definitions are from Federal Standard 1037 (FED-STD-1037), *Glossary of Telecommunication Terms*, which, in turn, is based on MIL STD 188-120.

7. Robert R. Moeller, *Computer Audit, Control, and Security* (New York: John Wiley, 1989), pp. 353–500.

8. S. Rao Vallabhaneni, *Auditing Computer Security* (New York: John Wiley, 1989), Parts III and IV.

9. Ibid. pp. 57–93.

10. M. Durr, "Ins and Outs of Data Integrity." *Micro Communications* Vol. 2, No. 1, Jan. 1985, pp. 18–22.

11. These definitions are taken from Vallabhaneni, pp. 57–58.

12. Note John Markoff, "Computer Intruder is Put on Probation and Fined $10,000," *The New York Times National*, Saturday, May 5, 1990, pp. 1, 9. For detailed background on this case see the following: Eugene H. Spafford, "The Internet Worm: Crisis and Aftermath," *Communications of the ACM*, Vol. 32, No. 6, June, 1989, pp. 678–687; Jon A. Rochlis and Mark W. Eichin, "With Microscope and Tweezers: The Worm from M.I.T.'s Perspective," *Communications of the ACM*, Vol. 32, No. 6, June 1989, pp. 689–698; and Ted Eisenberg, et al., "The Cornell Commission: On Morris and the Worm," *Communications of the ACM*, Vol. 32, No. 6, June 1989, pp. 706–709. This event also triggered new interest in codes of ethics. See, for example, *Communications of the ACM*, Vol. 32, No. 6, June 1989, pp. 688 (David J. Farber, Chair, DNCRI, DAP, National Science Foundation), 699 (Gary Chapman, Computer Professionals for Social Responsibility), and 710 (Vint Cerf, Internet Activities Board).

13. National Computer Security Center, *Trusted Computer Systems Evaluation Criteria* (Orange Book), DOD Standard 5200.28.

14. James Kobielus, "On the Net Manager's Role as Guardian of Privacy," *Network World*, July 1, 1991, Vol. 8, No. 26, p. 25(1).

15. Stephen T. Irwin, "What Corporate Users Should Know About Data Network Security," *Telecommunications*, Vol. 25, No. 5, May 1991, p. 49(3).

16. Donn B. Parker, "Information Security Myths Explained," p. IS09-150-105.

17. *Datapro Reports on Information Security* have a subsection on "planning," a part of which is a report on "Security Job Descriptions." Although it is not entirely clear that they have focused on all the correct personnel issues, this report is a good starting point in designing an information security department.

CHAPTER **3**

The OSI Security Architecture

To understand some of the issues involved in network planning and to lend credibility to the project itself, it is useful to take a quick look at some of the relevant standards available. There are several standards organizations in North America and Europe that seek to rationalize electronic systems. Among those organizations are the International Standards Organization (ISO) and the Institute of Electrical and Electronics Engineers (IEEE). Standards of any kind for networks are of recent origin, a situation that has led to an almost chaotic array of network products. The OSI Security Architecture is part of the Open System Interconnection Model (OSI). Thus, in order to understand some of the issues dealing with this architecture, it may be helpful to briefly review the OSI model.

Open System Interconnection Model (OSI) *

In 1977 the ISO chartered a committee to study the compatibility of network equipment, a development that eventually led to the publication of the Open System Interconnection Reference Model (OSI). In this context, "open system" refers to a network model open to equipment from competing manufacturers. As Frank Derfler and William Stallings have noted, the OSI "reference model is useful for anyone involved in purchasing or managing a...network because it provides a theoretical framework..." by which networking problems and opportunities may be understood.[1] The OSI model divides networking issues into functions or layers. These layers are depicted in Table 3.1.

Each layer in the OSI Reference Model defines a level of function. Compatibility of equipment can be defined within a layer, or lower-level implementations can be hidden to achieve compatibility at some higher level. The dual purposes of the model are to insure information flow among systems and at the same time permit variation in basic communications technology. Moreover, in any given organization, it might be possible to have one network take care of the lower levels and another network the higher levels, using gateways among the networks.

In the ISO Model, Layer 1 is the hardware base for the network. Layers 2 through 7 are implemented in software. The Application Layer (Layer 7) provides services for network users. The responsibility for the initiation and reliability of data transfers takes place in Layer 7. General network access, flow control, and error recovery are, in part, a function of this layer. Tasks are performed at the level of Layer 7, and all lower levels are designed to support the applications. Electronic message systems, terminal emulation

---

*This section rests heavily on similar discussions in prior works by this author including *Local Area Networks: Application of IEEE/ANSI802 Standards* (Wiley, 1989, *Local Area Networks: The Next Generation* (Wiley, 1990), and *Enterprise-Wide Computing* (Wiley, 1991).

TABLE 3.1. OSI Reference Model—Open System Interconnection

Layer	Function
Layer 7 Application	End-user and end-application functions, such as file transfer (FTAM), virtual terminal service (VTP), and electronic mail (X.400).
Layer 6 Presentation	Data translation for use by Layer 7, such as protocol conversion, data unpacking, encryption, and expansion of graphics commands.
Layer 5 Session	Provides for the establishing of a session connection between two presentation entities, to support orderly data exchange.
Layer 4 Transport	Transparent transfer of data between session entities, relieving the session layer of concerns for data reliability and integrity.
Layer 3 Network	Contributes the means to establish, maintain, and terminate network connections among open systems, particularly routing functions across multiple networks.
Layer 2 Data Link	Defines the access strategy for sharing the physical medium, including data link and media access issues.
Layer 1 Physical	Definition of the electrical and mechanical characteristics of the network.

capabilities, and file transfer programs are illustrative of the software operating at Layer 7.

Translation of information for use by Layer 7 is accomplished in the Presentation Layer (Layer 6). Such services as protocol conversion, data unpacking, translation, encryption, character set changes or conversions, and the expansion of graphics commands take place in Layer 6.

Of particular importance to local area networks is Layer 5 (the Session Level). Recall that one major reason for implementing a LAN or other network is connectivity—the ability for any two (or more) devices to connect with one another. When a link is made between two devices, a session is established. In a somewhat more technical sense, the Session Layer provides for the establishment and termination of streams of data from two or more LAN connections or nodes. When a network maps network addresses on specific connections, a Level 5 function is taking place.

The purpose of the Transport Layer (Layer 4) is to provide an additional, yet lower, level of connection than the Session Layer. Within the Transport Layer, issues dealing with a fundamental level of reliability in data transfer are confronted. These issues include flow control, error handling, and problems involved with the transmission and reception of packets. We will return to a more detailed discussion of packets in a later chapter, so suffice it to say that a packet is composed of user-originated data plus information the network needs to transport user data from one network node to another.

In many local area networks a functional Layer 3 (Network Layer) is not needed. Networks that require routing mechanisms among nodes require Layer 3. LANs, however, in some implementations, have data broadcast to every node and a particular connection collects those packets properly addressed to it. Baseband LANs, such as Ethernet, typically broadcast on only a single "channel" and require no routing. Broadband systems, however, are frequently designed with frequency agility (the ability to use more than a single "channel") and therefore require some bridging mechanism—that mechanism requires some routing technique.[2] When LANs are connected via gateways to one another, however, a functional Layer 3 is required.

The Data Link Layer (Layer 2) defines the access strategy for sharing the physical medium (the cable of whatever variety). We will discuss such access strategies at greater length later in this chapter, but common LAN techniques include Carrier Sense Multiple Access/Collision Detection (CSMA/CD) and token passing schemes. Techniques for network specific information in data packets, such as a node address, are functions of Layer 2.

Layer 1 is the Physical Layer—the layer that defines the electrical and mechanical characteristics of the network. Modulation techniques, frequencies at which the network operates, and the voltages employed are all characteristic of Layer 1. Because all networks must implement Layers 1 and 2, they have received the most attention from network vendors. If the attention paid to these layers results in compatible components, then we will know if the concept of standards has been useful. Standards are often less a technical accomplishment than they are the illustration of some vendors' ability to lobby a standard to success.

The development and implementation of OSI standards promises to make new and expanding networks easier and less expensive in multi-vendor environments. With increasing frequency, OSI is the model being followed by manufacturers and by requirements of governments and user organizations worldwide. In the United States, OSI standards have been incorporated into the National Institute for Standards and Technology (NIST, formerly the National Bureau of Standards fNBSg) "Federal Information Processing Standards" (FIPS). OSI is a key factor in the development of the Manufacturing Automation Protocol (MAP), developed by General Motors. Also the U.S. Department of Defense has reviewed OSI protocols for suitability for its requirements, although it supports its own Transport Control Protocol (TCP). Other standards, such as those of the IEEE (see Chapter 4), are integrated into the OSI scheme.[3]

Overview of OSI

The Reference Model was devised to allow "standardized procedures to be defined enabling the interconnection and subsequent effective exchange of information between users."[4] "Users," in this sense, means systems consisting of one or more computers, associated software, peripherals, terminals, human operators, physical processes, information transfer mechanisms, and related elements. These elements together must be capable of "performing information processing and/or information transfer."[5] The importance of the Reference Model is that it will permit various networks of the same or different types to easily communicate with one another as if they constituted a single network.

At the outset it is important to keep in mind that conformance with the Reference Model does not imply any particular implementation or technology. It does not, in other words, specify a medium (such as fiber optic cable, twisted pair, or coax), nor a specific set of recommendations such as the IEEE 802.3, 802.4, or 802.5 networks in the United States. The Reference Model is designed to support standardized information exchange procedures, but provides neither details nor definitions or interconnection protocols.[6] The Model, therefore, is a frame of reference for open systems with implementation details being left to other standards. Because the Model is a frame of reference, it provides the framework for the definition of services and protocols that fit within the boundaries established.

Open Systems Interconnection Environment

It is important to understand that OSI is concerned with the exchange of information among open systems—not with the internal functioning of each individual "real" open system. This concept is depicted in Figure 3.1.[7] A "real system" in this context is one that complies with the requirements of the OSI Model in its communications with other "real systems." A real system is, therefore, a set of "one or more computers, associated software, peripherals, terminals, human operators, physical processes, information transfer means, etc., that forms an autonomous whole capable of performing information processing and/or information transfer."[8] Within an open system an application-process performs the information processing for a particular application.

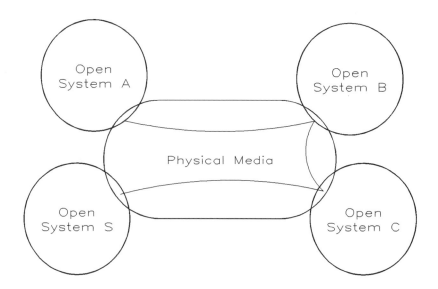

Figure 3.1 Open Systems Connected by Physical Media.

Aspects of systems not related to interconnection are outside the scope of OSI. This still leaves a broad scope for OSI, since for it is concerned not only with the transfer of information among systems but also with their ability to interwork to achieve a common or distributed task. This is implied by the expression "systems interconnection." The fundamental objective of OSI is to define a set of recommendations to enable open systems to cooperate. Cooperation involves a broad range of activities:

1. Interprocess communication—the exchange of information and the synchronization of activity among OSI application-processes.
2. Concern with all aspects of the creation and maintenance of data descriptions and data transformations for reformatting data exchanged among open systems.
3. Concern with storage media and file and database systems for managing and providing access to data stored on the media.
4. Process and resource management by which OSI applica-

tion-processes are declared, initiated, and controlled, and
the means by which they acquire OSI resources.

5. Integrity and security of data during the operation of open
   systems.

6. Program support for comprehensive access to the programs
   executed by OSI application-processes.

Since some of these activities may imply exchange of information
among the interconnected open systems, they may be of concern
to OSI.

Concepts of a Layered Architecture

In a layered architecture each open system is viewed as being
logically composed of an ordered set of subsystems.[9] The seven
subsystem layers of OSI have been depicted in Table 3.1. Subsystems that are adjacent to one another in the vertical hierarchy
communicate through their common boundary. Within each subsystem or layer are *entities*. Entities in the same layer, but in
different open systems, are termed *peer-entities*. Some conventional definitions have been developed to refer to the components
of the layered architecture:

(N)-subsystem—An element in a hierarchical division of an open
    system that interacts directly only with elements in the next
    higher division or the next lower division of that open system.

(N)-layer—A subdivision of the OSI architecture, constituted by
    subsystems of the same rank (N).

(N)-entity—An active element within an (N)-subsystem.

peer-entities—Entities within the same layer.

sublayer—A subdivision within a layer.

(N)-service—A capability of the (N)-layer and the layers beneath
    it, which is provided to (N11)-entities at the boundary be-
    tween the (N)-layer and the (N11)-layer.

(N)-facility—A part of the (N)-service.

(N)-function—A part of the activity of (N)-entities.

(N)-service-access-point—The point at which (N)-services are provided by an (N)-entity to an (N11)-entity.

(N)-protocol—A set of rules and formats (semantic and syntactic) that determines the communication behavior of (N)-entities in the performance of (N)-functions.

Layering and the method for referring to each layer (N, N11, N21, etc.) are depicted in Figure 3.2. The highest layer does not have an (N11)-layer above it, and the lowest layer does not have an (N21)-layer below it. The physical medium is not a part of the layered architecture.

When an entity communicates, it does so with a peer at the same layer at another open system. Not all peer (N)-entities need or even can communicate, however. Conditions that prevent such communication includes the possibility that they are not in interconnected open systems or that they do not support the same protocol subsets. A distinction is made between the *type* of some object and an *instance* of that object. A type is a

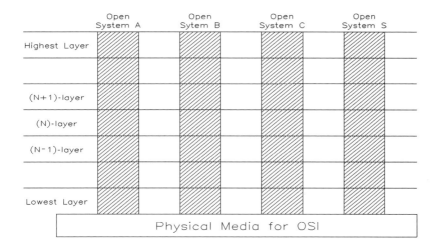

Figure 3.2 Layering in Cooperating Open Systems.

description of a class of objects, while an instance of this type is any object that conforms to this description. The instances of the same type constitute a class. A computer program, for example, is a type of something, and each copy of that program (running perhaps on different machines or concurrently on the same machine) are instances of the type. In the OSI Model, communication occurs only between (N)-entity instances at all layers. Connections are always made to specific (N)-entity instances.

As we noted earlier, a layer may have sublayers. Sublayers are small substructures that extend the layering technique to cover other dimensions of OSI. A sublayer, therefore, is a grouping of functions in a layer that may be bypassed, although the bypassing of *all* the sublayers of a layer is not allowed. A sublayer uses the entities and connections of its layer. We will later look at such sublayering in a discussion of the IEEE 802 standards, particularly the Logical Link Control (LLC) and Media Access Control (MAC), which are sublayers of the OSI Data Link Layer (Layer 2). Except for the highest layer, each (N)-layer provides (N11)-entities in the (N11)-layer with (N)-services. The highest layer represents all possible uses of the services that are provided by the lower layers.

It is important to understand that an open system can be OSI compatible without providing the initial source or final destination of data. In other words, an open system need not contain the higher layers of the architecture. The IEEE 802 standards, for example, apply only to the lowest two layers—data link and physical. This is often the source of significant confusion, since when we talk of 802.3 (commonly called Ethernet) or 802.5 (token ring) the discussion sometimes proceeds to commentaries on TCP/IP or XNS or some other "protocol." TCP/IP and XNS exist at layers beyond the physical and data link (although TCP/IP and XNS are not OSI standard protocols). Peer entities communicate through peer protocols at the appropriate layer of the OSI architecture, as seen in Figure 3.3.

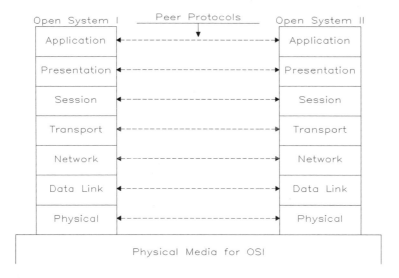

Figure 3.3 Seven-Layer OSI Reference Model and Peer Protocols.

The OSI Security Architecture

As part of its set of OSI standards, the International Organization for Standardization (ISO) has produced a standards proposal (DIS 7498-2, *OSI Reference Model Part 2: Security Architecture*) that can provide significant guidance for security.[10] Among the things DIS 7498-2 contains are the following:

- A checklist of important security features;
- Assistance for organizing the task of providing security;
- Guidance for implementors and purchasers; and
- A means for standardizing security implementations.

Two fundamental purposes served by the ISO standard are:

- To provide a functional assignment of security features to OSI layers that will guide future enhancements of OSI-based standards.

- To provide a structured framework within which vendors and customers can evaluate security products.

Within the OSI framework the proposal standard also defines security services and mechanisms. In order to understand the approach taken by the ISO, we will need to address three concepts: *security threat, security service,* and *security mechanism.*

Security Threat

Any action that compromises the security of information owned by an organization or individual is a security threat. Two types of threats have been identified—passive and active—and are dealt with in somewhat different ways. A *passive threat* is one in which there is interception and exploitation through the monitoring and/or recording of data while those data are being transferred over a communications facility. With *release of message contents* an attacker can read user data in messages; with *traffic analysis* the attacker can read user packet headers to identify source and destination information as well as the length and frequency of messages. An *active threat* is one where there is the unauthorized use of a device attached to a communications facility to alter transmitting data or control signals, or to generate spurious data or control signals.

Passive Threats

Passive threats do not, in general, alter any data in the system. Rather, these threats involve the reading of information for the purpose of profiting from knowledge of the information. Because there is no tampering with the information, audit trails of access are often sparse or nonexistent. Passive threats are therefore difficult to detect. Passive threats, however, can often be prevented, and prevention is fundamental to fighting such hazards.[11] In general, passive threats can most often be defeated through the use encryption methods. The use of encryption as a security mechanism will be discussed in some detail in Chapter

5. Suffice it to say here, however, that *encryption* may be defined as the translation of one character string into another by means of a cipher, translation table, or algorithm, in order to render the information contained therein meaningless to anyone who does not possess the decoding mechanism. It is the reverse of *decryption*. An encryption algorithm is a group of mathematically expressed rules that render information unintelligible by producing a series of changes through the use of variable elements controlled by the application of a random key to the normal representation of the information. In an information security environment, encryption is used at a number of points to maintain confidentiality and data integrity and to authenticate data and users.

Release of Message Contents

In a network, passive threats consist of the release of message contents to an attacker, or the attacker can read a packet header (traffic analysis) in order to determine the location and identity of either the communications source or destination. If a message has already been filed on a host system, of course, access to that system can result in an attack on the system in order to obtain the release of information already stored. To understand this issue in a network environment, take a look at Figure 3.4. Figure 3.4 depicts the way in which a network packet or frame is developed across the several layers of the OSI protocol stack. Other layered network architectures, such as TCP/IP, SNA, or DECNet, operate analogously.

The original data generated by the user is at the top—this is the base data. As a packet or frame is formed, for transmission on the network, certain control (C(n)) or header information is added, thus making up a new data segment for the next lower layer. The data for each (n21)-Layer is the accumulation of the data and control information of all preceding layers. In principle, at least, there is no reason why each new data segment could not be encrypted. If a security threat were actually passive (eavesdropping on a communication line for example), it would be all but

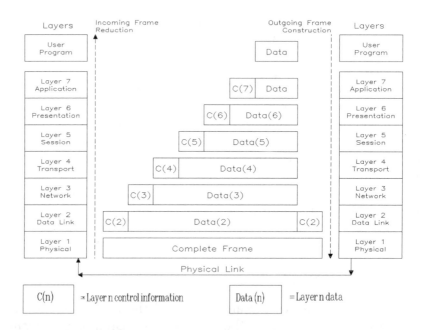

Figure 3.4 Nesting of Layer Protocols.
Source: MAP 3.0 Implementation Release, June 22, 1987, p. C3-2.5. Copyright by General Motors Corporation. All rights reserved.

impossible to decode the contents of the data segment, thus precluding the release of the contents of that segment. The control or header information will include information pertaining to peer communication and, in the data link layer, physical addresses for the source and destination of the packet/frame.

Traffic Analysis

Although we can protect message contents from unauthorized release, a second form of passive threat revolves around a traffic analysis attack. If an attacker can read the packet header, then the source and destination of the message is known, even when the message is encrypted. If encryption and decryption takes place only in end-nodes, then the source and destination addresses cannot be encrypted. End-to-end encryption is the encryption of data in a communications network at the point of origin, with decryption occurring at the final destination point. When link encryption is employed, however, that possibility is decreased or eliminated. Link encryption is the application of on-line crypto-operations to a communications system link, so that all information passing over the link is encrypted completely. The term also refers to end-to-end encryption within each link in a communications network. Figure 3.5 is a representation of communications involving relay open systems. The relay system, which may consist of a device in which only the first three layers are implemented, may be necessary when the end-systems are part of different networks or part of the same network where the different segments use different physical media. In such a system encryption and decryption would take place not only at the end-nodes but also in the relay node. The need for this is a function of the

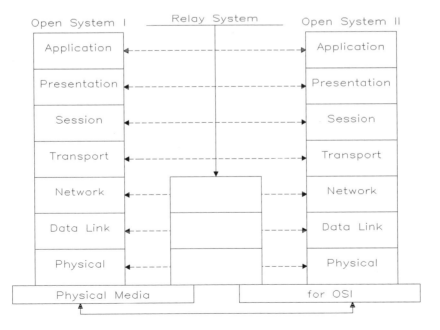

Figure 3.5 Communication Involving Relay Open Systems.

network needing the information in an encrypted source and/or destination address.

Encryption can only limit the reading of header information and messages. Considerable information can be inferred from traffic analysis itself, (the total volume and the amount of traffic entering and leaving selected nodes). Encryption cannot address this issue. One possible countermeasure would be to pad the communications link by generating a continuous stream of random data or ciphertext. An attacker would, therefore, find it difficult to distinguish between usable data flow and noise, thus making it difficult or impossible to count the amount of real traffic. If there is fear concerning an active threat, then a message authentication procedure can be used (see below). Traffic padding may be inappropriate with some network architectures or so inhibit the throughput of a network as to be unusable.

Active Threats

As might be anticipated, active threats are often thought to be more serious than passive threats. The reason why we might think this is that active threats are often designed to alter or to generate spurious data or control signals rather than to simply read the content of those signals. Loss can obviously be caused when the information flow is seriously altered, but whether an active threat is more serious than a passive threat is a function of cost of the harm caused by whatever threat occurs. Stealing trade secrets or national defense secrets, even when no alteration takes place, can turn out to be very costly. In any event, the active threats with which we must be concerned include *denial of message service, masquerading,* and *message stream modification.*

Keep in mind that active attacks can occur almost anywhere across the communications route: cable (both copper and fiber optic), microwave links, satellite channels, routing nodes, host or client computer systems—anywhere. Unless a very large amount of money is available for security, as in a military establishment for example, then it is unlikely that extensively guarded physical facilities along an entire route is feasible. In fact, even for military organizations, 100% coverage is probably impossible. In some way or another, however, an active threat can only be made if "physical" access is achieved. In this case we should understand "physical" somewhat metaphorically for physical access might well be through a dial access terminal hundreds of miles away from the target, or through radio channels also distant from the target. Even active wiretapping—the unauthorized attachment of a device to a communication circuit in order to obtain illegitimate access to data—may not physically require a device spliced into a cable. Cables can be tapped through the use of inductive, magnetic, capacitance, or other unobtrusive techniques. As might be imagined, preventing active attacks can prove to be very difficult, and the security goal to thwart active attacks might well be to detect quickly and recover from any disruption or delays caused by such attacks.

Denial of Message Service

Perhaps the most obvious active threat faced by a communication system is an attack that can destroy or delay most or all messages. In a modern, information-based society, such an occurrence could easily lead to the loss of large sums of money or worse. Such a threat need not even arise as a conscious plot of a gang of terrorists. If a major switching node on a switched network, such as a telephone system, were to go out of service, it could jeopardize the telephone service for hours or even days (as happened with AT&T in 1989 and again in 1991). Unless there is sufficient redundancy in the switch, it is unlikely that the device will never crash. Consequently, neglect of a system in the sense of no provision of redundant alternatives can be the source of an active threat. This concept can be expanded to include physical attacks by hostile forces that can have similar results. An example of a somewhat different physical attack on a system was that by Robert Morris with his Worm on Internet in 1987. Perhaps the most important contemporary example is the theft of money each year through electronic means by somehow infiltrating the system of electronic funds transfers and/or bank accounting systems.

In other words, any activity that can potentially destroy or sub-stantially delay most or all messages constitutes an active threat.

Masquerading

A more subtle approach to active interference with a network is through masquerading. Masquerading is the attempt to gain access to a system by posing as an authorized client or host. In this scenario an attacker poses as an authentic host, switch, router, or similar device in order to communicate with a peer to acquire data or services. Anyone who has ever been around a university knows that students (and sometimes faculty) share user IDs and passwords, even when cautioned against the practice. That is the most benign form of masquerading because it is usually not done to damage anyone else. As any university computing center director can attest, however, there are always some students who will willfully destroy what others have built. Another classic example from a university environment is the occasional attempt to access administrative systems to alter grade records. This is sometimes accomplished by simply noting user IDs and passwords that staff members have pasted to their terminals as a memory aid (but as a security breech). The effort, in other words, to masquerade as an authentic user is an old, if not honored, pastime. The effort to make a target system actually believe it is communicating with the desired host or client system, however, requires far more sophistication, but is not beyond the technical capabilities of many. Masquerading, as a technique, may be used for either passive or active purposes, but has been described under "active threats" because the objective is often interventionist in character.

Message Service Modification

The third way we noted that active threats might occur is through message stream modification. Here an attacker might selectively modify, delete, delay, reorder, and/or duplicate real messages or insert counterfeit messages. Even encrypted messages can be damaged in transit in ways that will not thwart CRC error-checking codes in transport packets. As a packet for transmission is formed by the protocol software (see "Concepts of a Layered Architecture" on pg. 54 and Figure 3.4), it acquires one or more cyclic redundancy checksums calculated by the sender and recalculated by the receiver. If those checksums are different, then a retransmission of the packet is usually requested. In a similar way, a manipulation detection code (MDC) can be generated on only the plaintext of the message contents prior to encipherment under the theory that, even if a packet is manipulated so that it is changed but passes the error correction tests, the actual encipherment of the plaintext will be altered sufficiently to produce a different checksum on it.[12] The MDC is one method of detecting message stream modification, and there are several different checksums used for the purpose. The ISO version of this approach is contained in the international standard ISO 8731-2, known as MAA (message authenticator algorithm)[13].

Security Service

A security service is an activity or provision of an activity that enhances the security of information systems and an organization's information transfer. In the OSI model the defined services consist of five groups: confidentiality, authentication, integrity, non-repudiation, and access control. In a layered communication architecture, such as the OSI Model, security could be built in almost anywhere. The OSI security architecture is more explicit, however, in that it specifies the layers in which specific services are to be provided. The relationship between security services and OSI layers is found in Table 3.2. Although some security services can be provided in most of the layers of the OSI protocol stack, there have been arguments made for focusing on security service in the application layer.

Ken Rossen, for example, has pointed out that the military has typically spent heavily to install security measures at ISO Layers 2 and 3. Most corporations do not need nor can they afford such high levels of security; for them, ISO Layer 7, the application

TABLE 3.2. Location of Security Services in OSI Layers

Layer of OSI:	Security Services				
	Confidentiality	Authentication	Data Integrity	Non-repudiation	Access Control
Application	Y	Y	Y	Y	Y
Presentation	Y	Y	—	—	—
Session	—	—	—	—	Y
Transport	Y	Y	Y	—	Y
Network	Y	Y	Y	—	Y
Data Link	Y	—	—	—	—
Physical	Y	—	—	—	—

layer, makes more sense. Recent developments that have made Layer 7's security possibilities more attractive include the CCITT's passage of X.509, a standard for distributing public encrypting and decrypting keys; new software tools for developing public key security features; growing availability of directory server installations and implementations; and the development of secure applications, such as the Kerberos project from the Massachusetts Institute of Technology.[14]

Confidentiality

Confidentiality or *data confidentiality* guarantees that information is not made available or disclosed to unauthorized individuals, entities, or processes. This service category provides mechanisms that, in general, protect transmitted data from passive attacks. The concept of confidentiality can be applied to an entire message or to fields within a message. In the latter case the term often used is *selective field confidentiality*. Data confidentiality is affected by whether the communication protocols use connection-oriented or connectionless services. A connection-oriented service is one that establishes a virtual connection that appears to the user as an actual end-to-end circuit, and is sometimes called a virtual circuit or virtual connection. Thus, there can be defined *connection-oriented confidentiality,* which effects end-systems.

Contrasted to a connection-oriented service is a connectionless service, which is a class of service that does not establish a virtual or logical connection and does not guarantee that data units will be delivered or will be delivered in the proper order. Connectionless services are flexible and robust and provide connectionless application support. Connectionless applications are those applications that require routing services, but do not require connection-oriented services. *Connectionless confidentiality* applies to connectionless data flows and may affect mid-points in a network as well as end-points. Finally, there is the issue of *traffic flow confidentiality.* Traffic flow confidentiality constitutes concealment of the quantity of users' messages in a communication system and their sources or destinations, to prevent traffic analysis.

Authentication

Authentication ensures that a message is genuine, has arrived exactly as it was sent, and came from the stated source. It may also involve the verification of the identity of an individual, such as a person at a remote terminal or the sender of a message. Authentication itself is composed of two types: *data-origin authentication* and *peer-entity authentication.* The emphasis in OSI is more explicit than in other contexts in that authentication refers especially to the certainty that the data received comes from the stated source. Data-origin authentication operates in conjunction with connectionless service, whereas peer-entity authentication usually refers to an operation with connection-oriented services. In other contexts the idea of authentication might be made synonymous with data integrity, but with OSI the two are clearly separate and distinct.

Some would suggest that authentication is the most basic security service a network can offer. It protects against fraudulent transactions by establishing the validity of messages, stations, individuals, or originators. Authentication is essential for data integrity, and network designers need to know the strength of authentication security, what is being authenticated by the service, and at what level in the OSI framework it should be provided. Peer-entity authentication supports connection-oriented networks. It provides confidence in the identities of end-points by means of two-way or three-way exchanges. Authentication that relies on cryptographic techniques is known as "strong authentication" because, unlike passwords, the cryptographic key resides in a device or computer and is therefore not easy to replicate. According to Michael Fecko, the primary issues in choosing an authentication method are price, strength, and technique infrastructure.[15] With Fecko we might ask, "How strong is network authentication security? At what level in the OSI framework should it be provided, and what does it really authenticate?"

Data-Origin Authentication

Data origin authentication is the corroboration that the source of data received is as claimed. When authentication supports connectionless networks using the various OSI connectionless protocols (ISO 9576, Layer 6; ISO 9548, Layer 5; ISO 8602, Layer 4; and ISO 8473, Layer 3) or the Defense Department's Internet Protocol (IP), it is known as data-origin authentication. In such cases each datagram carries the information necessary to authenticate its source. Authentication mechanisms are generally based on some combination of three types of information:

- Who you are, based on information such as a fingerprint or signature.
- What you possess, such as an ID card or physical key.
- What you know, such as a personal identification number or mother's maiden name or the responses to other "questionnaire" items.

The strength of authentication depends on this information and its immunity to duplication.

The simplest form of authentication relies on user IDs and passwords and is known as "simple authentication." There are various methods for enhancing simple authentication, such as including a random number or by password time-stamping, followed by applying a one-way (encryption) function to the entire message. From the one-way function output it is impossible to determine the original input. Thus, even if an intruder can intercept the authentication message, he or she cannot determine the user's password. Nor can he or she replay the intercepted message by pretending to be the user at a later time, because of the time stamp. Data-origin authentication can be done in relay systems or end-systems (Layer 3 or below). Authentication at Layer 4 or above, on the other hand, applies strictly to end systems. The choice of authentication mechanisms is necessarily a compromise between the strength of the authentication procedure and the cost of implementing and managing it.

Peer-entity Authentication

Peer-entity authentication is the corroboration that a peer-entity in an association is the one claimed. When authentication supports connection-oriented networks it is known as peer-entity authentication. Peer-entity authentication provides confidence in the identities of end-points by means of two-way or three-way exchanges. Throughout the set of standards discussed in this book, two concepts recur and need to be defined here: *connectionless* and *connection-oriented* services. These are also sometimes referred to as *datagram* and *virtual circuit* services, respectively. Generally, a datagram may be defined as a finite-length packet with sufficient information to be independently routed from source to destination without reliance on previous transmissions. Datagram transmission typically does not involve end-to-end session establishment and may or may not entail delivery confirmation acknowledgment. A connection-oriented service establishes a virtual connection that gives the appearance to the user of an actual end-to-end circuit. The virtual connection contrasts with a physical circuit in that it is a dynamically variable connection where sequential user data packets may be routed differently during the course of a virtual connection. A connectionless service does not set up a virtual or logical connection between hosts and does not guarantee that all data units will be delivered or that they will be delivered in the proper order. The advantages of connectionless service are flexibility, robustness, and connectionless application support. Connectionless applications are those that require routing services but do not require connection-oriented services.[16]

A datagram service, such as that provided by the U.S. Department of Defense Internet Protocol, is a connectionless service. Likewise, in the context of OSI, some protocols provide connection-oriented services, while others provide connectionless services. Moreover, both these services can exist at several levels. The ISO 8473 standard, for example, is a connectionless protocol for the Network Layer and functions similarly to IP, while ISO 8073 is a connection-oriented protocol at the Transport Layer. The IEEE

Std 802.2 (ISO 8802/2) Logical Link Control standard can be implemented as either a connectionless or connection-oriented service in the Data Link Layer. Typically, if a network is configured to handle connection-oriented services at, say, the Transport Layer, the protocols at the Network and Data Link Layers would likely be implemented as connectionless services.

Data Integrity

Data integrity ensures that data have not been altered or destroyed in an unauthorized manner. The two concepts of data integrity and authentication remain closely allied even within OSI, however. This alliance extends to the mechanisms used to support the services. Note from Table 3.3 that the same mechanisms apply to both services. Moreover, they are usually required together. Both data integrity and authentication rely heavily on encryption as a primary security mechanism. Just as with authentication, data integrity services can be applied to the entire message or only to selected fields. Integrity issues vary somewhat, depending on whether the message is being transmitted in the context of a connection-oriented or a connectionless service. If it is being used with a connection-oriented protocol, then the data integrity mechanism can be provided with a form of recovery mechanism.

Repudiation and Non-repudiation

When one of the entities involved in a communication denies or repudiates participation in whole or in part of that communication, we have *repudiation.* The security service defined by the OSI architecture called *non-repudiation* is the precise opposite of repudiation and can be provided in two forms: with proof of origin or with proof of delivery. One of the mechanisms by which these forms of non-repudiation can be provided is through the use of a digital signature. A digital signature is a number that depends on all the bits of a message and also on a secret key. Its correctness can be verified by using a public key (unlike an authenticator, which needs a secret key for its verification). A second mechanism for providing proof of origin or with proof of delivery is through notarization by a trusted third party.

Access Control

Finally, *access control* can be applied at either the source or destination of a communication or somewhere along the route. Access control protects a network against deliberate saturation by an opponent or unauthorized access to an information service. Access control typically takes place in the application layer, but may also be accomplished in the transport or network layers. Sometimes it is desirable to provide protection for a subnetwork by allowing only authorized entities access to it. Access control services in the transport layer can handle such a problem.

Security Mechanisms

Many of the standard security mechanisms were encountered during the preceding discussion of security services. *Security mechanisms* are operating procedures, hardware and software features, management procedures, and any combination of these that are designed to detect and prevent either passive or active threats on any component of an information system. Security mechanisms are related to security services in that the mechanisms are the procedures used to implement a security service. The relationship between OSI-defined services and selected mechanisms may be clearly seen in Table 3.3. The service "Confidentiality," for example, can be implemented through the use of encryption, traffic padding, and/or routing control. "Encryption," on the other hand, can be a component of the implementation, not only of confidentiality, but also of "integrity" and "authentication" services.

Encryption

Of all the security mechanisms, encryption is perhaps the single most important technique because of its wide applicability. Be-

TABLE 3.3. Security Services and Mechanisms

Services			Mechanisms					
	Encryption	Digital Signature	Access Control	Data Integrity	Authentication	Traffic Padding	Routing Control	Notarization
Confidentiality	✓	⊗	⊗	⊗	⊗	✓	✓	⊗
Integrity	✓	✓	⊗	✓	⊗	⊗	⊗	⊗
Authentication	✓	✓	⊗	⊗	✓	⊗	⊗	⊗
Access Control	⊗	⊗	✓	⊗	⊗	⊗	⊗	⊗
Non-repudiaton	⊗	✓	⊗	✓	⊗	⊗	⊗	✓

✓Considered Appropriate ⊗ Not Considered Appropriate

cause of that wide applicability an entire chapter (Chapter 5) is devoted to the topic. Suffice it to say at this point that if there was only a single security mechanism available, encryption would be the mechanism of choice. We have already defined *encryption* as the translation of one character string into another by means of a cipher, translation table, or algorithm, in order to render the information contained therein meaningless to anyone who does not possess the decoding mechanism. In Chapter 5 we will explore more closely the meaning of this definition.

Digital Signature

An increasingly important technique for authentication is the digital signature. A digital signature is a number that depends on all the bits of a message and also on a secret key. Its correctness can be verified by using a public key (unlike an authenticator, which needs a secret key for its verification). While digital signatures are used for authentication purposes, they are also used to implement integrity and non-repudiation services as well. When used for non-repudiation, digital signatures may be used in conjunction with notarization, which is the verification (authentication) of a message by a trusted third party, similar in logic to classic notarization procedures, although in this context it is normally an automated procedure.

Access Control Mechanisms

The most common security experience of end users of networks is access control through the use of passwords. A password is a unique word or string of characters used to authenticate an identity. A program, computer operator, or user may be required to submit a password to meet security requirements before gaining access to data. The password is confidential, as opposed to the user identification, which is often known to many, much like a telephone number. An alternative to a password might be a passphrase, which is a phrase used instead of a password to control user access. Unfortunately, password systems can often be circumvented. Closely akin to the use of passwords are questionnaires. A *questionnaire* is a method of identity verification that makes use of information known to the authorized user but unlikely to be known to others. A common and widely used example is to request a grandmother's maiden name. The advantage of the questionnaire is that it uses memorable information. The disadvantage is that it may involve a rather lengthy dialogue.

There are a variety of products that allow identity verification by more esoteric means than those described thus far. It is possible, for example, to design a system using smart cards (credit card–sized cards with at least some memory) or cards with magnetic strips (such as credit cards) for verification by token. It is also possible to design systems requiring comparisons with file copies of voice, hand-written signatures, fingerprints, and/or retinal patterns. These various technologies all find some use, but can be expensive to implement. Before embarking on a security program requiring such techniques, it would be well to do the analyses suggested in Chapter 4.

A better approach might be to isolate sensitive data and its access on "private" concurrent networks, using an alternative communications protocol along with encryption and call-back techniques. A call-back system can often be implemented in a straightforward fashion. Such systems use either a specialized modem or the computer to break the connection to a user, after the user has properly logged on an application, and then call the user back at one or more authorized terminals from which the application might be accessed. Like many other security systems, however, call-back techniques are vulnerable to determined efforts to undermine them. Even advances in related communications technology, such as call forwarding in telephone systems, have implications for security systems.

Data Integrity Mechanisms

Although data integrity is treated as a separate concept in the context of OSI, in practice it is closely related to data authentication. They employ the same security mechanisms, for example, and are usually required together. Therefore, note the following authentication mechanisms.

Authentication Mechanisms

There are a number of authentication techniques available for network security. The scope of authentication in network security can be very wide. When a unit of information (a message, file, or document) is genuine and came from its reputed source, it is said to be authentic. Some questions to be asked might include:

- Did the source have the authority to issue the unit of information?
- Does a payment correspond to a genuine invoice?
- Is the sender who he, she, or it claims to be?

Authentication extends from data entry through the safe arrival of information at its destination.

Data entry is sometimes checked through the use of checksums, a summation of a set of data items for error detection or, a bit more narrowly, a sum of digits or bits used to verify the integrity of data. Cyclic redundancy checks (CRC) are often used to identify when there have been accidental errors in data transmission. A CRC is an algorithm designed to generate a check field used to guard against errors that may occur in data transmission. The check field is often generated by taking the remainder after dividing all the serialized bits in a block of data by a predetermined binary number. Greater security is often needed, however, and that is the function of systems designed to check data integrity through the use of secret parameters. The ISO has recognized the need for more than one type of authenticator, and this has led to several authenticator algorithms or methods, including the Decimal Shift and Add (DSA) and the Message Authenticator Algorithm (MAA).

It should be understood that authentication mechanisms within the OSI framework do not necessarily authenticate the person who originates a message. Protocol data units are sent by a computer, not a person. That means origin authentication within the communications protocol stack is traceable only to the point at which some security mechanism provided it. Network authentication at Layer 4 or below can ensure only that data came from a certain end-system. The result of the foregoing is the suggestion that authentication at the application layer is better, but the possibility still exists for an illegal application to invoke the authentication mechanism. The National Computer Security Center's Trusted Network Interpretation of the "Orange Book" deals with this issue.

At the risk of some redundancy, please note the National Computer Security Center (NCSC) of the U.S. National Security Agency (NSA) levels of security listed in Chapter 2, each of which involve security models of varying formality.[17] Each of NCSC's levels adds more features and requirements and extends from *D* (nonsecure system) to *A1* (highest security):

D. Nonsecure system.

C. Provides discretionary control. The owner of the data determines who has access to it.

C1. Requires user log-on, but allows a group ID.
C2. Requires individual user log-on with password and an audit mechanism.

B. Provides mandatory control. Access is based on standard DOD clearances.

B1. DOD clearance levels.
B2. Guarantees path between user and the security system. Provides assurances that system can be tested and that clearances cannot be downgraded.
B3. System is characterized by a mathematic model that must be viable.

A. Provides mandatory control. Access is based on standard DOD clearances.

A1. Characterized by a mathematical model that can be proven, thus providing the highest security.

At the C2 level and above, the trusted network interpretation specifies that, when a network trusted computer base mediates the actions of hosts acting on behalf of users, the trusted computer base may authenticate the hosts instead of the users, so long as each host can identify the set of users active in the host when the authentication is performed.

Most current host log-on procedures are password-based because cost-effective alternatives to the "what-you-know" identification technique have not been available in the past. The "what-you-know" identification can be improved by using questionnaire systems rather than a simple password, but it is still the "user-agent" being authenticated rather than the user. Current technology, however, allows users to be associated directly with their cryptographic keys through smart cards similar to credit cards. Smart cards typically carry a microprocessor, RAM and ROM memory, a lithium battery, and a liquid crystal display. A smart card directly associates the authentication source for a strong mechanism with the user. In addition, a personal identification number (PIN) identifies the user by two of the three potential identifiers: who you are, what you possess, what you know. Smart cards may come to play a larger role in authentication mechanisms of new systems, establishing a basis for other security concerns, such as user accountability.

Traffic Protection Mechanisms

If an intruder can tap into a communications channel (a cable, radio signal, etc.), traffic flow analysis can take place. When communication traffic is in cipher form and cannot be understood, it may still be possible to get useful information by detecting who is sending messages to whom and in what quantity by analyzing the traffic flow. Traffic flow security is the protection resulting from features, inherent in some cryptoequipment, that conceal the presence of valid messages on a communications circuit, normally achieved by causing the circuit to appear busy at all times. This technique of making the circuit appear busy at all times, is called *traffic padding*. Traffic padding is a function that generates a continuous stream of random data or ciphertext, thus making it (1) very difficult for an attacker to distinguish between true data flow and idle traffic; and (2) making it very difficult to deduce the amount of traffic. Traffic padding precludes the simple counting and compiling of statistics on data flow. *Link encryption* can be used to protect the message headers, in order to prevent analysis of source and destination of messages. Traffic padding is a more general technique and can probably be applied in a wider variety of networks.

Routing Control

Some threats can be avoided by routing messages to avoid particular networks or systems. National security and intelligence agencies, as well as large multi-national corporations, for example, might wish to avoid routing through some countries. These and others might wish to avoid network nodes that have a history of security problems or are suspicious for some reason. Routing control is a mechanism that is used primarily to ensure connectionless confidentiality, connection-oriented confidentiality, and traffic flow confidentiality. Security techniques include network configuration control and periodic deletion or modification of messages.

Notarization

Notarization is the verification (authentication) of a message by a trusted third party, similar in logic to classic notarization procedures; it is normally an automated procedure. Notarization is a mechanism to implement the security service called non-repudiation. Notarization is essentially a technique of arbitrated authentication requiring a third party for the determination of the authenticity of a message and the identity of its sender and receiver.

Concluding Notes

The importance of this discussion of OSI security concepts cannot be overstated. Even though other network architectures may not use the same vocabulary (although they will come to do so over the next few years), to secure those networks it is necessary to be concerned about the same categories of issues found in OSI. In this review I have attempted to set forth the OSI security architecture in a systematic and easily understood manner. Fundamentally, in order to plan for security in a network it is necessary to understand what kind of security services are needed and then determine what mechanisms are available to implement those services. Other issues may intrude, to be sure. For example, the speed of the security mechanisms will affect response time. In some implementations, public key cryptography may be relatively slow compared with DES, and DES may be slow compared with protected passwords. Other considerations are product availability, standardization, interoperability, and cost.

Notes

1. Frank Derfler, Jr. and William Stallings, *A Manager's Guide to Local Networks* (Englewood Cliffs, NJ: Prentice-Hall, 1983), p. 79.

2. Gregory Ennis, "Routing Tables Locate Resources in Bridged Broadband Networks," *Systems & Software*, March 1983.

3. The state of OSI development can be followed in various places. See, for example, Jean Bartik, "OSI: From Model to Prototype as Commerce Tries to Keep Pace," *Data Communications*, March 1984, pp. 307–319; Jerrold S. Foley, "The Status and Direction of Open Systems Interconnection," *Data Communications*, Feb. 1985, pp. 177–193; Sunil Joshi and Venkatraman Iyer, "New Standards for Local Networks Push Upper Limits for Lightwave Data," *Data Communications*, July 1984, pp. 127–138; and Kevin L. Mills, "Testing OSI Protocols: NBS Advances the State of the Art," *Data Communications*, March 1984, pp. 277–285.

4. The actual text of standards are sometimes difficult to obtain. An easily accessible compilation of many of the more important standards can be found in Harold C. Folts, ed., *McGraw-*

Hill's Compilation of Data Communications Standards, Edition III (New York: McGraw-Hill, 1986), 3 volumes. The ISO 7498 standard (OSI) was adopted from the CCITT Recommendation X.200. X.200 has been used as the basis for the discussion in this chapter, and references are made to that document, designated as *Fascicle VIII.5-Rec. X.200.* In references following the identification of the actual standard, volume and page references to the standard, as found in *McGraw-Hill's Compilation of Data Communications Standards, Fascicle VIII.5-Rec. X.200,* p. 3 (Vol. 2, p. 2235).

5. Ibid.

6. Ibid. p. 3 (Vol. 2, p. 2235).

7. Figures 3.1, 3.2, and 3.3 may be found in International Telegraph and Telephone Consultative Committee (CCITT), Recommendation X.200, *Reference Model of Open Systems Interconnection for CCITT Applications, Fascicle VIII.5-Rec. X.200* (1984), pp. 5, 8, and 26, respectively.

8. Ibid. p. 4 (Vol. 2, p. 2236).

9. The concepts of a layered architecture are given in p. 40, Ibid. pp. 6ff (Vol. 2, p. 2238ff), Section 5.

10. This section loosely follows William Stallings, "A Network Security Primer," *ComputerWorld,* Vol. 24, Jan. 29, 1990, pp. 63–66, 70. Stallings piece was also reprinted in *Datapro Reports on Information Security* (Delran, NJ: McGraw-Hill, 1990), Vol. 2, IS35-110-101 through IS35-110-107.

11. For an interesting, more-or-less popular account of a serious "passive" threat, yet one that was tracked down, see Clifford Stoll, *The Cuckoo's Egg: Tracking a Spy Through the Maze of Computer Espionage* (New York: Doubleday, 1989).

12. See Davies and Price, pp. 123–125.

13. Banking—*Approved algorithms for message authentication Part 2: Message authenticator algorithm,* International Standard ISO 8731-2, International Organization for Standardization, Geneva, 1987.

14. Ken Rossen, "Network Security: Just Say 'Know' at Layer 7; Application-Layer Encryption Is the Key to Secure Corporate

Communications," *Data Communications,* Vol. 20, No. 3, March 1991, p. 103(3).

15. Michael Fecko, "Authentication Checks Who You Are, What You Know," *Government Computer News,* Vol. 7, No. 21, Oct. 10, 1988, p. 97(2).

16. See Thomas Wm. Madron, *LANS: Applications of IEEE/ANSI 802 Standards* (New York: John Wiley & Sons, 1989), p. 30 and elsewhere for a more extended discussion of connection-oriented and connectionless services.

17. National Computer Security Center, *Trusted Computer Systems Evaluation Criteria* (Orange Book), DOD Standard 5200.28.

CHAPTER 4

Recognizing
Security Risks

The typical response in many MIS or network installations to discussions regarding security is likely to be either one of panic and paranoia or one of incredulity that anyone would waste time and effort to do damage to the system. Neither of these extreme responses is appropriate, of course. The former is inappropriate because reasonable security precautions will, in most instances, be sufficient for those security threats that do arise. The latter is equally inappropriate, however, because in a networked environment there are always some security threats, including the fact that most of the serious threats are not external to the organization. Similarly, in seeking corporate funding for security, a network/MIS manager may be told to secure his or her system, but also told to do it cheaply (and probably inadequately).

Apart from the situation in which a breach of security actually happens and some problem occurs as a result, security risks are not always easy to recognize beyond the few basic ones that are common to every installation. There are three basic techniques, however, that have been developed to assist management to assess either the lack of security or the cost of the lack of security. These techniques are the *security audit, qualitative risk analysis,* and *quantitative risk analysis.* A security audit is an examination of data security procedures and measures for the purpose of evaluating their adequacy and compliance with established policy. Risk analysis, by way of contrast, is a process of studying system assets and vulnerabilities, to determine an expected loss from harmful events, based upon probabilities of occurrence of those harmful events. The object of risk analysis is to determine the degree of acceptability of each risk to system operation.

The Security Audit

A more detailed definition of a security audit suggests that it is an independent evaluation of the controls employed to ensure:

1. The appropriate protection of the organization's information assets (including hardware, software, firmware, and data) from all significant anticipated threats or hazards;

2. The accuracy and reliability of the data maintained on or generated by an automated data processing system; and

3. The operational reliability and performance assurance for accuracy and timeliness of all components of the automated data processing system.

These issues can perhaps be best understood by examining the typical control objectives suggested by auditors assessing network security and the audit procedures that can be taken to assess each objective. One list of objectives suggests the following:[1]

1. The information systems telecommunications network should be controlled through a central administrative function.

2. Inventory and identification controls should be maintained for all terminals on the telecommunications network.

3. All system access should be controlled through passwords and authorization codes that are validated by security software.

4. All telecommunications accesses to the computer system should be logged, and logs should be reviewed periodically by data processing or telecommunications management.

5. The use of dial-up lines to the computer systems should be controlled or not used at all, to prevent unauthorized access attempts.

6. Master terminals, which can change the access rights of other terminals or users, should only be located in secure locations.

7. Sensitive data should be encrypted or otherwise protected when transmitted, to prevent message interception.

8. Manufacturer, software vendor, and third-party access lines to the computer system should be monitored, with frequent changes to lines and access codes.

9. All requests for uploads or downloads of data or programs from distributed processors, such as microcomputers, should be subject to management review and approval.

10. Telecommunications billings should be monitored, to identify potential efficiencies and to detect unauthorized users.

The list just presented is clearly geared for a more-or-less private network. Moreover, when we recognize that "terminals" are probably microcomputers, procedures may be required to ensure that the attached micros are not actually doing more than acting as limited terminals, such as subverting controlled dial-access. The lists of procedures that often go along with such lists of objectives are essentially a set of instructions for auditors, telling them how to measure each objective.

What a security audit can do is to suggest where the holes are in an installation's security system. The audit, however, is only as comprehensive as the understanding of the auditors allow. The audit is unlikely to turn up problems unearthed by questions never asked or objectives never stated. If the audit is comprehensive, however, what the results can suggest are the areas where attention must be paid in order to have more effective security. The audit does not specify *how* to accomplish the objectives. It merely specifies *what* needs to be done. The methodologies used to plug security holes is a function of how aware of the appropriate software and hardware technologies those responsible for maintaining security are.

Although we cannot give a detailed treatment of how to do a security audit, any such audit should include taking a look at the network management function and physical and logical network controls.[2] The management function is concerned with the overall management and operation of the network, including the setting of standards and the maintenance of a network inventory, monitoring network problems and use, the review of the network to achieve balanced loads, and active participation in the systems development process. The physical controls are concerned with the physical security of network equipment, and logical controls are those that involve the functioning network, such as error checking, audit trail logging, and encryption.

The point is that a security audit can provide the organization with part of the information needed to improve network security. It is some form of risk analysis, no matter how informal, that will ultimately determine how much attention we pay to the plugging of holes in our security structure.

Risk Analysis

As we noted earlier, *risk analysis* is a process of studying system assets and vulnerabilities, to determine an expected loss from harmful events, based on probabilities of occurrence. The object of risk analysis is to determine the degree of acceptability of each risk to system operation. Risk analysis can include both quantitative and qualitative approaches. The key reason for using risk analysis is to determine what is a sufficient level of security in a particular situation. Because the cost of security can be high, it is important to come to some conclusion about when the costs of security exceed the value of the information and physical environment being secured. Alternatively, because the cost of loss or failure can also be high, it is important to understand the real costs incurred in losses due to insecure systems.

Qualitative Risk Analysis

The objective of *quantitative* risk analysis, as will be seen below, is to evaluate security risks in terms of probable expected losses. With such information, assuming it is valid to begin with, decisions can be made in a rational manner that balance the cost of securing systems against the potential cost of not securing them. If quantitative risk analysis could be accomplished reliably, with valid data, there is little doubt that it would be the superior method for determining the potential loss factors for a particular organization as a result of having inadequate security. Critics have pointed out, however, that there are a host of problems with quantitative risk analysis, including the length of time it takes and lack of reliable data. I would add to that the lack of people who understand either how to accomplish quantitative analysis or the associated research. Furthermore, there is an unwillingness on the part of many to admit to the need for the conclusions that can be drawn, even if all other issues were solved.

The alternative to quantitative risk analysis is qualitative risk analysis. Qualitative techniques, in contrast, avoid much of the detailed statistical analysis characteristic of the quantitative methods. Some qualitative risk analysis may be nothing more than the intuitive understanding of security risks that any good MIS or data communications manager may have. It is unfortunately true, however, that many people would prefer to go with "intuitive understandings" than with any systematic efforts to determine security risks. The difficulty with intuitive understandings is that they are difficult to communicate and, even when written down, are difficult to relate the same way twice in a row. Moreover, insistence on "intuitive analysis" is often an argument to avoid the hard work necessary to do decent research and analysis.

There are, however, systematic techniques available that can capture qualitative information about security risks. Such methods include extensions of the auditing objectives and procedures noted in the section above ("The Security Audit"), sometimes called "Auditor Risk Assessment Reviews." A second technique might be *security reviews by management* through the use of focused discussions among the members of a risk analysis team. Akin to the use of discussion groups, a third approach might well be derived by using a *threat scenario case study* method. Fourth, an organization could use highly structured techniques, such as the *Delphi Method*; often associated with technological forecasting, it also uses a group of experts as the basis for making judgments, resulting in interpretations about the likelihood of some event actually taking place. Fifth, with the recent improvements of *expert systems*, it might be possible to use such artificial intelligence (AI) systems to capture what a group knows or thinks about security risks (as some contemporary risk analysis software seeks to do). Each of these approaches provides alternatives in situations where quantitative data are unavailable, too expensive to collect, or of suspect validity when collected. The disadvantage is that these techniques do not provide the cost comparisons between having and not having decent security systems. Brief discussions of each of these methods follow. The references should be consulted for detailed methodological treatments.

Auditor Risk Assessment Reviews

As the subtitle implies, this approach is basically an auditing procedure that management might request during standard auditing periods.[3] In a typical audit the concern would be largely directed toward general controls reviews. In some cases either the auditors or management may wish to have more specialized or detailed audit reviews of specific security attributes, such as physical security. Under such circumstances an additional, more detailed set of objectives and procedures would be established.[4] The result of such a review might be either a standard audit report or a less formal management report designed primarily to assist MIS or network management to improve security. This kind of assessment does not contain detailed probability estimates characteristic of quantitative risk analysis. Moreover, auditors are usually counseled against drawing extreme conclusions. In other words, care is generally taken not to overinterpret minor control weaknesses. On the other hand, such an assessment may be very useful as the starting point for a management security review. The primary problem with the use of auditors, especially those outside the organization, is that they may not understand the organization that is being audited nor the real security risks involved. While most auditors would likely disagree with this point of view, I have dealt with few auditors in an information processing environment that had the practical or academic experience necessary to provide much guidance.

Management Security Reviews

An effective nonnumerical risk analysis can frequently be accomplished through surveys and detailed discussions. Such procedures require that the group of managers responsible for computing and networking attempt to survey security exposures. On the basis of the information collected, those managers can then make recommendations regarding the course of action to limit security risks. The first step in such a review consists of gathering some standard data so that each participant will have access to the same information. Such data might include a brief inventory of equipment and procedures in each data processing or network center within a large organization. The process also works best when a security risk analysis team is assembled. The members of the team will usually, although not necessarily exclusively, be appropriate managers in the organization. The difficulty with this approach is that MIS and/or network managers may not be able to identify most or all risks. Data processing managers, for example, fearing physical damage from disgruntled employees often recognize that access controls to the physical environment of computers or network equipment can be effective in limiting potential sabotage.

It may not be so readily understood, however, that an uninterruptible power supply (UPS) may be more important to physical security than control of disgruntled employees. Power fluctuations and outages, for example, may be far more common than sabotage. Even if the expense of a UPS is accepted, independent air conditioning of the battery room may not be considered, even when the desirability of independent air conditioning of the entire computer facility is recognized. A large room full of storage batteries may, for example, give off considerable hydrogen. If there is a loose connection on the wiring to one or more battery, sparks may occur. The result of those two facts may be a fire or explosion. Even if the fire is contained with standard fire-fighting techniques, soot may be sucked into a common air conditioning system, thus contaminating one or more machine rooms. This story is not hypothetical, by the way—I was once the manager of a system in which this particular circumstance took place. The point is that total security concerns are not only problems for MIS or network managers. Rather, they are the concern and responsibility of those managers *and* selected vendors and users of the service.

Threat Scenario Case Study

An extension of the focused discussion groups already mentioned might be the threat scenario case study method. A wide range of possible threats can be played out theoretically. The participants can be a group of system experts, and it would be done with the full knowledge and cooperation of all the people who could be affected by a threat. SRI, for example, uses a seven-step threat scenario based on real loss experience.[5] This technique covers a wide range of vulnerabilities under a wide variety of conditions. Its success depends on the "honesty and integrity of the target system staff and experts," but "honest cooperation is forthcoming, motivated by self-interest and the opportunity to participate rather than operate in an adversary relationship."[6] The strength of this method is that it allows some testing of the adequacy of current security measures and draws those in the team into a systematic consideration of the problems. The disadvantage is that this technique, also, may miss significant problems.

The Delphi Method

The classic Delphi Method,[7] while using a group of "experts" similar to the discussion methods already outlined, is more dependent on paper and pencil or automated survey techniques. A target group of experts must first be chosen. In the case of network security risk analysis this group would probably consist of people in an MIS and/or network department, related managers, selected vendor representatives, and selected user representatives. These people would be presented first, with essentially a blank piece of paper and asked to list three to five security threats, in short declarative sentences, that they each think the organization might be most likely to encounter. Out of a group of 20 people, therefore, a total of 60 to 100 statements might be forthcoming. After eliminating nonsense issues and redundant statements, the result might well be a list of 40 or more statements. Those statements are then converted into items to be used in a questionnaire to be sent back to each participating expert. Each person would be asked to rate each item (often on a 1 to 7 scale) in terms of the likelihood of its occurrence and of the importance to the organization if the event actually occurred. Other ratings might also be requested as appropriate, such as the time frame in which the events might take place, the cost to the organization (in time, money, or some other unit) if the event took place, and so forth. Those results are then tabulated. A second questionnaire is prepared that again asks each member of the panel to rate each item, but before doing so to consider where they stand in relationship to the others. The latter information is made a part of each item by furnishing each individual the range and median of the ratings of all members of the panel as well as the respondent's own previous responses. The individual respondent is then asked whether he or she wishes to change his or her original rating and, if so, to what. This iteration process may continue until consensus is reached or until distribution changes cease.

Part of the purpose of Delphi is to come up with reliable ratings through achieving consensus or by demonstrating disconsensus on particular items. The notion here is that through consideration of the feedback given each respondent, each successive iteration will produce a more reliable estimate of group opinion. Of course, it may be that the technique, under some circumstances, simply fosters consensus where none actually exists. The output of the method, however, for purposes of risk analysis, would be subjective ratings of the probability of occurrence of a security threat and estimates of the importance of such a threat to the organization. It would be possible then to sort the threats into descending sequence, thus producing a list of threats considered both likely and important. Especially if the staff is far flung, one advantage of this technique is that face-to-face meetings can be eliminated. On the other hand, Delphi can also be used in the context of group discussions to further focus those discussions. While there are numeric summaries of the results available, the technique is still qualitative rather than quantitative in character, if by quantitative we mean the use of rigorous mathematical techniques applied to validly measured data.

Expert Systems

An expert system is an artificial intelligence application that uses a knowledge base of human expertise to aid in solving problems. The degree of problem solving is based on the quality of the data and rules obtained from the human expert. The expert system derives its answers by running the knowledge base through an inference engine, a software program that interacts with the user and processes the results from the rule and data in the knowledge base. Expert systems are relatively new to risk analysis, but are becoming an essential ingredient. Access control is one area of security management where expert systems are in use. Such a system reads violation reports and makes decisions on whether the violations are worthy of notice. Especially for the analyst or organization that does not have a risk analysis expert, expert systems can be very useful and cost-effective. Products such as MicroSecure Self Assessment (Boden Associates) and RiskWatch (Expert System Software) ask a user a set of questions, which are then analyzed, providing a list of vulnerabilities and possible ways of controlling them. Expert systems are only as good as the rule and knowledge base of the system, but if used as part of an overall risk assessment suite it could provide considerable opportunities for dealing with security risks.

Quantitative Risk Analysis

A subsidiary question is, how much is your information worth to the operation of your organization? Or even, how much of the worth of your organization is dependent on your information? The late Rear Admiral Grace Murray Hopper, until recently one of the oldest persons on active duty with the United States Navy, had an appropriate answer to that question. She was, in her words, the "third programmer on the first computer," and was one of the original authors of COBOL. Admiral Hopper, in a speech a few years ago, made the point that information processors have frequently placed emphasis on the "processing" of information to the exclusion of an understanding of the worth of the information itself.[8]

With the deployment of microcomputers as workstations the issue of the value of information has become more apparent than it was previously. Micros have proved to be catalysts for this issue, because one primary reason people want micro-based workstations is to be able to download subsets of organizational data for further local processing, analysis, and reporting. Database administrators concerned about the "integrity" of their data, as a result of these changes in the way data are used, have had to learn new practices. It is becoming more apparent than ever that, if information is to be used as the basis of organizational decision making, the information must be timely and accurate. Part of an assessment of the value of information is how much it costs to ensure that it is "timely" and "accurate."

Even though timeliness and accuracy have always been an objective of data processors, in the old days that often meant generating the data in machine-readable batches (cards or something equivalent), producing an initial report, checking the report for accuracy, making corrections, and then producing a final report—a process that could take days or weeks. In today's environment, where the end user may control much of the process, a file or record may be updated one moment from some terminal, and downloaded the next moment to a micro by some other user, massaged, and a report generated in an hour. Technology has provided timeliness—people still provide accuracy.[9] The result of the differences in timeliness between development and/or report generation time on a mainframe and on a micro is not solely one of easier-to-use technology on the micro, nor of the obtuseness of mainframe systems developers. At least some of the difference is that over the years mainframe development people have been required to adhere to a greater degree of corporate accountability than is typically true of so-called "end-user" computing.

In a mainframe environment, procedures have often been established over a period of years in cooperation with all sorts of interests within an organization. Such procedures are usually absent with micro-based computing. Furthermore, many of the procedures required in a mainframe environment are tied directly to security concerns—something that is only superficially recognized, if ever, with micro-based computing. An illustration of this is the question of how we store the data after we have massaged it on our micro. If we do the analysis on the mainframe, all the standard security measures typical of large systems are taken to ensure that we don't lose the analysis or at least do not lose the data on which the analysis was based. We can replicate it if necessary because standard backup procedures ensure that it will always be available. How many of us have standard backup procedures for our micros? Therein lies the problem. A way of looking at the mainframe as a microcomputer peripheral is to regard it as a secure and cost-effective file server for backing up microcomputer files. If the files we generate on the micro are important means for making organizational decisions, then those data are every bit as important to the organization as any generated on the mainframe. Yet they are not as secure and are not usually in any audit trail that anyone can find.

The effort to answer the question of how much security is enough has led to the development of various techniques, both quantitative and qualitative, to assess the risk involved in *not* establishing appropriate security. In general, as the risk of a security failure increases, and as the cost of the system increases, the cost of doing damage control increases. This is illustrated in Figure 4.1. The general answer to the question is, therefore, to establish sufficient security procedures so that both security and corrective costs are minimized. A low-cost, low-risk system is less in need of heavy-duty security than is a high-cost, high-risk system. Yet these are still relative terms, since a $5,000 system for IBM or AT&T or the federal government may be trivial, while a $5,000 system for an

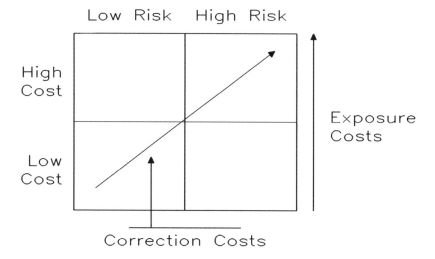

Figure 4.1 Security Costs vs. Risks.

independent consultant, an author, or a one-person law firm may be catastrophic.

In any event it is still useful for an organization to attempt to assess the risk involved in security or the lack thereof. The credit for the first application of quantitative risk analysis techniques probably goes to Robert Courtney. It was in 1977 that Courtney, then with IBM, first presented the technique. In this context risk is defined in terms of probable loss dollars per year, according to the relationship:

$$R \, 5 \, P \, 3 \, E$$

where R is risk, P is the probability that a security threat will occur a given number of times per year, and E is the exposure cost attributed to any such loss. The difficulty with this formulation is that the assignment of probabilities is subjective and costs are often difficult to determine. The exercise itself is instructive, however, for it forces the members of an organization to think through their risk exposure.

P is not a simple statistical probability estimate. The probable exposure is known as the Loss Multiplier (P_L), which annualizes the rate of occurrence of a given risk. For example, if something happened once every 300 years, then the P_L would be .00333 (365/109,500, not counting leap days during leap years). If it happened once a day, the P_L would be 365 (365/1), and if it happened 100 times per day, the P_L would be 3650 (365/.1). In other words, the P_L is calculated as follows:

$$\text{Loss Multiplier } 5 \, \frac{\text{(No. of Days per Year)}}{\text{(No. of Days between Events)}}$$

For example, a given piece of equipment might have a Mean Time Between Failures (MTBF) of 10,000 hours. If that item operated 24 hours per day, then the number of days between events would be 10,000/24 5 416.67 days per event. One year 5 365 days, so the P_L for this device is 365/416.67 5 .876. Some other device has a failure rate of two per day: 1 (day) / 2 5 .5 days per event. P_L 5 365/.5 5 730. Something that fails once about every three months (90 days) would produce P_L 5 365 / (90/1) 5 4.06. There are other techniques available for estimating rates of occurrence, but where possible those estimates should be based on hard data rather than on subjective estimates. If subjective estimates of future rates are necessary, then the Delphi Method may be employed to provide those estimates in a systematic manner.

Just as it can be difficult to estimate the Loss Multiplier, it is also difficult to precisely calculate the costs of expected losses. Losses are not simply a function of replacement cost of equipment. Many other factors can increase costs, due to failure of a computer/communication system. Some of the factors to be considered are:[10]

1. Personnel productivity time resulting from an outage—This includes the salary per hour of the employees concerned, as well as the cost of fringe benefits for those hours lost but paid. Employees here include anyone whose job is dependent on the existence of the system, whether technical support or end user.
2. Personnel time required to correct the outage, including direct salary and benefits.
3. Value of business lost due to outage.
4. Cost of using alternative methods, if at all possible.
5. Legal liability costs.
6. The cost of hazard protection and business interruption insurance.
7. The costs of backup and recovery capabilities, including annual testing costs.
8. Equipment replacement costs, including ordering and shipping, installation, and testing and startup processing time.
9. Damage repair costs less insurance recoveries.
10. The current replacement cost of the asset.

A simple example will suffice. Suppose that a data entry operator, using a microcomputer, has an equipment failure. It takes one full day to get the failing device fixed or replaced. The costs would be something like the following:

1. Cost of operator's time, including fringes: $12.30/hour x 8 5 $98.40.
2. Repair costs (personnel): $30.00/hour 3 4 5 $120.00.
3. Lost business (operator billed at $20/hour): $20.00 3 6.8 5 $136.00. The 6.8 hours is the maximum amount of billable time an operator is likely to have in a normal 8-hour day. That is calculated by excluding coffee breaks and providing a time for backing up the work accomplished at the end of the day.
4. No alternative methods available.
5. No legal liabilities in this case.
6. Some small proportionate share of insurance overhead costs (?).
7. Backup and recovery costs: $22.30.
8. The hard drive failed; replacement cost: $800.00 (including ordering, installation, and startup time).
9. No other damage costs.
10. Cost of replacement of asset covered in (8).

When these costs are totaled, the cost of expected losses comes to $1,056.70. The P_L for this problem is .876. The risk, or annualized probable loss, is therefore, $1,056.70 x .876 5 $925.67. There are limits to the usefulness of this kind of risk analysis, but it can be a valuable technique. Obviously, doing a risk analysis for a network would be more difficult, and network failure could cause very large probable losses.

The list of ten factors used to calculate the "actual" costs of expected losses could also be applied to problems caused through malice. When Robert Morris sent his virus across the

Internet, the cost of expected losses probably looked something like the following.

Assumptions:

1. Several hundred computer systems were involved. Assume the number was 500 (some estimates ran as high as 6,000).
2. Assume an average of 10 users per system were precluded from using those systems for 24 hours, at an average personnel cost of $50.00 per hour at a maximum pay of 8 hours for each 24-hour period 5 $400.00/person 3 10 3 500 5 $2,000,000.
3. An average of two technical people per installation to clean up the system affected at $800.00/day for one day 5 $800 3 500 5 $400,000.
4. Cost of lost revenue from connect-time charges at $10.00 per hour for an average of $800.00/day per installation for the average of 10 users 5 $800 3 500 5 $400,000.

The cost of losses caused by Morris were, using these assumptions, about $2,800,000. The foregoing calculations are very conservative, since, as we noted earlier, Morris' worm may have hit as many as 6,000 computer systems across 500 to 700 institutions. Jay Bloombecker, Director of the National Center for Computer Crime Data, estimates that the cost to the Los Alamos National Laboratory alone was about $250,000. It required two days to restore service at NASA's Ames Research Center in Mountain View, California—a facility that services 52,000 on-line users.[11] These are the reasons why many computer professionals thought that the fine of $10,000 and some community service was an inadequate punishment. Just because most of the institutions involved were government or university systems does not reduce the loss calculations. Because of the nature of Morris' virus there was no permanent damage to software systems or data, thus minimizing the losses, but substantial losses were nevertheless incurred, even though they may not be exactly the numbers presented above.

Donn B. Parker, in "Seventeen Information Security Myths Debunked," argues quantitative risk assessment techniques are invalid and excessively costly. Moreover, according to Parker, "Experienced security practitioners already know most of what they need to do to reduce risk and also realize that valid data on information value and probability of loss are too costly, if not unobtainable." This assertion falsely assumes that all installations have pretty much the same risk and that, whatever the risk may be, expertise can be a substitute for data. Parker goes on to use an anecdote to "prove" his case. He tells the story of an information security officer who used quantified risk software to "artificially produce numbers that would support his previously developed security plans, because his management insisted on numbers to back his proposals." When Parker suggested that this procedure was deceptive, the security officer replied "that the fabricated number were simply a means of expressing his opinion, which was based on years of experience."[12] The lesson to be drawn from this story is not that we should forego attempts to do quantified risk analysis, but that results should not go unquestioned.

Indeed, it appears that the employee was clearly not a team player and was more concerned that his own prejudices be accepted than to learn whether there were valid alternatives. The point is that quantified risk analysis is difficult and the data are sometimes unavailable, although reasonable and sufficient estimates of missing data can frequently be made by knowledgeable people within the organization. It takes considerable time and money to fully secure a computer/network/information base. Just because it is difficult to come up with is no excuse not to try to estimate the cost of security vs. the cost of potential losses, as well as to make *estimates* of the likelihood of loss. Moreover, there is a discipline imposed on management if a formal risk assessment is undertaken, although it should not be done solely by the MIS department nor by a security officer. In fact, most installations, even if they have designated a security officer, will not have an "experienced security practitioner."

Risk Analysis Software

At least 11 vendors are marketing risk analysis software, ranging in price from under $100 to over $10,000. Price is generally related to the number of threats identified and the depth of analysis. Software that enhances both qualitative and quantitative risk analysis are available. Through the use of risk analysis software, it is possible to reduce the time expended in making a risk analysis, although if it is a typical quantitative analysis the output is only as good as the input ("garbage in garbage out"). The benefits also include the easy recording, manipulation, and accessing of information stored on databases, the capability to see the effects of loss of combinations of safeguards; consistency in the determination of loss; and the ability to quickly change the risk environment. Risk analysis products may range from a security checklist to expert systems; NIST and NCSC are considering the development of standards for risk analysis software. It is important to understand that risk analysis software is not a substitute for the ignorance of the user. It is a tool, not a solution.

All the current systems provide for a data gathering function, including input to questionnaires dealing with various risk components in an organization. Many of the packages also assess the degree of risk a threat poses. They may, in addition, provide an estimate of a company's loss if such threats were to occur. Costs of implementing security measures can be weighed against potential losses should a security threat occur. Once threats and costs have been established, some of the packages then assist the decision-making process, regarding what to do about the security threats. When evaluating risk analysis software some care should be taken. First, acquire a list of references and check the way in which the package has been used in similarly sized organizations. Second, select the vendor with some care about how the company does business, how long it has been in business, how experienced the vendor is in risk analysis, and if the product can be customized. Third, check out the documentation and training available. Fourth, how does a new release affect your work schedule? And fifth, is the source code and associated documentation placed in escrow (against the vendor going out of business); is escrow placement standard with the software's contract?[13] One of the more convenient places to go for finding the current software vendors and software evaluations of risk analysis software is the *DataPro Reports on Information Security* (Delran, NJ: McGraw-Hill, updated monthly). *DataPro* provides the product's name, the name and address of the vendor/manufacturer, a description of the product, and its price. Bear in mind, however, that whatever is published in a book will be out of date by the time the book is published.

Concluding Notes

The answer to the question, "how much security is enough?" is dependent on the cost of potential loss to the organization. Spending nothing on security is too little, while spending enough to ensure total redundancy is likely too much for most purposes. An automobile assembly plant employing several hundred workers and manufacturing a large number of automobiles per day, with a factory floor controlled by a MAP (Manufacturing Automation Protocol) network, may require very substantial security systems to preclude unscheduled outages. A bank would clearly require substantial security to preclude unwanted intrusions for the purpose of electronically misappropriating funds. In these cases substantial expenditures for security would be warranted.

How much damage can occur if there were unauthorized disclosure or alteration of sensitive data, and how much is an institution willing to pay to protect the information? These are the critical questions in designing a security system. One answer is to keep a truly sensitive processor and its data off a network under the assumption that the only secure computer system is one that is electrically and physically isolated. Even in such an isolated system, however, issues of physical security exist. We can make some networks more secure than others, but total security may not be possible.[14] It is also increasingly difficult to maintain a computer system not connected or networked to other such systems, particularly in organizations of any substantial size.

Other issues also intrude into the discussion of security. The size of a network may preclude problems of security or may increase those problems. A small LAN, totally contained in a single office, probably has different security problems than a large LAN spread across a campus environment. In a small LAN, data integrity may be compromised more as a result of inadvertence than of malice, and relatively simple techniques might be appropriate. In a large LAN, encryption or other strong techniques might be needed. With a small LAN it may be possible to control what is attached to a system; in a large LAN such control may be more difficult. In a large, highly connective system, for example, an individual with a LAN connection may simply plug in a cheap auto answer modem and a new point of semi-public access is created that would be difficult to detect even if rules against such connections were in effect.

Notes

1. Robert R. Moeller, *Computer Audit, Control, and Security* (New York: John Wiley, 1989), pp. 73–76.

2. In addition to Moehler, already cited, see also S. Rao Vallabhaneni, *Auditing Computer Security* (New York: John Wiley & Sons, 1989), and Charles Cresson Wood, et al., *Computer Security: A Comprehensive Controls Checklist* (New York: John Wiley & Sons, 1987), for examples of current books on security auditing.

3. Moeller, pp. 376–394, describes both "Auditor Physical Security Risk Assessment Reviews," and "Management Oriented Physical Security Reviews," and includes some useful lists of objectives and procedures to aid the process.

4. See, for example, Moeller, Figures 8.7, 8.8, and 8.9, pp. 378–391, for examples of lists of objectives and procedures for a more detailed audit of physical security.

5. Note Donn B. Parker, "Seventeen Information Security Myths Debunked," pp. 43–46.

6. Ibid. p. IS09-150-106.

7. The Delphi Method is explained in detail in Harold A. Linstone and Murray Turoff (eds.), *The Delphi Method: Techniques and Applications* (Reading, MA: Addison-Wesley Publishing Company, 1975), particularly note page 78.

8. For a more complete account, see T. W. Madron, "Just A Reminder: Data is Priceless." *ComputerWorld*, July 16, 1985.

9. A discussion of this issue as applied to the contemporary trend to move software development from mainframes to high performance micros may be found in Steven W. Mann, "The Art of Building Computer Programs," *PCToday*, Vol. 4, No. 10, Oct. 1990, pp. 29–34.

10. This list goes beyond, but is based on, Moeller, p. 371.

11. As reported by Dave Powell, "Fighting Network Infection," *Networking Management*, Vol. 7, No. 9, Sept. 1989, p. 38ff. (8 pages).

12. Donn B. Parker, "Seventeen Information Security Myths Debunked," *ISSA Access*, Vol. 3, No. 1, first-quarter 1990, pp. 43–46; also reprinted in *Datapro Reports on Information Security* (Delran, NJ: McGraw-Hill, 1990), pp. IS09-150-101:107.

13. These questions were derived from Anon., "Risk Analysis Software: Technology Overview," *DataPro Reports on Information Security* (Delran, NJ: McGraw-Hill, 1990), pp. IS21-001-123, 124.

14. Dave Powell, "Fighting Network Infection," *Networking Management*, Vol. 7, No. 9, Sept. 1989, pp. 38ff (8 pages).

CHAPTER 5

Encryption as a
Security Mechanism

The primary method used to thwart passive threats are encryption techniques to make the information unusable without possession of the encryption key necessary for decoding the data. Of all the mechanisms used to protect information, encryption is the most powerful. Please recall that in Chapter 2 a brief security model was presented that suggested that layers of security protection extended from simple terminal access, with little or no access control to a fully encrypted data file and communication system. Figure 5.1 briefly reiterates that notion of a continuum of increasingly strong security mechanisms. The strongest of those mechanisms is encryption.

Encryption is accomplished through the use of either a code or a cipher. With a code, a predefined table substitutes a meaningless word or phrase for each message or part of a message. In contrast, a cipher uses a computable algorithm that translates a bit stream into an indecipherable cryptogram. Encryption is the translation of one character string into another by means of a cipher, translation table, or algorithm in order to render the information con-

Figure 5.1 Encryption as a Maximum Security Mechanism.

tained therein meaningless to anyone who does not possess the decoding mechanism. Cipher techniques can often be more readily automated than codes and are, therefore, used more frequently in computer and network security systems. Because the vocabulary of encryption is somewhat arcane, a short encryption vocabulary is presented in Glossary 5.1 (these terms are in the more general Glossary at the end of this book, as well).

Cipher—An algorithm for disguising information according to a logical principle by working within the elements of whatever alphabet is in use, such as by shift substitution of the letters of the alphabet by other letters a certain number of places toward the beginning or end of the alphabet. Not to be confused with a *code.*

Ciphertext—Encrypted text that cannot be read without decryption; data in its encrypted form that is cryptologically protected; the opposite of *plaintext* or *cleartext.*

Code—A technique by which the basic elements of language, such as syllables, words, phrases, sentences, and paragraphs, are disguised through being replaced by other, usually shorter, arbitrarily selected language elements, requiring a codebook (table) for translation. A term not generally used in relation to encryption. Not to be confused with *cipher.*

Cryptochannel—A complete system of cryptocommunications between two or more holders. The basic unit for naval cryptographic communication. It includes: 1) the cryptographic aids prescribed; 2) the holders thereof; 3) the indicators or other means of identification; 4) the area or areas in which effective; 5) the special purpose, if any, for which provided; and 6) pertinent notes as to distribution, usage, etc. A cryptochannel is analogous to a radio circuit.

Cryptogram—The ciphertext.

Cryptography—The branch of cryptology devoted to creating appropriate algorithms.

Crypto-information—Information that would make a significant contribution to the cryptanalytic solution of encrypted text or a cryptosystem.

Cryptology—The science that deals with hidden, disguised, or encrypted communications. It embraces communications security and communications intelligence. The art of creating and breaking ciphers.

Cryptomaterial—All material, including documents, devices, or equipment that contains crypto-information and is essential to the encryption, decryption, or authentication of telecommunications.

Data encryption standard (DES)—An algorithm to be implemented in electronic hardware devices and used for the cryptographic protection of digital, binary-coded information. For the relevant publications see "Data Encryption Standard," *Federal Information Processing Standard (FIPS) Publication 46,* January 15, 1977, also published as *American National Standard Data Encryption Algorithm,* American National Standards Institute, Inc., December 30, 1980, and supplemented with "DES Modes of Operation," *Federal Information Processing Standard (FIPS) Publication 81,* December 2, 1980; "Telecommunications: Interoperability and Security Requirements for Use of the Data Encryption Standard in the Physical Layer of Data Communications," *Federal Standard of the General Services Administration,* August 3, 1983, FED-STD-1026; "Telecommunications: General Security Requirements for Equipment Using the Data Encryption Standard," *Federal Standard of the General Services Administration,* April 14, 1982, FED-STD-1027; and "Telecommunications: Interoperability and Security Requirements for Use of the Data Encryption Standard with CCITT Group 3 Facsimile Equipment," *Federal Standard of the General Services Administration,* April 4, 1985, FED-STD-1028.

Encryption—The translation of one character string into another by means of a cipher, translation table, or algorithm, in order to render the information contained therein meaningless to anyone who does not possess the decoding mechanism. It is the reverse of *decryption*.

Encryption algorithm—A group of mathematically expressed rules that render information unintelligible by producing a series of changes through the use of variable elements controlled by the application of a key to the normal representation of the information.

End-to-end encryption—The encryption of data in a communications network at the point of origin, with decryption occurring at the final destination point.

Key—A piece of digital information that interacts with cryption algorithms to control cryption of information and, thus, must be protected from disclosure.

Key distribution center (KDC)—The element in a system that generates and distributes cryptographic key variables.

Key generator—An object for encrypting-key generation.

Key hashing—The method in which a long key is converted to a native key for use in the encryption/decryption process. Each letter number of the long key helps to create each digital bit of the native key.

Key management—Control of key selection and key distribution in a cryptographic system.

Key notarization—A method for encrypting information at a terminal site before transmission to a host computer, over communications media that might not be secure. It is necessary for the host and the terminal to maintain the same encryption key and algorithm. This is frequently accomplished by *downloading* (sending information) from the host to the terminal on key changes. The downloaded information must also be encrypted.

Link encryption—Application of on-line crypto-operations to a communications system link so that all information passing over the link is encrypted completely. The term also refers to end-to-end encryption within each link in a communications network.

Plaintext—Text that has not been encrypted (or has been decrypted) and can be easily read or acted upon.

Private key cryptosystem (encryption)—A type of encrypting system that uses a single key to both encrypt and decrypt information. Also called *symmetric,* or single key, encryption.

Public key—A cryptographic key used for encipherment, but not usable for decipherment. It is therefore possible to make this key public.

Public key cryptosystem—An encryption methodology that depends on two keys: a public key—made available to anyone who wants to encrypt information—is used for the encryption process, and a private key—known only to the owner—is used for the decryption process. The two keys are mathematically related. Also termed *asymmetric encryption.*

Symmetric encryption—see *private key cryptosystem.*

Glossary 5.1 An Encryption Vocabulary

Private Key Cryptosystems

With conventional encryption the original data, or "plaintext," is converted into an unintelligible "ciphertext." The conversion is accomplished using an algorithm and a random key composed of a bit string that controls the algorithm. In symmetrical cryptographic processes the key must be in the possession of both the sender and receiver, so key management becomes an issue. The algorithm must be sufficiently powerful to preclude decipherment of the message based solely on the ciphertext. Lest it still be unclear concerning the encipherment/decipherment process, note Figure 5.2. The system depicted, in Figure 5.2 is called a *private key cryptosystem* (encryption). A private key system is one that uses a single key to both encrypt and decrypt information. It is also called *symmetric,* or single-key, encryption. The primary disadvantage of symmetric algorithms is that, while the key must be kept secret, it must also be shared between sender and receiver. Because sharing is required, the key must be communicated from one person (sender) to another (receiver), thus creating a security threat. Hybrid techniques employ public key cryptography dissemination, but still use an electronic symmetric algorithm. A major advantage, however, is that some systems of authentication can be established so that problems involving bogus information can be reduced. The most widely publicized and used private key cryptosystem is the Data Encryption Standard from the National Institute of Standards and Technology (NIST) of the U.S. Federal government.

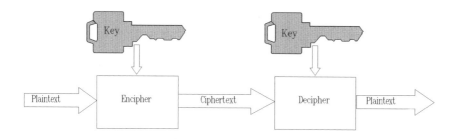

Figure 5.2 The Encipherment/Decipherment Process.

The Data Encryption Standard (DES)

While there are proprietary encryption algorithms in use, one of the most widely used and discussed algorithms is the data encryption standard (DES) supported by the National Institute of Standards and Technology (NIST) of the U.S. government, formerly (prior to 1988) the National Bureau of Standards (NBS).[1] DES is an algorithm to be implemented in electronic hardware devices and used for the cryptographic protection of digital, binary-coded information. DES is set forth in an assortment of federal standards, primarily Federal Information Processing Standards Publications (Fips Pub) No. 46, January 15, 1977. The Data Encryption Algorithm (DEA), which underlies DES, is described in Fips Pub 46. The algorithm is the result of a search made by NBS for an appropriate encryption technique. IBM submitted the winning methodology, which was then processed by the National Security Administration (NSA), to become DES. The DES algorithm is a block-oriented (as opposed to bit-oriented) invertible encryption algorithm. A single 64-bit (56 bits 1 8 bits parity) key is used to encrypt the data, and the same key is required to decrypt the cipher text. The algorithm, in its basic form, accepts data blocks of 64 bits and produces 64 bits of ciphertext per "cycle." The algorithm is invertible in the sense that the same algorithm runs "backwards" with the same key thus undoing the encryption. Since the algorithm is invertible, the security of the cryptographic system rests on the protection and security afforded the key.[2] From the beginning, however, there have been challenges to the extent to which the DES algorithm can protect anything.

Of all the security mechanisms noted in Table 3.3 (Chapter 3), encryption has the broadest application as well as providing the greatest degree of security. The primary use of encryption mechanisms is to prevent breeches of confidentiality, integrity, and authenticity. It was intended that DES be implemented in hardware, rather than simply as free running software in a computer's main memory. Such a system can provide a high degree of security even on dial-up lines. The data encryption device for a personal computer uses a plug-in board completely encased in epoxy inside a metal box so that the encryption chip cannot be removed or, more recently, a tamper-proof chip technology.[3] Considerable effort has been expended creating encryption systems for data transmission and storage. Those without the key to the encrypted information cannot access the content of the data, although the files themselves might be vulnerable.[4] The purposes of the standard were to ensure a high level of protection and to foster compatibility among users. Diffie and Hellman demonstrated in 1976 that the proposed standard was deficient on both grounds. They suggested, however, that the deficiency could probably be corrected by increasing the key and block sizes from 64 bits to 128 or 256 bits. It is alleged that the NSA, in fact, cut the key size down from IBM's original specification from 128 bits to 64 bits.[5]

DES Past and Present

At one time all computer security systems in the United States were certified for use by the U.S. Government by the National Security Agency (NSA). The data encryption standard was scheduled for decertification by NSA in 1988. Had NSA actually decertified DES, it would have effectively brought its use to an end. Although public outcry kept DES alive,[6] NSA did get out of the certification business other than for classified and certain sensitive applications for the U.S. government, especially the Defense Department. NSA's perspective was that DES, while very good, was not secure enough for classified national security applications. Today it certifies security products only for the U.S. Department of Defense (DoD) or other classified and/or sensitive systems. The result of all this is that the fate of DES in the future is in the hands of NIST rather than NSA. At this writing, however, DES continues to be used in the private sector with new, DES-based products coming to the market with some frequency.[7] The public support for DES caused NIST to recommend to the Secretary of Commerce that DES be reaffirmed for an additional five years—a term that will require reconsideration in 1992.

Since the Data Encryption Standard (DES) was published in

January 1977, as a Federal Information Processing Standard (FIPS), it has become the basis for the development of several security and integrity standards. Seven DES-based security standards have already been approved, and several others are in development. Five standards-making organizations are now involved with DES-based standards: the American Bankers Association (ABA), the American National Standards Institute (ANSI), the General Services Administration (GSA), and the National Bureau of Standards (NBS). The International Organization for Standardization (ISO) was originally looking at DES as a possible international standard, but has stepped back from its original concept of a single cryptographic standard. While these standards are all based on the DES, future standards may make provision for using other cryptographic algorithms. For example, public key cryptographic algorithms could offer some advantages over the traditional, secret key cryptographic algorithms in certain applications. In anticipation of this future requirement, NBS (now NIST) published a Solicitation for Public Key Cryptographic Algorithms to be based in special application standards.[8]

Modes of Operation

Four modes of operation for the DES are defined that may be used in a wide variety of applications. The modes specify how data will be encrypted (cryptographically protected) and decrypted (returned to original form). The modes included in this standard are the Electronic Codebook (ECB) mode, the Cipher Block Chaining (CBC) mode, the Cipher Feedback (CFB) mode, and the Output Feedback (OFB) mode. A DES mode of operation is a technique, external to the cryptographic algorithm, for incorporating the DES into a cryptographic system.[9]

The basic block encryption method in DES is called the Electronic Codebook (ECB). Each block in DES is 64 bits of plaintext. In effect, DES acts like a codebook for each block. A code (as distinguished from a cipher) is a technique by which the basic elements of language, such as syllables, words, phrases, sentences, and paragraphs, are disguised through being replaced by other, usually shorter, arbitrarily selected language elements, requiring a codebook (table) for translation. Although this is a term not generally used in relation to encryption, it is helpful in understanding ECB. In this mode of operation DES always produces the same block of ciphertext for a given key and block of plaintext. It does not interfere with the structure of the plaintext. Thus, an intruder, seeking to understand the encrypted message and having some sense of the organization of the plaintext document, may be able to make significant inferences based on an ECB-encoded plaintext.

In order to limit the extent to which an intruder can make inferences from plaintext altered with ECB, a second mode was developed called Cipher Block Chaining (CBC). In CBC mode, DES encrypts each block using the plaintext, the key, and a third value based on the previous block. This repetitive encryption or *chaining* tends to hide the structure of the plaintext. An enhancement of ECB is Cipher Feedback (CFB), which uses randomly generated ciphertext as input to generate pseudo-random intermediate output. This intermediate output is combined with plaintext to produce chained ciphertext. Even individual characters can be encrypted with CFB mode, although this can cause a loss of efficiency. The need to encrypt individual characters is essential in data organized by fields. The last mode, Output Feedback (OFB), is an enhancement related to CFB. Rather than randomly generated ciphertext, previously generated ciphertext is used as a means for encrypting subsequent plaintext.

The Future of Private Key Cryptosystems

Because of the usefulness of private key systems and because of investments already made in DES, it appears that these cryptosystems will be around for at least some time into the future. In fact, some form of private key encryption, such as a subsystem in a larger cryptographic system, will likely be around for the foreseeable future. The public outcry over NSA decertification did not keep NSA in the encryption certification business for the general public. Rather, it simply assured that there would be some continuing support by the U.S. federal government for DES. It is not today, nor has it ever been, approved to protect sensitive, classified materials, and that in itself can influence at least the defense industry. Moreover, the scheduled review of DES in 1992 may result in new modifications. Possible variations include extending DES to a block-size of 128 bits rather than its current 64 bits.

The applications of DES have been numerous and apply to a wide variety of information communication systems. It is used not only to encrypt "normal" network data flows and files, but also facsimile documents,[10] packet radio packets, and host passwords,[11] among other forms of information. With the increasing popularity of FAX, the issue of information security has become important. Any FAX message being transmitted across public networks is capable of being intercepted and copied. Similarly, packet radio in recent years has been gaining popularity as a transmission medium for digital traffic. It provides its user with the capability of accessing computer resources while in a mobile configuration or in a remote location, where access to cable based computer networks are either unreliable or nonexistent. As with any communications network, communications protocols must be in place to manage the transmission of data. Unfortunately, when using the protocols such as TCP/IPs Telnet to communicate with a computer, passwords are often transmitted in the clear. Any station monitoring the frequency can acquire a user's password to a particular system. In such an environment, DES has been used to provide encrypted strings as passwords. Notwithstanding these developments, DES does have its problems. The major alternative to private key cryptosystems, in general, and DES, in particular, are public key cryptosystems.

Public Key Cryptosystems

An alternative to private key encryption is a *public key cryptosystem* (PKC). The newer alternative methodology uses an *asymmetric* system, first reported in 1976.[12] Public key encryption is the outgrowth of this development. The advantage of an asymmetric system is that the second, private key is known only to the receiver who calculates it. In such a system, the encryption/decryption algorithms and the encryption (public) key may be made public. The decipherment key is related to the encipherment key, but is actually a random sample of one from a large universe of potential key values.[13] More formally, a public key cryptosystem is an encryption methodology that depends on two keys: a public key—made available to anyone who wants to encrypt information—is used for the encryption process, and a private key—known only to the owner—is used for the decryption process. The two keys are mathematically related.

The obvious advantage of public key over private key cryptosystems is that a secret key need not be carried from the sender to the receiver. Moreover, not only is a single secret key not necessary, it is not necessary to keep the enciphering algorithm secret in order to help preserve the security of the encrypted text. The process for using public key encryption is the following:

1. The *receiver* generates both a public (K_1) and private (K_2) key.
   a. A random seed number (K_0) is used to generate both (K_1) and (K_2) through the use of two public algorithms.
   b. The random seed number is discarded, unrecorded. The reason for this is that random number generators can reproduce a "random" number sequence if the same seed number is used.
   c. The highest security is achieved if this process takes place in hardware that is in a secure location.
2. The public key is then given to the sender.
3. The sender, using the public key (K_1) encrypts and sends the message.
4. The receiver, using both the public and private keys $((K_1 \ 1 \ K_2)$, decrypts and reads the message.

This process is depicted graphically in Figure 5.3. The reason

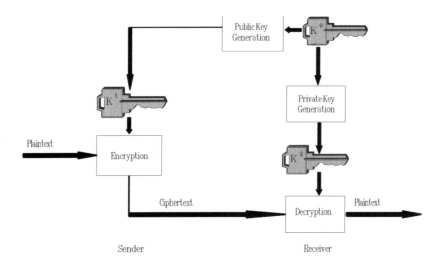

Figure 5.3 Public Key Encryption Process.

why this is more secure than single key encryption is that the public key very literally need not be kept secret. Nor does the algorithm behind the system require secrecy. Such a system can be made so well that it would, in principle at least, be possible to send the public key to the sender via a postcard.[14]

Although public key systems are coming to be more widely used, at this writing there was no public key standard. In 1976 Diffie and Helman proposed a public key algorithm to be used for encrypting keys for other cryptosystems rather than for directly encrypting messages or files. Later, in 1978, Merkle and Hellman suggested a more general PKC called the trap door knapsack encryption method,[15] although it was broken in 1982.[16] An alternative algorithm, RSA (from its authors, Ronald Rivest, Adi Shamir, and Leonard Addleman), is very powerful and has resisted all attempts to break it to date. RSA has often been proposed as a standard for PKC, but this has presented some difficulty because it is patented and sold in the United States as a commercial product. The keys for RSA are large numbers generated mathematically at least in part by combining prime numbers. One of the problems with this approach is the computing power necessary to generate the keys.

Encrypting Network Flows

From a network perspective there are two fundamental types of encryption: *link* and *end-to-end.* Link encryption implies that data are encrypted independently on each vulnerable communication link, which for a simple network may be end-to-end, but for a more extended network may be from packet switch (router, bridge, etc.) to packet switch. In this situation the data are in the clear at each switch, so there is a separate problem of node security over which the user may have little or no control. The advantage of this scheme, however, is that the entire packet, including the header information, can be encrypted. End-to-end encryption, as the name suggests, takes place at the source and destination addresses of the packet. While this takes care of the vulnerability of the data at intermediate nodes, the header is in the clear. A hybrid system that employs both approaches is the most secure with the header being in the clear only at end and intermediate nodes and the substantive information never being in the clear. A slight variation of the end-to-end scheme is the permanent storage of data in encrypted files, which might be used in place of or in addition to the other two approaches to encryption. From its inception the DES has been the subject of discussion concerning its use in a networking environment.[17] In a period when network transmission speeds are increasing at a dramatic rate, a serious problem with encryption systems is that they originated in a period of very slow data communications and may not be at all adequate in high-speed networks.

In a network any of the encryption algorithms available will slow down the communications process. There are, however, at least two ways of looking at this problem. If files, as they are stored on disk at a computer site, are encrypted, then simply sending such a file across a communications channel is, in principle, no more of a problem than sending plaintext. If, however, encryption was done "on the fly" at several layers of a layered network architecture, throughput might well be slowed considerably. If the network is already slow (say, 19.2 Kb/s or slower), then this is not much of a problem, since encryption might be faster than the network anyway. On the other hand, if the network was a 10 Mb/s

IEEE 802.3 (Ethernet) or a 16 Mb/s Token Ring or 150 Mb/s MAN or FDDI, then there could be serious deterioration of throughput. To get some sense of the problem, note Figure 5.4. The drawing is similar to that found in Figure 3.5, but in Figure 5.4 we have shaded those layers in which encryption can be used. The situation is bad enough when only end-systems are involved, but if the network was to use link encryption as well as end-system encryption, then the encrypting process might take place multiple times at the lower three layers before getting from one end-system to another. I won't even attempt a calculation of the throughput degradation, but it could be substantial.

Key Management

The task of key management is the control of key selection and key distribution in a cryptographic system. A key is a piece of digital information that interacts with encryption algorithms to control

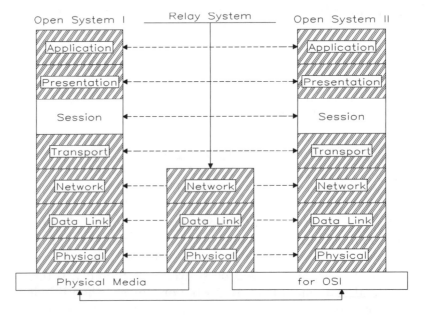

Figure 5.4 OSI Layers at Which Encryption Can Take Place.

encryption of information and, thus, must be protected from disclosure. With conventional encryption systems, both ends of the communication link must have a copy of the key, thus potentially compromising security. This is mitigated to some extent by frequent changes of the key as well as electronic public key cryptographic dissemination of private key material. The alternative is a public key cryptosystem that depends on two keys.

There are three basic approaches to key distribution: distributed, centralized, and hybrid. Even more basic, however, is the method of key transport. Will keys be distributed physically by a keyfill device or downline-loaded by transmission over the channel? Some would argue that the key should never be transported over the communication channel, but rather by a trusted courier. When this approach is used, a relatively large number of keys is usually transported in a keyfill device and loaded at each site. The key to be used for particular transmissions is selected by a real-time clock or index. The method of selecting keys and ensuring that crypto-devices are using the correct key is extremely important. A distributed approach to key management implies that each cipher device is loaded with one or more key-encrypting keys or with a number of session keys and that the session keys are exchanged on a periodic basis.[18]

A key distribution center (KDC) is the element in a system that generates and distributes cryptographic key variables. If a key distribution center exists, it will have the responsibility for key generation and distribution. Creation of keys may be centralized or in the cipher device, but selection is always controlled by the cipher devices; it's never under the control of a centralized key distribution center. In a centralized system the key distribution center will download the keys to each of the cipher devices on a periodic basis. These keys are encrypted with a key-encrypting key, which may be common to the system or unique to each cipher device. The methods used may also vary, of course, according to whether one is using a public or private key system.[19] A hybrid system distributes key-encrypting keys from a central location, and the session keys (keys used to encrypt data) are exchanged in a distributed manner between cipher devices. The fact of the matter is that when one uses a public key one needs to include certification or authentication. A certification center is needed to make sure that the parties exchanging keys are in fact authorized and that one of them is not an eavesdropper. Otherwise, an eavesdropper can use a public key to place two ciphering units in a link.

Applications at Risk

As has been documented throughout this book, data security and integrity are crucial issues for virtually every private corporation and government agency using data communications networks to transfer information from one point to another. This is especially true for agencies that employ distributed databases, electronic mail, and electronic funds transfers in their everyday activities. For most agencies, information is an asset to which value can be attributed, and the loss of assets that accompany the loss (through disclosure) of information can indeed be great. Data encryption is particularly effective in protecting the privacy of information.[20] With the growing use of electronic mail on a national and international level, the security of such mail is particularly important. The U.S. government is looking closely at the problems of abuse of electronic mail systems by outsiders as well as internal employees.

The National Security Agency is administering the Secure Data Network Standard program for development of network protocols to ensure the security of federal government Open Systems Interconnection networks. The program's Key Management Protocol and Message Security Protocol concern encryption of sensitive EMail messages. The Internet Activities Board Privacy Task Force is developing standards around authenticity, confidentiality and message integrity into Internet's electronic mail. The Protection of Logistics Unclassified/Sensitive Data (PLUS) program from the Department of Defense is advising more use of the Data Encryption Standard as well as other encryption systems for unclassified but still sensitive federal government applications.[21]

With the increasing popularity of electronic mail systems, users must come to understand that in most systems in use today there is very little attention paid to maintaining the confidentiality of mail messages. EMail systems, used by more than 10 million corporate and federal workers in 1990, are particularly vulnerable to abuse by outsiders and disgruntled insiders. A November 1990 survey by SoftSwitch Inc., a Wayne, PA, supplier of electronic mail and wide area networking software to the federal government, indicated that 88 percent of the respondents from Fortune 200 companies said the use of EMail within their companies increased significantly in 1990, and 69 percent said they would increase spending on EMail in 1991, despite the uncertain economic climate at that time.[22] In his book, *The Cuckoo's Egg,* Clifford Stoll cites the misuse of electronic-messaging systems as one of the leading techniques for gaining unauthorized access to computer systems.[23]

At the very least it is possible for systems programmers to browse through files of electronic mail. Anyone who has ever managed systems people has probably had to admonish one or more of them about such browsing. This problem arises largely when messages are stored rather than when they are enroute someplace. If it is important enough, however, it is clear that mail messages could be intercepted enroute and electronic mail itself be used to gain access to remote systems. Many of the problems regarding electronic mail can be solved through the use of some method of encryption, since encryption will protect the confidentiality of the information concerned.

Notes

1. Data encryption standard (DES)—An algorithm to be implemented in electronic hardware devices and used for the cryptographic protection of digital, binary-coded information. For the relevant publications see "Data Encryption Standard," *Federal Information Processing Standard (FIPS) Publication 46,* January 15, 1977, also published as *American*

National Standard Data Encryption Algorithm, American National Standards Institute, Inc., December 30, 1980, and supplemented with "DES Modes of Operation," *Federal Information Processing Standard (FIPS) Publication 81*, December 2, 1980; "Telecommunications: Interoperability and Security Requirements for Use of the Data Encryption Standard in the Physical Layer of Data Communications," *Federal Standard of the General Services Administration,* August 3, 1983, FED-STD-1026; "Telecommunications: General Security Requirements for Equipment Using the Data Encryption Standard," *Federal Standard of the General Services Administration*, April 14, 1982, FED-STD-1027; and "Telecommunications: Interoperability and Security Requirements for Use of the Data Encryption Standard with CCITT Group 3 Facsimile Equipment," *Federal Standard of the General Services Administration*, April 4, 1985, FED-STD-1028.

2. B. W. Burnham, *DES: Applications and Uses*, Report No.: SAND-85-0530C; CONF-850428-2, Department of Energy, Washington, DC, 1985, 2 pp., DOE Computer Security Group conference, Richland, WA, April 16, 1985. NTIS Accession Number: DE85010121/XAB.

3. Landgarten, pp. 16–18.

4. Thomas Wm. Madron, *Enterprise Computing* (New York: John Wiley & Sons, 1991), p. 99.

5. Whitfield Diffie and Martin E. Hellman, *Cryptanalysis of the NBS Data Encryption Standard* (Stanford, CA: Information Systems Lab., May 1976), 47 pp. Technical Report. NTIS Accession Number: PB-262 781/8. See also Michael Swaine, "Commercial Banks' Data Code Is Crackable, Expert Says," *InfoWorld*, Mar 22 1982, Vol. 4, No. 11, March 22, 1982 p. 37–38; and "Cryptographer Decries Inadequacy of Data-Encryption Standard," *InfoWorld*, Vol. 4, No. 11, March 22, 1982, p. 10.

6. See the following for some background on the controversy: Anon., "Encryption Standard To Get Reprieve," (Data Encryption Standard extended five years), *Computerworld*, Vol. 21, No. 42, Oct. 19, 1987, p. 1(2); Anon., "DES Issues Still

Unresolved after a Decade," (Data Encryption Standard) *Computers in Banking*, Vol. 4, No. 10, Oct. 1987, p. 12(2); Anon., "DES Gets an Encore," (the U.S. National Security Agency's Data Encryption Standard) (Computerworld Focus), *Computerworld*, Vol. 21, No. 22A, June 3, 1987 p. 47(1); Anon., "Bankers Get NSA to Agree to Extend the Life of DES," (data encryption standard), *Computer Decisions*, March 23, 1987, Vol. 19, No. 6, March 23, 1987, p. 16(3); The destiny of DES, (Data Encryption Standard), *Datamation*, Vol. 33, No. 5, March 1, 1987, p. 79(4).

7. See the recent standards documents already listed in Note 1. For a recent applied description of DES in which there is C code for doing encryption and decryption, see Al Stevens, "Hacks, Spooks, and Data Encryption," *Dr. Dobbs Journal*, Vol. 15, No. 9, Sept. 1990, pp. 127ff. For an explanation of DES see Asael Dror, *Byte*, Vol. 14, No. 6, June 1989, pp. 267ff.

8. D. K. Branstad and M. E. Smid, "Integrity and Security Standards Based on Cryptography," *Pub. in Computer Security*, Vol. 1, No. 3, Nov. 1982, pp. 255–260.

9. See Dennis Branstad, *DES Modes of Operation* (Washington, DC: National Bureau of Standards, 2 Dec 80), 31 pp., and Michael J. O'Brien, *Technical Specifications of a Proposed Federal Information Processing Standard on the Modes of Operation for the Data Encryption Standard* (Washington, DC: National Bureau of Standards, April 1980), 40 pp., Report No.: NBSIR-80-2019. NTIS Accession Number: PB80-183189.

10. *Computer Simulation of Group 3 Facsimile Encryption*, Final technical information bulletin, Delta Information Systems, Inc., Horsham, PA, sponsored by the National Communications System, Washington, DC, Report No.: NCS-TIB-87-10, March 1987, 70 pp., NTIS Accession Number: AD-A199 330/2/XAB.

11. T. N. Lebano, *TCP/IP Gateway Interconnecting AX.25 Packet Radio Networks to the Defense Data Network*, Master's thesis (Wright-Patterson AFB, OH: Air Force Inst. of Tech., School

of Engineering, Dec. 1988), 106 pp., NTIS Accession Number: AD-A202 733/2/XAB.

12. W. Diffie and M. E. Hellman, "New Directions in Cryptography," *Transactions of the IEEE on Information Theory*, IT-22, No. 6, 644-654, Nov. 1976.

13. See Chapter 8 in D. W. Davies and W. L. Price, *Security for Computer Networks*, 2nd Edition (Chichester, UK: John Wiley & Sons, 1989) for a more detailed description of how key systems operate. For an applied approach to cryption algorithms, see Rick Grehan, "Cloak and Data," *Byte*, Vol. 15, No. 6, June 1990, pp. 311ff.

14. This description is derived from D. W. Davies and W. L. Price, *Security for Computer Networks*, 2nd Edition (New York: Wiley, 1989), pp. 209ff.

15. R. Merkle and M. E. Hellman, "Hidden Information and Signatures in Trapdoor Knapsacks," *IEEE Transactions in Information Theory*, Sept. 1978.

16. Deborah Russell and G. T. Gangemi, Sr., Computer Security Basics (Sebastopol, CA: O'Reilly & Associates, Inc., 1991), p. 188.

17. Stephen Thomas Kent, *Encryption-Based Protection Protocols for Interactive User-Computer Communication*, Master's thesis April 1975–May 1976 (Cambridge, MA: Mass. Inst. of Tech. Cambridge Lab for Computer Science, 1976), 124 pp. NTIS Accession Number: AD-A026 911/8. This thesis developed a complete set of protocols, which utilize a block cipher, e.g., the NBS data encryption standard, for protection interactive user-computer communication over physical unsecured channels. The protocols include facilities for key distribution, two-way login authentication, resynchronization following channel disruption, and expedition of high-priority messages.

18. Arnold M. McCalmont, "Lock Your Data Network," *Communications News*, Vol. 27, No. 7, July 1990, p. 45(1).

19. Ibid.

20. G. D. Wishon, *Data Security and Integrity in Open Networks:*

A Prototype Implementation of Internet Standard Privacy-Enhanced Electronic Mail, Master's thesis (Wright-Patterson AFB, OH: Air Force Inst. of Tech., 1990). Report No.: AFIT/CI/CIA-90-045, 339 pp. NTIS Accession Number: AD-A224 641/1/XAB.

21. J. B. Miles, "E-mail Systems Are Vulnerable, But Security's Winning Attention," *Government Computer News*, Vol. 10, No. 3, Feb. 4, 1991, p. 29(2).

22. As reported by J. B. Miles, "E-mail Systems Are Vulnerable, But Security's Winning Attention."

23. Clifford Stoll, *The Cuckoo's Egg: Tracking a Spy Through the Maze of Computer Espionage* (New York: Doubleday, 1989).

CHAPTER 6

Methods for Preventing Unauthorized Access

In a network or its components, access control is constituted by the tasks performed by hardware, software, and administrative controls to monitor a system operation, ensure data integrity, perform user identification, record system access and changes, and grant access to users. An early method developed for maintaining the integrity of information was the use of user identification numbers and passwords. Early use of these techniques sought to prohibit unauthorized access to computer systems per se. Later uses of passwords applied the method to files, subsystems, and other information resources that needed protection. Besides IDs and passwords, there are hardware techniques, such as call-back systems, biometric devices, and encryption techniques, that limit access. In this chapter we will survey the various methods of preventing or limiting unauthorized access, and assess the effectiveness of those methods.

The responsibility for security, of course, resides with the people responsible for corporate networks. Network managers often maintain that they scrupulously employ every security feature available to them and want more features to be added. At the same time, vendors of security software decry the difficulty of selling into the private sector. The discrepancy here has its roots in the major gap between what network management perceives as vital and what corporate management will foot the bill for. Allowing levels of security to be dictated by purely financial considerations is foolhardy. The corporate environment is rife with opportunities for unauthorized access to corporate data. Users neglect proper log-off procedures and share passwords. Security levels are not fully enforced. Local area networks are particularly vulnerable. A single workstation or communications device that is added to the network without the proper security measures can open a gateway for the theft or loss of information worth millions.[1]

Introduction

Communications security provides data protection through access control. Most systems use the basic communications channel for cryptographic key management, but some configurations and protocols are simplified by "using a third port" for crypto-management. Protection is also gained through backup crypto-variable distribution centers connected to the main distribution center by a secure link. Cryptographic ciphering devices should be located where they can be physically protected, observed, and interfaced. Security equipment and systems use keys, or secret codes and crypto variables, to protect information from different users.[2] As was noted in Chapter 3, access control can take place in the OSI model at the application, transport, and/or network layers. A form of access control can also take place (although this is outside the OSI model) between a host system (a computer or terminal server on a network) and an incoming modem (this is on the digital side of the loop); or between the host-side modem and the physical communications line (usually, though not exclusively, a telephone line). The problem with the latter notion is that it applies almost exclusively to dial access systems and ignores networks of interconnected LANs and other modern networking systems.

The trend in computing to move away from centralized mainframe computers and mid-range systems to microcomputer-based networks opens up the access of information to undesirables and makes data security a more pressing issue. Accessing information on a microcomputer-based network can be done at any workstation, and tracing the origin of intrusion is often impossible. Some mainframes and minicomputers offer security provisions based on granting and tracking user privileges; microcomputers have no such system. Local area networks (LANs) began as an innovative way of linking several related microcomputers, but has blossomed into a much larger program where it is not strange to see over 500 microcomputers linked on a LAN.[3] The increasing reliance on LANs is, in fact, forcing many organizations to reinvent processes and procedures that are well known in mainframe computer environments. Moreover, it is also requiring that LAN operations start to resemble the older, more traditional multi-user computer operational environments.

Another way of thinking about access control is that we may wish to control access to a network, to a host (a computer, a terminal server, a router, or some similar device), to an application running on a computer, to a database, or to some other undefined resource. That is why in the OSI model access control is defined at three different layers. Access through a terminal server, for example, may be controlled at the OSI network layer. That would not, however, take care of all users—only those who dialed in from the outside. Thus, access control might be implemented at the transport layer of a host system, thus catching anyone who got past a router or terminal server. Once past access control mechanisms at the transport layer, however, it is probable that not all users should have access to all applications. Thus, a second level of access control might be implemented at the application layer to prohibit access to user applications or data.

One way to limit access, regardless of the layer at which access testing takes place, is through authentication techniques. Authentication mechanisms 1) ensure that a message is genuine, has arrived exactly as it was sent, and came from the stated source; and/or 2) verifies the identity of an individual, such as a person at a remote terminal or the sender of a message. In OSI nomenclature, authentication refers to the certainty that the data received comes from the supposed origin; it is not extended to include the integrity of the data that are being transmitted. Basically, authentication is protection against fraudulent transactions by establishing the validity of messages, stations, individuals, or originators. Authentication is essential for data integrity, and network designers need to know the strength of authentication security, what is being authenticated by the service, and at what level in the OSI framework it should be provided. Peer-entity authentication supports connection-oriented networks. It provides confidence in the identities of end-points by means of two-way or three-way exchanges. Authentication that relies on cryptographic techniques is known as "strong authentication" because, unlike passwords, the cryptographic key resides in a device or computer and is therefore not easy to replicate.[4] The primary issues in choosing an authentication method are price, strength, and technique infrastructure. Simple testing of user IDs and passwords is the most elementary form of authentication.

There are, however, other techniques of access control. With the prudent use of access controls, most secure areas or systems can be regulated. A very popular method for controlling access is through the use of hand-held password generators (HPG).[5] HPGs, or tokens, are pocket-sized devices, similar in appearance to pocket calculators, that generate unique one-time passwords for each access attempt to a properly equipped host or network. A related technique is the use of identification cards encoded with access information. Cards can be encoded with information in a number of ways—the most common, and most easily copied, is the magnetic strip. A barium ferrite card is factory programmed and more difficult to copy, and a Wiegand Effect card is more expensive, but nearly impossible to copy. Card access is often coupled with personal identification numbers to make it more difficult for stolen cards to be used. Most systems will destroy a card that has been reported as stolen. Biometric devices are more esoteric; they are machines that measure unique physical traits such as fingerprints, palm prints, retinal patterns, and voice patterns. When combined with identification codes, biometric devices may provide a higher level of security than most other techniques.[6]

Biometric systems are most frequently associated with physical access to physical facilities rather than to electronic access to networks (see Chapter 9). Because security threats can come from inappropriate physical access, however, it is an issue to be considered. Physical access control systems use one or more of three basic methods to identify a person: combination lock, portable key, or physical attribute. Combination locks, or stored-code systems, use a series of numbers stored in the human brain and in the lock mechanism; portable keys, in the form of a metal key, an ID card, or a badge, are held by the person and inserted in a reader that senses the code; and physical attributes, such as a human face, are recognized by a guard, who compares the actual face with a picture-badge. All three techniques have basic weaknesses, however, and the best security systems combine features of two or all three. Among the options available with keypad systems are combination time, error alarm, time penalty, door delay, hostage alarm, remote indication, and code storage.[7]

The basic lesson of this book is that computer security is no stronger than the weakest link in the chain. A fundamental "law" of security is that users should only receive the amount of system access required to accomplish their specific tasks.[8] Don Gurski has suggested that four key principles should be addressed when securing a network:

1. It must be possible to validate the network configuration, so there are no unknown weak links;
2. The network should only allow access from authorized locations;

3. Disclosure of sensitive data during transmission should be prevented; and

4. Electromagnetic radiation from devices on the network should be minimized.

In single-level defense, user attributes are used to identify all users. Examples are passwords, questionnaires, card-keys, and biometric systems such as fingerprint monitors. The latter are effective but expensive and not easy to move. In a two-level defense, location identifiers as well as user attributes can be used.[9] In the remainder of this chapter, we will take a closer look at some of the issues just introduced.

Techniques of Access Control

It was once the case that the primary means of access control to a computer system was the key to the front door of the computer room. With the growth of networking during the 1980s, however, "access" came to be associated with electronic rather than physical entrance to computers. Certainly, issues of physical security and physical access are important in the 1990s, but the more insidious problems revolve around electronic access. Some of the techniques of access control are similar to, or identical with, user authentication methods. Remember that access control consists of the tasks performed by hardware, software, and administrative controls to monitor a system operation, ensure data integrity, perform user identification, record system access and changes, and grant access to users. Authentication ensures that 1) a message is genuine, has arrived exactly as it was sent, and came from the stated source; and 2) verifies the identity of an individual, such as a person at a remote terminal or the sender of a message. In OSI nomenclature, authentication somewhat more narrowly refers to the certainty that the data received comes from the supposed origin; it is not extended to include the integrity of the data that are being transmitted.

Some of the mechanisms used for authentication may also be used for access control, particularly where the objective is to identify a legitimate user. Once having identified a legitimate user, it is the task of access control (rather than authentication) to grant access to that user. Thus, as we have already noted in Chapter 3, legitimate users are usually identified through determining who the user is, what the user possesses, and/or what the user knows. If access to a network is based only on a User ID and password, then these two items of information, for that network, provide the information for all three forms of user identification. Simple User IDs and passwords may not provide sufficient security, however.

Back in 1978 a unique approach to the solution of computer network security problems was suggested in a research report sponsored at that time by the U.S. National Bureau of Standards.[10] The approach was based on a network resource, called a Network Security Center (NSC), that would perform the functions of user identification/authentication and access request authorization. The NSC would work in concert with Network Cryptographic Devices (NCDs) to enforce access control policy through the creation or denial of logically separate cryptographic connections between subjects (users) and objects (resources). According to the author, Frank Heinrich, the use of an NSC in a network would provide effective control over network access, provide for audit data collection, and provide protection against tampering or modification of the access control database. For the most part, such suggestions have been ignored, partly because of the cost of implementation and partly because most organizations fail to provide adequate support for security. The point is that concern for network access control is not a new problem, but it is one that has taken on more urgency in the 1990s.

Who You Are

Depending on the level of security required for a particular network, the determination of who you are may be as simple as the use of a user identification number or name (the User ID), or as complex as digital signatures or various forms of biometric scanning devices. Since User IDs are not usually designed to be kept secret (as are passwords), only the use of a User ID would be completely inadequate as a security mechanism. A User ID in combination with other techniques, however, might prove to be adequate in a given situation. If the determination of who you are is important in a given situation, however, it may be necessary to use more sophisticated approaches.

Network and computer access control can be made very secure by biometric security devices verifying such characteristics as thumb prints, retinal patterns, voice prints, or other physically unique attributes.[11] Biometric techniques are usually associated with physical access to a facility, although the same approaches could easily be used for access to a computer system. Thumb-Scan, Inc., for example, markets a device called the ThumbScanner specifically designed for network/computer access. ThumbScanner is a fingerprint device that compares the current print to a previously stored fingerprint image of the user. When logging on to a network, the user at a remote workstation first enters the usual User ID and password, and then places the enrolled finger on a glass platen. The newly read fingerprint is then compared with the previously enrolled print before access is granted. This particular device works on a workstation that is IBM/PC/XT/AT compatible. Similar systems include those from Identix, Inc. (Touchsafe) and Fingermatrix, Inc. (Ridge Reader Mint). The verification times claimed by these manufacturers varies from one to three seconds and prices (in 1992) begin around $1,500 (and up). Thus, there are at least two inhibitions to the use of these devices: cost and time.[12]

What You Possess

There are various ways in which access can be controlled through what a user possesses. The use of a magnetic card with an associated reader is one of the techniques now coming into use. More often found in physical security systems as a replacement for a physical key, the card reader is considered an additional layer of security, and using a computer memory adds the option to lock or open all doors in the event of a power failure. Just as other technologies developed primarily for physical access control have been adapted to network access systems, so too are cards that carry or generate passwords or phrases difficult to duplicate.[13] More sophisticated than an encoded card is the hand-held password generators (HPG), sometimes called tokens, which are pocket-sized devices that generate a unique one-time password for each access attempt to a properly equipped host or network.

One of the major problems in the use of passwords is password management. Once a password has been issued or devised, keeping it secret becomes a problem. The best clear password would be one that is a randomly generated sequence of numbers and/or alphabetic characters. This, in fact, is the approach being taken by some of the long distance telephone companies in their attempt to thwart the theft of telephone credit card numbers (which, in addition to being an aid to accounting, is also a kind of password). Unfortunately, many people find it difficult to memorize such passwords and consequently have it written or printed in various places, as well as permanently encoded in login scripts used by many terminal emulators. Various encryption techniques have been developed to encrypt the password itself so that it is not in the clear. This requires, however, possessing a key to decrypt the password, and this can present the same security problem as did the original password. A way of dealing with even clear passwords is to require users to change passwords on a regular basis (every month, for example).

Another way of dealing with the problem is to use HPGs. With such a system, every user must possess an HPG for use with each access attempt. The HPG itself has an appearance similar to a hand-held calculator and generates passwords from a user-unique "seed." The seed is often packaged in the form of a key, calculator, or card. In order to work, a standard or proprietary algorithm resides at both the access point (which may be in the HPG itself or in a stand-alone reader) and in the access control software at the host site. Each device will generate a different password from user key data. Some variable data may also be introduced which changes for each access attempt. It is apparent that there must be a key management system for generating and securing the seed data.

There are two typical methods of operation used by HPGs: asynchronous, one-time password generation or challenge-response operation; and synchronous password generation. Asynchronous password generation, which is the most frequently used, generates passwords on the basis of a response to a challenge sent by the host. The host has access to the same algorithms operating in the HPG, as well as knowledge of what keys have been encoded in the HPG. A variation of this approach is to use it in conjunction with a memorized personal identification number (PIN), thus resulting in a hybrid PIN/asynchronous system. With synchronous systems there is no challenge-response formula. Rather, the HPG and the host synchronize themselves via some commonly known item of information, such as time or use history. A PIN is sometimes combined with synchronous systems as well, producing a PIN/synchronous password generation. Automatic teller machines (ATM) are the most widely used access devices to banking networks that combine PINs and magnetic cards.

What You Know

The traditional "what you know" technique, still the most widely used access control method, is the password. A password may be assigned by the system or may be user generated. Repeated breaches of network security have demonstrated many times over that the memorized password is often far from secure. In order to improve security, passwords must be changed frequently, be long and obscure enough to resist acquisition, and must be maintained in absolute secrecy. As any MIS or network executive will attest, however, it is not at all unusual for users to paste User IDs and passwords written on a scrap of paper to a remote terminal device. Moreover, most people use easily remembered passwords, such as the names of spouses or children, birth dates, middle names, or something similar. Thus, guessing at passwords becomes a feasible way of breaking into a system. These problems have caused the development of HPG systems as well as other, more complex access methods.

We have already noted that some additional security for passwords can be achieved if they are encrypted. At least the file of passwords is much more difficult to read, even if it is breached. But encryption requires the possession of a key of some sort, and a key can be lost or stolen. Access to passwords may be controlled by the use of a personal identification number, and may be used in conjunction with encryption systems. In effect, however, this simply adds a second password to the process and still carries with it all the problems involved with passwords in the first place.

A variation on the "what you know" motif is the use of several items of information presumably possessed only by the user. Requests for such information as mother's maiden name constitute a "questionnaire," with the resulting data presumably uniquely identifying the user. While far from foolproof, the addition of a questionnaire for access control is less expensive than HPGs or an encoded card system. While an entry questionnaire can improve security, it also lengthens the access time. Moreover, the comparative data must be stored in some file, so the file itself may have to be encrypted and further secured from access. All of this further reduces the friendliness of the system and increases the frustration of the user.

Public Networks

One of the elements of the U.S. infrastructure that is often taken for granted is the integrity and reliability of the public networks on which virtually all wide area networks (WANs) are based. Unfortunately, public telecommunications networks, which handle a tremendous amount of traffic, are not secure. Because of an increasing number of major failures of the AT&T public telephone network, the FCC in November 1991 issued orders to that company to take care of their reliability problems. Thus, there is the possibility on the one hand that public networks will simply fail, and on the other hand that the confidentiality or privacy of information carried over them is not assured. As Michael Bacon has noted, international communications, because they pass through international exchanges, are particularly vulnerable to security breaches and compromise. It is often easier to intercept and exploit public communications than private systems. Microwave communications and other technological advances, such as satellites, facsimile, videoconferencing, and cellular radio, are also susceptible to compromise, particularly interception (eavesdropping). "The truth is," according to Bacon, "that public networks are not secure; information carried over them cannot be confidential and integrity is not guaranteed."[14]

If international links are used, the problem is magnified because points of access are relatively easy to identify and messages easy to intercept. In some areas of the world it is apparently common for a friendly telephone employee to assist in the interception of various forms of telecommunications traffic, especially telex. Even in the United States, however, conventional transmission media are quite simple to tap. The tap can be passive (i.e., it only receives) or active (i.e., it can also transmit information). Connections can be direct or inductive: direct taps involve a connection to the transmission medium; inductive taps do not. Moreover, the cost to establish such taps is trivial. Even fiber optic cable, once thought to be less vulnerable to tapping, can be accessed with repair kits costing under $2,000. Standard twisted pair telephone connections can be tapped for next to nothing. Unfortunately, wiretapping public communications is frequently easier than tapping private systems; the medium is more accessible, the risk of detection is lower because of the wide geographical area of coverage, and the return is often as great, particularly with international calls.[15] While X.25 public data networks (PDNs) may take some research in order to access a targeted user, even this can be accomplished. Partly because of the rapid development of technology, legislation has failed to keep abreast with increasing security concerns, and severe penalties are frequently exacted only for a breech of government security.

The increasing use of non-wire media (microwave, satellite, cellular radio, and packet radio systems) open up an entire new arena for security failures. Cellular and packet radio systems in particular can be accessed with relatively inexpensive equipment often available from consumer outlets. Microwave communications is only a little more complex and expensive. The interception of satellite signals, which not long ago presented significant cost and technical problems to access, have also become vulnerable. Cellular radio, in particular, is susceptible to "tapping" with inexpensive equipment. In fact, most cellular systems are now sold with a warning that cellular communications is not a "private" medium and may be overheard. When cellular radio is used for data communications, security can be problematic.

With the increasing integration of facsimile (FAX) systems with data communications, and since virtually all FAX transmissions take place over public networks, FAX is also a target for interception. FAX systems are based on international standards that are well known. Fundamentally, FAX is a standardized system for transferring FAX graphics files. Once a FAX "file" has been captured, it can be printed with cheap, easily available hardware and software.

How do we protect transmissions of the sort just described? Confidentiality or privacy is maintained through encryption systems. How much do we have to be concerned about such intrusions? As with all such questions, the answer is, "it depends." The competitive advantage that can come from the rapid communication of information is lost, of course, when others intercept that information. Thus, a security audit of potential security threats should reveal how much a particular organization should be concerned. All systems need some level of protection. Governments and large, multinational corporations may need to be more concerned than a small business or a university or a religious organization, even though the latter organizations may have other legitimate security concerns.

Private Network Access Control

As with many other distinctions in the networking world, that between "public" and "private" networks is becoming less and less a reality. Even that paragon of the private network, the LAN, is no longer immune from the issues that have for many years confronted WANs. Especially with the growing popularity of electronic mail and with its growing use in business and government, the ability to send and receive messages from a local private network to someone on the other side of the world is becoming popular. CompuServe, among other services, for example, offers global connectivity. CompuServe allows you to communicate easily and economically to users all over the world from, among other places, a Novell LAN through MHS. MHS (Message Handling Service) is an electronic mail system developed by Action Technologies, Inc., and licensed by Novell for its NetWare operating systems. It allows for the transfer and routing of messages between users and provides store and forward capabilities. MHS also provides a gateway into IBM's PROFS, Digital's All-in-1 office automation system and X.400 message systems.

MHS version 1.5C contains all of the capabilities to connect to CompuServe and send and receive messages with CompuServe. No additional software or hardware is needed to use the CompuServe Mail Hub. To access the CompuServe Mail Hub, a CompuServe User ID must first be obtained. Many hubs have special hub services installed on them, using MHS's gateway feature. Typically, users have reached these services by addressing messages to some "user @ gtwname", where "gtwname" is the name assigned to the gateway. The administrator of the workgroup where these gateways are installed must decide whether the gateway can be reached through the CompuServe hub. One strategy for the use of the Hub is to define as a workgroup on CompuServe the name of the gateway (or a workgroup name routed via the gateway) and define on CompuServe the route to reach this workgroup via a host in your workgroup that can access the gateway.

Before messages can be sent via the CompuServe Mail Hub, the MHS network must be registered with CompuServe. Each workgroup name registered must be unique. CompuServe will prompt you for the name of the host to which CompuServe will send messages when the messages are addressed to your workgroup and have not yet been routed to users. On CompuServe this is called the default hub. The default hub will most likely be the workgroup-wide router, since the logical place to send messages that have not yet been routed to users is the place where this service is performed. (If the workgroup-wide router will not connect directly to CompuServe, the default hub may be an intermediary hub through which the workgroup-wide router can be reached.)

The point of this rather detailed description, drawn from CompuServe documentation, is to demonstrate that even LANs can now be easily interconnected through commercially available services as part of world-wide electronic mail systems. Through the CompuServe Hub, for example, an MHS user on a Novell LAN would be able (or will be able) to not only send messages to CompuServe mail addresses, but also to a wide variety of other mail services accessible from CompuServe Mail, such as the Internet, MCIMail, and ATTMail. Thus, it is difficult to suggest that even small LANs may not be connected to a worldwide information network. Even with a small, private workgroup-based LAN, there is the potential for worldwide connectivity, thereby requiring some rethinking of security needs, particularly with respect to access security.

LAN Access Control

The example of potential LAN connectivity given above illustrates that even LANs may be susceptible to external access in some form. Even if this were not the case, however, and no external connectivity existed, there can still be problems with uncontrolled access. Computer "viruses," for example, are often distributed when microcomputer users exchange programs that may have been posted on bulletin boards or other connectivity services. Thus, a trusted employee with access to an LAN not externally connected may unwittingly bring in an "infected" program, not knowing its destructive force. A *virus* is a program that may be used to "infect" a computer. After virus code is written, it is buried within an existing program. Once that program is executed, the virus code is also activated, and it attaches copies of itself to other programs in the system. Whenever an infected program is run, the virus copies itself to other programs. A virus cannot be attached to data. It must be attached to an executable program that is installed on a computer. The virus-attached program must be executed in order to activate the virus. See *logic bomb* and *worm* in the Glossary and the more extended discussion of viruses, worms, and logic bombs in Chapter 7.

There have occasionally been some unwarranted claims that have excited owners of LANs. Jon David, an independent consultant, for example, claims the existence of a Novell Netware–specific virus that can bypass Netware's read-only access controls and infect the server by allowing nodes to write to and delete files on the server without the usual privileges. David claims the virus is a version of Jerusalem B, a virus that deletes every file executed on any Friday the 13th, as well as slowing system performance by a factor of 10. The only independently reported case was at the University of Indiana where a NetWare network was shutdown for four days by the virus. Novell has disputed the claim, pointing out that the virus is (IBM/compatible) DOS-based and cannot bypass the NetWare security measures.[16] Such claims as David makes must be taken with a grain of salt, although reasonable precautions should be taken.

The key to LAN access security is to use techniques appropriate for the organization and for the level of security threats that might be posed for a specific installation. Not all organizations have the same level of risk or exposure, nor do all LANs within the same organization. Recall, however, that most threats come not from external sources (notwithstanding virus scares), but from those who already have some sort of access within the organization. LAN access security must, therefore, focus on real rather than imagined problems and threats. As with most multi-user computer environments, LAN network operating systems (NOS) provide as a basic access control the use of user names or User IDs, along with passwords. This approach has all the advantages and disadvantages discussed previously. If dial-access is required, a second level of User ID/Password protection is often provided. When more sophisticated access control is required, then other techniques may be used.

There are at least three solutions for access control that are more extensive than passwords: hardware keys, tokens, and encrypted passwords. Peter Craig has described the hardware key as devices that can be "assigned to authorized users in the same manner as keys to the front door—with security management efforts commensurate to key management. This simple solution does away with the complicated process of administering user rights by class and work group."[17] With a physical key system, the user must plug the key into the PC before he or she can successfully log on to access controlled files and programs. A *token* is a hand-held password generator designed to provide a unique password for each access attempt to a LAN (or other network) or multi-user computer system. A third level of security is provided by a public or proprietary algorithm to automatically encrypt/decrypt data files and sub-directories on individual PCs or file servers. Craig has pointed out that "Only the owner of the key, or his or her manager holding a master key, can decrypt, or open, the files protected in this manner."[18]

An important part of Craig's comment is "his or her manager holding a master key,...." It is often forgotten that the data that reside on an individual workstation or LAN in an organization belongs essentially to the organization rather than to the employees. The problem with encryption methods that are solely under the control of a single employee is that, when that individual leaves, his or her data may no longer be available to the organization, no matter how strategically or operationally important it may be. Consequently, an important aspect of access control is to ensure that management can gain access as well as an individual worker can, although this admonition carries with it an implied reduction in security, since more than one copy of the encryption key is now in use.

WAN Access Control

OSI Networks

The OSI network security architecture was discussed extensively in Chapter 3, and we will not belabor the approach here. At this point it is important to recognize that access control problems can crop up even within a system that has a well thought out security control strategy. For example, there have been concerns evidenced in OSI compliant networks revolving around the X.500 network directory. X.500 network directories designed are to be central repositories for all X.400-based (OSI message standard) network address information, including electronic mail addresses. Bob Brown has noted that users want to make their X.500 directories widely accessible, to provide employees with quick access to useful information, as well as enhance relations with trading partners. They would like to include as much information as possible. However, they do not want competitors to be able to scan directories for the purposes of gaining employment history information to hire employees away or to target employees for sales pitches. Managers need to determine how to coordinate access among directories, without providing too much access. In some cases, companies will be amenable to giving others access to their directories but will draw the line at directories of customers.[19] The point is that access issues can crop up in unexpected places, and the management of networks and computer systems need to understand this phenomenon.

IBM Mainframe Networks

OSI and TCP/IP network architectures were designed to enhance connectivity. Consequently, access to such networks may come through a variety of devices. Moreover, computers in such networks operate primarily as peers. Consequently, the issue of access can be approached from a wide variety of network access points, including connected computer systems, terminal servers, and perhaps other hardware. By contrast, IBM's System Network Architecture (SNA) was originally designed with a private centralized star network in mind and with intermediate device controllers (such as the 3374 terminal controller) were essentially passive devices. While SNA is undergoing substantial change and modification, along with the attached devices, it is still primarily an architecture for a private, centralized system. The consequence of this is that for IBM mainframe networks security has traditionally been thought of as access to the central mainframe on the system. Both IBM and other software competitors have for many years produced security software that runs under both the MVS and VM operating systems. These systems all have in common the feature that they provide security primarily through access control.

There are five commonly used security software products: CA-ACF2 (Computer Associates), Omniguard, RACF (IBM), CA-Top Secret (Computer Associates), and VMSECURE (Systems Center), all of which run on IBM operating systems.[20] Managers of IBM mainframe systems have long been critical of IBM's RACF because the onus is on the user organization to explicitly identify security areas of concern. By way of contrast, CA-ACF2, one of the most widely used security systems, protects much of what is on the system by default. ACF2, Omniguard, RACF, and Top Secret are wedded to the MVS operating system, while VMSecure is specific to the VM operating system. The software determines access by referring to a logon id database. The logon id is a record or system identifier that defines a user's identity and privileges. VMSecure offers users an open or closed system. Prior to 1990, Top Secret, RACF, and ACF2 all achieved a C2 (see Chapter 2) security rating from the U.S. government, although with increasing security concerns, higher levels of rating were acquired by 1990.[21] C2 level security has been deemed adequate in the past for systems without classified information to protect, while systems dealing with classified material are optimally of B1 clearance rating.

In November 1990, IBM made RACF available for VM as well as MVS.[22] The Resource Access Control Facility (RACF) 1.9 software package restricts access to mainframes by dictating what functions various users can perform. The program is licensed for about $927 a month. Encrypted messages can be routed to System/370 mainframes and decrypted by the 4753 Network Security, which sells for $37,675. The $1,115 4755 Cryptographic Adapter allows remote PS/2s to send the encrypted messages to the mainframe, and the $1,035 4754 Security Interface Unit includes a 12-digit keypad for entering personal identification numbers.[23] The essential strategy is to protect through a sequence of passwords, for both initial access to the computer system as well as access to specific applications. Variations on RACF are being made available by IBM for its AS/400 minicomputers and OS/2-based microcomputers.[24] This will extend RACF-like facilities to many of the variations on SNA brought about by connected LANs and newer modifications of the 3270 Display System.

In IBM mainframe environments, security concerns have extended from simple access to the mainframe computer system to access to specific database software systems, such as IBM's DB2. Methods of securing the DB2 database are improving with products from both IBM and Computer Associates International, Inc. (CA) competing and pushing technology forward as a result. CA, as noted above, has two access control products for IBM mainframes, Top Secret and ACF2, both of which are undergoing enhancements to control DB2. As the systems have classically worked, a mainframe runs an access control facility, which validates a user's ID and password and gives the user access to specific system resources. If one resource is a DB2 database, the procedure has to be performed again, this time checking the database's own internal authorization tables. Security managers want DB2 to work with RACF or the CA products so that they will not have to define authorizations and privileges twice, which is expensive and difficult.[25]

It has often been thought that IBM MVS systems were more or less immune to a virus attack. Although there have been no reported virus cases involving an MVS operating system, the danger does exist. At least one publication, *Abacus,* has printed technical information on MVS virus design by the German author B. Fix. Security loopholes like those used to invade UNIX and VM systems exist in many MVS environments and may go unnoticed and uncorrected until the system is attacked. Martin L. King, writing in *Computer Security Journal,* has examined these loop-holes and explored the techniques that viruses use to attack systems. King describes specific steps for protecting MVS systems by making use of the facilities built into commercial access control software, such as CA-ACF2, RACF, and CA-Top Secret.[26] If an IBM mainframe is interconnected to a large national or global network, such as the Internet, it may be worthwhile to at least explore the methods for protecting the system from an IBM-specific virus. However, it should be understood, that, because of the differences in the operating system structure of MVS and because IBM systems use a character coding system called EBCDIC (rather than ASCII), the *same* viruses that have attacked UNIX systems cannot be successful.

DEC Networks

Like IBM, Digital Equipment Corporation has long been concerned with the security of its VMS operating system and DECNet networks.[27] DEC's VMS and Digital Network Architecture (DNA) provide their users with many powerful features that can help to make DECnet-VAX networks more secure. When a communications circuit between two nodes is established on a DECnet network, the local node will try to initialize the DECnet-VAX software at the remote node. An added measure of security can be added to this process by requiring a password at the remote node. The use of a proxy log-in is one way of limiting user access to restricted areas in a network.[28] Because of recent security scares and because of demands from customers, DEC has recently been enhancing its security offerings, even though it has "long bragged about the internal security features of its VMS operating system."[29] DEC is now offering a full security review program, to operate in conjunction with its security software tools, to aid customers in evaluating their security requirements. VAX and MicroVAX customers can now take advantage of a new VAX/VMS Security Review Service (SRS) that includes DEC-designed software tools that cover such procedures as password implementation, disk space quota, file protection, user account implementation, proxy access procedures, DECnet installation and use, and audit procedure use. Like IBM, however, DEC security is heavily dependent on the use of password protection to control access to DEC facilities.

Access Policies

How should an organization go about dealing with network access? In many organizations in business, government, and education, the potential limitation on network access can become a serious political problem. The reason for this is that there will, even in small organizations, be many different perceptions of the "real" security threat to a network and its resources. Except in the most authoritarian of organizations, it is at least distasteful, and perhaps impossible, to implement an extensive security system without reference to the "customers" that use those resources. Actually, the establishment of an access control policy may be even a bit more complicated than just noted. Jonathan D. Moffett and Morris S. Sloman have noted that models for access control have not addressed the problem of the source of authority for access control decisions that arise, particularly in commercial organizations. An access control policy needs to be developed, and authority for permitting access must be defined in the policy model. Moffett and Sloman identify five components of an access control policy: users, resources, operations, authority, and domain.[30]

Moffett, Sloman, and Kevin Twidle have proposed a framework for specifying access control policy for very large distributed processing systems. Distributed systems typically consist of multiple interconnected networks and span the computer systems belonging to different organizations. A result of distribution has been the need for cooperation between independent managers to specify access control policy. An organization's security policy specification should permit interaction between organizations, while limiting the scope of what objects can be accessed and what operations can be performed on them. The large numbers of objects in such systems make it impractical to specify access control policy in terms of individual objects. Domains can be used to group objects and structure the management of access control policy. Access rules are introduced as a means of specifying the access rights between a domain of user objects and a domain of target objects, in terms of the permitted operations as well as constraints such as user location and time of day.[31]

Even when the organization is relatively small, a written access policy is advisable so that users will understand the need for and the meaning of network security. Access control is, after all, designed not only to protect the organization, but also to protect the individual user and his or her data. In other words, access control problems are not solved simply by buying a security package. Rather, the security package should be the end result of consultations based on an effort to identify real security access needs, rather than being based on hypothetical issues.

Notes

1. Peter Stephenson, "It's Time To Get Serious About Network Security," *LAN Times*, Vol. 8, No. 9, May 6, 1991, p. 68(1).

2. Arnold M. McCalmont, "Lock Your Data Network," *Communications News*, Vol. 27, No. 7, July 1990, p. 45(1). The concern about access control has been around for a number of years. See, for example, E. Springer, "Current Status of Link Access Control and Encryption Systems," Department

of Energy, Washington, DC, Los Alamos National Lab, NM, Report No.: LA-UR-84-465; CONF-8404117-2, 1984, 5 pp., NTIS Accession Number: DE84009604.

3. Peter Craig, "Individual Access Control Will Secure Data in a Network," *Computing Canada*, Vol. 16, No. 23, Nov. 8, 1990, p. 71(1).

4. Michael Fecko, "Authentication Checks Who You Are, What You Know," *Government Computer News*, Vol. 7, No. 21, Oct. 10, 1988, p. 97(2).

5. Anon., "Network Access Control Systems: Technology Overview," *Datapro Reports on Information Security* (Delran, NJ: McGraw-Hill, 1991), p. IS36-001-121.

6. Rick Friedman, "Access Control Systems That Are Hard To Beat," *The Office*, Vol. 111, No. 3, March 1990, p. 79(3).

7. Anon., "Principles of Access Control," *Modern Office Technology*, Vol. 34, No. 11, Nov. 1989, p. 44(3).

8. George W. Muller, "User Access Control," *Data Base Monthly*, Vol. 7, No. 9, July 1987, p. 42(1).

9. Don Gurski, "How To Attain Network Security," *Canadian Datasystems*, Vol. 19, No. 3, March 1987, p. 68(4).

10. Frank Heinrich, *Computer Science and Technology: The Network Security Center: A System Level Approach to Computer Network Security* (Santa Monica, CA: System Development Corp., Jan. 1978), sponsored by the National Bureau of Standards, Washington, DC Inst. for Computer Sciences and Technology, Report No.: NBS-SP-500-21-Vol-2; Contract No.: NBS-5-35934; NBS-6401112, 74 pp. NTIS Accession Number: PB-276 772/1.

11. Averil Reisman, "Biometric Devices Offer Data Access Control," *Computer & Software News*, Vol. 5, No. 48, Nov. 30, 1987, p. 49(1).

12. Anon., "Biometric Access Control Systems: Comparison Columns," *Datapro Reports on Information Security* (Delran, NJ: McGraw-Hill, 1990), pp. IS42-001-356, 357.

13. John Naudts, "Access Control Market Gives Clients Many

Options," *Government Computer News*, Vol. 6, No. 3, Feb. 13, 1987, p. 40(2).

14. Michael Bacon, "Assessing Public Network Security," *Telecommunications*, Vol. 23, No. 12, Dec. 1989, p. 19(2).

15. Ibid.

16. Michael Alexander, "Netware Virus Threat Disputed," *Computerworld*, Vol. 24, No. 47, Nov. 19, 1990, p. 67(1).

17. Peter Craig, "Individual Access Control Will Secure Data in a Network," *Computing Canada*, Vol. 16, No. 23, Nov. 8, 1990, p. 71(1).

18. Ibid.

19. Bob Brown, "Users of X.500 Directories See Access Control Problem; Security Concerns May Slow X.500 Acceptance," *Network World*, Vol. 7, No. 44, Oct. 29, 1990, p. 4(2).

20. For a comparison of these products see Stuart C. Henderson, "A Comparison of Data Access Control Packages: Part II," *Computer Security Journal*, Vol. 5, No. 1, Summer 1988, p. 67(38); and David Bicknell, "Hack Through the Security Labyrinth," *Computer Weekly*, No. 1163, May 11, 1989, p. 10(1).

21. Rick Vizachero, "IBM Keeps Up with Competition By Achieving B1 for MVS/ESA," *Government Computer News*, Vol. 9, No. 25, Nov. 26, 1990, p. 32(1).

22. Robert Moran, "IBM Spices Up Batch Offering," *Computerworld*, Vol. 23, No. 45, Nov. 6, 1989, p. 27(2). Note also the operating system security enhancements coming from IBM: Anon., "IBM Adds C1 Security Features to VM-SA Release 2," *Computergram International*, No. 1219, July 13, 1989, p. CGI07130001.

23. Tom Smith, "IBM's New Release of RACF, Other Security Tools Bow," *Network World*, Vol. 6, No. 43, Oct. 30, 1989, p. 4(2).

24. Jean S. Bozman, "RACF's Reach To Include PCs, Minis," *Computerworld*, Vol. 23, No. 20, May 15, 1989, p. 108(1).

25. Vin McClellan, "The Coming Battle Over DB2 Security: IBM,

CA Face Off in Efforts To Meet Customer Demand for Streamlined DB2 Protection," *Information Week*, No. 240, Oct. 9, 1989, p. 78(4).

26. Martin L. King, "Do We Have a Virus Problem with MVS Systems?," *Computer Security Journal*, Vol. 5, No. 2, Winter 1990, p. 57(7).

27. Note the comparisons of VMS and MVS in Robert A. McKosky, "Security Features of VMS and MVS with Emphasis on Their Vulnerability to Computer Viruses," *Computer Security Journal*, Vol. 6, No. 2, Winter 1991, p. 89(8).

28. Bill Brindley, "Controlling access to VMS: Halt—Who Goes There?," *Digital Review*, Vol. 6, No. 19, May 15, 1989, p. 13(2).

29. David Gianatasio, "DEC Tightens VMS Security Another Notch," *Digital Review*, Vol. 6, No. 22, June 5, 1989, p. 6(1).

30. Jonathan D. Moffett and Morris S. Sloman, "The Source of Authority for Commercial Access Control," *Computer*, Vol. 21, No. 2, Feb. 1988, p. 59(11).

31. Monathan Moffett, Morris Sloman, and Kevin Twidle, "Specifying Discretionary Access Control Policy for Distributed Systems," *Computer Communications*, Vol. 13, No. 9, Nov. 1990, p. 571(10).

CHAPTER 7

Dealing with
Worms and Viruses

There is abroad in the world of networks and computers a considerable amount of nonsense regarding the realities of security threats from worms and viruses. The fear of a threat from viruses has been exacerbated by claims that eventually almost all networked systems will be hit with a computer virus.[1] That such claims may be gross exaggerations should not keep managers from taking steps to prevent problems associated with viruses, however. This chapter is designed not as a technical evaluation of viruses, for there are many other sources available to obtain that information in more detail than could be provided here. Rather, here we will try to develop a realistic management strategy for preventing the onslaught of viruses in the first place.

Although, for the sake of literary simplicity, I will use the word *virus* as the generic designation for any security threat that executes in such a way so that computer resources are damaged, lost, or tied up so that they cannot be used, you should keep in mind that there are different forms of "infection" from external sources. The use of biological terms as analogies for problems with networks and computers sometimes seems a bit over dramatic, but I will continue to use that terminology in this chapter simply for consistency with what others are talking and writing about. There are three different terms that are commonly used to distinguish among differing forms of network/computer infection: *virus, worm,* and *logic bomb.* In addition to these three, other similar security assaults have been given equally colorful names: bacterium, rabbit, rogue, time bomb, and Trojan Horse. It is helpful to understand the distinctions among the three more common terms, although in the popular and managerial literature the logic bomb is less often discussed than are viruses and worms. All of these terms may be found in the glossary, as well.

The definitions used here are distilled from a variety of sources, but seem to be in common use. A virus, therefore, is a program that may be used to infect a computer. After virus code is written, it is buried within an existing program. Once that program is executed, the virus code is also activated and it attaches copies of itself to other programs in the system. Whenever an infected program is run, the virus copies itself to other programs. A virus cannot be attached to data. It must be attached to an executable program that is installed on a computer. The virus-attached program must be executed in order to activate the virus. In comparison, a worm is a destructive program that replicates itself throughout disk and memory, using up the computer's resources and eventually putting the system down. The adoption of the word "worm" to designate an "infection" of a network or computer system is somewhat unfortunate, for worm also has at least two other meanings within the industry: 1) a program that moves throughout a network and deposits information at each node for diagnostic purposes, or causes idle computers to share some of the processing workload; and 2) a storage device (WORM, Write Once Read Many) that uses an optical medium that can be recorded only once. Finally, there is the logic bomb, which is a program routine that destroys data. It may, for example, reformat the hard disk or randomly insert garbage into data files. Once executed, it does its damage right away, whereas a virus keeps on destroying.[2] Although a number of sources are cited in this chapter, it should be noted that the organization of this chapter is heavily dependent on an excellent IBM research report by Steve R. White, David M. Chess, and Chengi Jimmy Kuo, and on the National Institute of Standards and Technology (NIST) Special Publication, *Viruses and Related Threats: A Management Guide,* by John P. Wack and Lisa J. Carnahan.[3] The interpretations of the material are, of course, my own.

Vulnerabilities

Any discussion of virus threats needs to remind the reader why viruses are successful in the first place. Certainly the reason is that people and systems are vulnerable to attack. One of the better lists of vulnerabilities is that set forth by John P. Wack and Lisa J. Carnahan, on behalf of the U.S. Department of Commerce, National Institute of Standards and Technology:[4]

- *Lack of user awareness*—Users copy and share infected software, fail to detect signs of virus activity, and do not understand proper security techniques.
- *Absence of or inadequate security controls*—Personal computers generally lack software and hardware security mechanisms that help to prevent and detect unauthorized use. Existing controls on multi-user systems can sometimes be surmounted by knowledgeable users.
- *Ineffective use of existing security controls*—Using easily guessed passwords, failing to use access controls, granting users more access to resources than is necessary.
- *Bugs and loopholes in system software*—Enabling knowledgeable users to break into systems or exceed their authorized privileges.
- *Unauthorized use*—Unauthorized users can break into systems; authorized users can exceed levels of privilege and misuse systems.

- *Susceptibility of networks to misuse*—Networks can provide anonymous access to systems; many networks are only as secure as the systems that use them.

Much of what virus protection is all about is reducing or eliminating these vulnerabilities.

How Viruses Infect Networks

The point of networking is to improve productivity and to achieve organizational goals more efficiently, effectively, and easily—in other words, to improve an organization's competitive advantage or to make it work better. A formal definition can be found in the glossary, but fundamentally, whether networking is used in a human context or to delineate a set of interconnected computers, it means improving interactions among the participants. As a result, modern networks of computers perform both a technological task and a sociological task. While all these purposes are laudable, they are not necessarily consistent with the goal of securing computers and networks. The spread of viruses is a case in point.

There are many ways in which a system can become infected with a virus. Modern computer systems, even single-user desktop computers, are complex devices. If a program is run that can alter one or more other programs, the potential for viral infection exists. When a user runs a program written by someone else, compiled by a compiler, or linked to run-time libraries, use is made of code written by a large number (mostly unknown) of people. All computing is a cooperative enterprise, even on a stand-alone workstation.

The introduction of an infected program can occur in a variety of ways:[5]

- Software introduced into or used on the system by an outsider who had access to the system;

- Software used at home by an employee whose home computer system is, unknown to the employee, itself infected;
- Software purchased from a commercial software company whose production facilities are infected;
- Software that turns out to be infected that has been downloaded from public bulletin boards for business use or by employees;
- Software intentionally infected by a malicious or disgruntled employee;
- *Any* other time that a piece of software (including programs, operating systems, and so on) is created within the organization, or brought in from *any* outside source; and
- A program attached to other messages in a network, such as electronic mail, that takes advantage of computer operating system and/or network operating system flaws.[6]

In others words, a virus or other infection can come through the door via almost any route. The most widely publicized incident, that of Robert Morris and the Internet Worm in November 1988, resulted when Morris took advantage of flaws in the UNIX operating system and in the Internet protocols TCP/IP and SMTP (Simple Mail Transfer Protocol). While many of the openings that Morris's Worm used have since been closed, the case is quite instructive. Briefly, the Morris Worm took advantage of the standard *finger* program in networked UNIX systems, the *sendmail* program, designed to route mail in a heterogeneous internetwork, and the file(s) used to contain UNIX passwords (which are user readable on a world-wide basis, although the passwords themselves are encrypted). By exploiting services provided by these elements, Morris's Worm was able to propagate itself across some 6,000 BSD (Berkeley) UNIX systems. Please note that the Worm infected *only* BSD UNIX systems, *not* MS/DOS (on PCs), UNIX V, VM, MVS, or VMS operating systems. One unfortunate aspect of this incident, among others, was that in exploiting what previously were thought of as features rather than flaws, some degradation of connective service will eventually be the outcome.

Viruses spread to microcomputers most frequently by sharing software among users. This is particularly a problem with public-domain software acquired from sources such as bulletin boards. This threat should probably not deter a person from the genuine pleasure of using the many bulletin board services, but care should be taken in the acquisition and use of the software. Even commercial products are not immune from virus attacks, however. A computer virus program that corrupted the software master disk of a new program released by Aldus Corp alarmed the software publishing industry in 1988, for example. The Aldus incident was the first cited case of a virus infecting commercial software. Apparently, it entered the company's new graphics program for the MacIntosh, Freehand, after unintentionally being passed to the company by a contractor, who picked up the program in a user group's game; the virus was embedded in the game, entered the contractor's computer, and contaminated the training disks prepared for Aldus. The virus was copied by Aldus in commercially distributed copies, which were replaced. Aldus changed its production procedures by introducing "fail-safe" data security methods.[7]

Viruses and Other Security Threats

As we have seen throughout this book, there are many kinds of threats to security. Many threats, when identified, can be prevented or at least traced back to their source. Viruses often have the capacity to be substantially untraceable, however, and this makes them different from other security threats. Often, the only way a virus's author becomes known is when the author admits to ownership. Morris was ultimately identified through standard (not technological) investigative techniques that found persons to whom he had spoken concerning the writing of the worm. Morris, a graduate student at Cornell University at the time, phoned Andy Sudduth of Harvard who, in turn, tried to post a warning to the TCP/IP mailing list. In that message, posted anonymously from "foo@bar.arpa", stipulated that "There may be a virus loose on the internet," followed by three brief statements suggesting ways to stop the worm, followed by "Hope this helps, but more, I hope it is a hoax."[8] It did not turn out to be a hoax.

With current technology there are only two ways in which a computer system might be completely protected against a virus (or worm): by isolation and by reducing functionality. If a system can run only one fixed program (with verification code) and cannot have new programs loaded to it or created on it, except through very elaborate procedures, then access control is complete. This approach is not only not very useful, it obliterates the point of networking in the first place. The consequence is that there is always some exposure. At this point the issue comes down to the same one we confront with other security threats: "it is a matter of weighing benefits, practicality, and potential risks, and then taking cost-effective action to help control those risks."[9]

Although viruses exhibit elements of many other security threats, they are also peculiar in their behavior. As White, Chess, and Kuo summarize the situation:

> But a virus is more than the part that replicates itself. There is usually also a potentially damaging portion. This portion could be a "time bomb" (on November 11th, display a political message), a "logic bomb" (when it sees a certain write to disk, it also corrupts the file structure), or anything else the virus author can design. The variety of possible effects is part of the reason why the notion of a virus is so confusing to many people. The term "virus" is sometimes misused to refer to anything undesirable that can happen to a computer. This is incorrect. The thing that makes viruses and related threats different from other problems is that they spread.[10]

As with other security threats, however, the solution to the problem (if a problem exists) involves the cooperative efforts of people and technology. Certainly some effort should be made by an organization before the threat becomes a reality. This means putting in place a *policy* designed to limit infection by a virus, and to have an *understood procedure* for detecting and dealing with a virus, should one be suspected or occur.

Elements of a Viral Infection Policy

It is probably the better part of valor to include a viral infection policy as part of the general security policies for an organization. Several times throughout this book we have noted the importance of having a *written* security policy. If the office in question is larger than one person (and perhaps even then, as a reminder), a written security policy is desirable. Basically, a virus infection policy should include standard methods for *deterring* attacks by viruses and related threats; *detecting* attacks when they occur; *containing* the attacks to limit damage; and *recovering* from attacks in a reasonable period of time.[11] The basic methodology for accomplishing these goals are the following, as listed by (and quoted from) Wack and Carnahan:

- *Educating users* about malicious software in general, the risks that it poses, how to use control measures, policies, and procedures to protect themselves and the organization;
- *Software management* policies and procedures that address public-domain software, and the use and maintenance of software in general;
- *Use of technical controls* that help to prevent and deter attacks by malicious software and unauthorized users;
- *Monitoring of user software activity* to detect signs of attacks, to detect policy violations, and to monitor the overall effectiveness of policies, procedures, and controls; and
- *Contingency policies and procedures* for containing and recovering from attacks.

User Education

White, Chess, and Kuo have reemphasized the point made else-where in this book: "Good security policies depend on the knowledge and cooperation of the users."[12] Moreover, as Wack and Carnahan have noted, "In situations where technical controls do not provide complete protection (i.e., most computers), it is ultimately people and their willingness to adhere to security policies that will determine whether systems and organizations are protected."[13] Particularly with malicious software, end users are at least as likely to recognize an attack as are the technical caretakers of the system. Thus, it is important that users be trained to understand the issues involved in virus security proce-dures. Such training should include at least the following:

- Awareness of the dangers that exist—This may include addressing the way in which malicious software operates, the methods by which it is planted and spread, and the vulnerabilities exploited by malicious software and unau-thorized users.

- What to do if they suspect they have found a security problem—An important element of a security policy will be some specification of what to do when a problem occurs. This may include phone numbers of whom to call, software for technical control of the problem, or proce-dures for isolating a workstation from a network. Not all, in fact not most, anomalies discovered in a computing environment are the result of viruses. It is, therefore, important for users to be able to either distinguish be-tween problems brought about by malicious software and "normal" behavior of a system. Having someone to call, a system administrator or security officer, is important.

- Who to call if they have questions or suspicions—User education must inform users who to call if they see a system problem that may be the result of a virus. Someone in the organization should be designated as the person responsible to work with others in determining if a prob-lem exists, and to report the problem to a central source of information if it is serious. The ability to inform the necessary people of the problem quickly and reliably and to set in motion the process of containing and solving the problem is the function of the central security information center.

- What to do, and what not to do, to minimize security risks—A part of this awareness should also be knowledge of general security policies and procedures and how to use them. These general policies will include those relating to backup, storage, and use of software, especially public-domain software and shareware.

- If an appropriate security policy has been established, there should be procedures in place—both organizational and technical—designed to protect systems and users from virus attacks. Thus, in order for such policies and procedures to be effective, the user must know and understand how to use them. It is particularly important that people know how to monitor their own systems and software in order to detect signs of abnormal activity (see "Monitoring," below).

It is important that users feel that security measures are established for their own benefit, rather than "make-work" projects. Although the kind of education described above can be expensive in time and resources, it is ultimately cost-effective if the organization is dependent on the work the individual is doing. User education will contribute to a better overall understanding of the need for security measures and policies, thus contributing to better security of the network. Nor should education be limited to end users. While it is very important to educate the end users, the first-level support people and management at all levels must also have a good understanding of the issues, since they must take the necessary actions quickly when a viral infection is detected.

Software Management

Although networks of computers provide unique opportunities for the spread of viruses and worms, the networking among people interested in the use of computers also provides many opportunities for viral infection. We have already noted above the ways in which viruses are spread. The problem is to manage software in such a way so that infection does not become a problem across an organization. There are many instances when technical controls cannot prevent the introduction of new software on a system. Under such circumstances some policy should be specified that deals with the introduction of new software. Some approaches might be the following:

- Prohibit the copying or use of public-domain software, or allow the use of public-domain software with appropriate management control and restrictions—"Appropriate" control might be the use of an *isolated system* (one not connected to a network and not used for any other purpose) to copy and test the software in question. An isolated system could also be used to test internally developed software as well as updates to vendor software.

- Purchase software from "reputable" sources and maintain it properly—This admonition is sometimes more easily stated than observed because a small, not well-known software house may produce a product that could be important to a specific organization. Even when software is purchased from a "reputable" company, as we saw above, it may not be immune from viruses.

- Don't use *pirated* software—In many organizations the inappropriate sharing of commercial software products is widespread. There are many problems with this, including the fact that it is illegal (since it is theft in the sense of copyright violation) and that it may have been modified to include a virus.

- Keep an inventory of software installations (system, location, version, etc.)—While this is good business practice under any circumstance, it is often not observed, since it is time-consuming and may be expensive to maintain. In fact, most micro software usually falls below the value of purchases required to be inventoried in most organizations. The value of such an inventory is that it can be used for contingency and recovery purposes.

- Store the original disks from vendors in a safe place, and ensure that vendors can be quickly contacted if problems occur.

- Use appropriate operating procedures to insure that "clean" software can be restored if a problem occurs—In other words, provide appropriate backup procedures that will allow restoration of software and data (see "Contingency Planning" in this chapter). This is a general policy that relates to general operating procedures, but is of particular use (and also presents peculiar problems) under a virus attack.

Technical Controls

Technical controls are the mechanisms used to protect the security and integrity of systems and associated data. There are a variety of technical controls available, depending on whether we are concerned with workstations, multi-user systems, or networks. In general, better technical controls are available for multi-user systems and networks than for stand-alone workstations. The reason for this is that network and multi-user managers have long had to contend with a variety of security issues simply because a number of different people use the system or network. This means that such systems have always been susceptible to problems—if not from malice, then from inadvertence. In general, there are a few general technical controls that can be applied to any system, as well as those specific for the different kinds of systems.

The most significant general control is to limit access to the system to those authorized to use it. For workstations this may be software or hardware locks, and for multi-user/network systems it may be the techniques used for user authentication in the access process. Of the more common methods for access control, good password management is the most important. Two technical controls that are often suggested, the use of *isolated systems* and of *limited-use systems*, I see as being of *very* limited value. In a contemporary organization, dependent on the widespread deployment of computer technology, the unconnected personal computer is becoming increasingly anomalous. In order to take advantage of services such as electronic mail, we want as many people as possible to be connected, rather than devising ways to disconnect them. And the need for such connectivity extends from an entry-level employee to the corporation's president.

Generally, for multi-user and network environments, several technical control guidelines might be observed:[14]

- Use the technical controls that exist.
- Change passwords periodically.
- Disable or remove old or unnecessary user accounts. In particular, the accounts of employees that have been laid off, fired, or who resign should be *immediately* disabled.
- Use a "least privilege" policy, where users are restricted to accessing resources on a "need-to-know" or minimum accessibility basis.
- Consider the use of tokens (magnetic access cards) as part of the management of passwords.
- Provide external access (through modems) only for specific uses. If dial-out is needed, provide only dial-out rather than both dial-in and dial-out. If dial-in is allowed, monitor those calling in or use some form of call-back (although, see the appropriate discussions in Chapter 6).
- Allow users to encrypt data files (although this will not specifically deter the impact of a virus).
- Give users software and/or hardware to lock local workstations or microcomputers used for access, and do not leave the workstation unattended while still on-line and unlocked.
- Boot the local workstation/micro from either a network file server or from a write-protected floppy disk, and

down-load all software from write-protected directories on the file server or multi-user system.

- Run virus detection software routinely on boot-up of the local workstation or microcomputer.

As with many security control mechanisms, there are problems with the use of these and other technical controls. First, some of these controls may be unduly obtrusive and actually decrease the productivity of end users. Second, at the very least, legitimate access is made more arduous. If such controls become too obtrusive, users will find ways to thwart them, regardless of how much education they may have.

Monitoring

There is no substitute for diligence. Managers can improve the chances that malicious software will be detected early through the appropriate monitoring of software, system activity, and sometimes user activity. Users also have a monitoring role in that they may detect anomalous system behavior first, and certainly that will be the case with their own workstation. In addition to the user education noted above, individuals should also be trained to watch for unexpected behavior of hardware and software. As long as we do not institute something fairly radical, like isolating all systems, there is always an opportunity for viral infection. There is no "one-time fix" for virus control, as there is for some other computer security problems. Because there is always the possibility of infection, virus *detection* is an important component of system security.

As White, Chess, and Kuo have observed, "the two most important resources available for the detection of viruses are watchful users and watchful programs. The best approaches to virus detection include both."[15] Users need to be aware of the possibility of viruses, just as they need to be aware of the necessity for backups. Simple "awareness" is insufficient, however, because they need to know what kinds of things to watch for. System programs and utilities should be available to help the users and the computer center or network staff to take advantage of this awareness.

When users are aware of the kinds of visible things that are known to happen in systems that are virus-infected, they can serve as an important line of defense. It is important that users know that odd behavior in a computer system may be a symptom of penetration by a virus. They should also know to whom such odd behavior should be reported. On the other hand, odd behavior is usually not caused by viral penetration. Software bugs, user errors, and hardware failures are much more common. It is important to avoid unfounded rumors of viral infections, as dealing with such "false alarms" can be costly. An actual infection, however, may require rapid action. So the group to which users report oddities must have the skill to determine which reports are almost certainly due to one of these more common causes, and which merit closer investigation for possible viral infection. One obvious choice for such a group is within the computing center or "help desk," since the computing center staff probably already has a good idea of what sorts of oddities are "business as usual."

Workstation Viruses

There is probably no exhaustive list of symptoms for malicious software. Moreover, whatever list we might adduce now is likely to change in the future, as authors of such software "improve" the way in which that software operates. Moreover, some of the things in the list that follows can occur only after a system is infected and some triggering action takes place. Other behaviors may occur only while the virus is spreading. White, Chess, and Kuo provided the following list of anomalous behaviors:[16]

- Unexpected changes in the time stamps or length of files, particularly executable files;
- Programs taking longer to start, or running more slowly than usual;
- Programs attempting to write to write-protected media for no apparent reason;

- Unexplained decreases in the amount of available workstation memory, or increases in areas marked as "bad" on magnetic media;
- Executable files unexpectedly vanishing;
- Workstations unexpectedly "rebooting" when certain previously correct programs are run, or a relatively constant amount of time after being turned on;
- Unusual things appearing on displays, including "scrolling" of odd parts of the screen, or the unexpected appearance of "bouncing balls" or odd messages;
- Unexpected changes to volume labels on disks and other media; and
- An unusual load on local networks or other communication links, especially when multiple copies of the same data are being sent at once.

Partly because there has been a significant virus problem with microcomputers, there are now on the market a number of virus detection programs available. Many universities—where the problem is sometimes acute—often have microcomputers organized in a lab automatically execute a virus detection program every time it is turned on or rebooted. This takes time away from the user and from the use of the workstation, but it also protects both.

Multi-User System Viruses

This section covers traditional IBM-style mainframes as well as super-minis, like DEC's VAX computers. The sorts of things that happen in multi-user environments concerning viruses are very similar to those that happen to workstations. Lengths or time stamps of executable files may change, programs may load or execute more slowly, unusual errors (especially relating to disk-writes) may occur, files may vanish or proliferate, and odd things may appear on displays. If the virus is attempting to spread between users, users may also notice "outgoing mail" that they did not intend to send, "links" to other user's information that they did not intentionally establish, and similar phenomena. In Chapter 6 I noted that it has often been thought that IBM MVS systems were more or less immune to a virus attack. At the risk of repeating myself, I believe my earlier observations need to be reiterated.

Although there have been no reported virus cases involving an MVS operating system, the danger does exist. At least one publication, *Abacus,* has printed technical information on MVS virus design by the German author B. Fix. Security loopholes like those used to invade UNIX and VM systems exist in many MVS environments and may go unnoticed and uncorrected until the system is attacked. Martin L. King, writing in *Computer Security Journal,* has examined these loopholes and explored the techniques that viruses use to attack systems. King described specific steps for protecting MVS systems by making use of the facilities built into commercial access control software, such as CA-ACF2, RACF, and CA-Top Secret.[17] If an IBM mainframe is interconnected to a large national or global network, such as Internet, it may be worthwhile to at least explore the methods for protecting the system from an IBM-specific virus. It should be understood, however, that because of the differences in the operating system structure of MVS, and because IBM systems use a character coding system called EBCDIC (rather than ASCII), the *same* virus programs that have attacked UNIX systems cannot be successful.

Many multi-user systems have technical resources for monitoring system activity not available on microcomputers or even high-performance workstations. Such a monitoring mechanism can be an important tool for detecting threats of malicious software. Just as users are important in monitoring their own workstations, so too are they important in monitoring multi-user systems. The NIST report by Wack and Carnahan recommends the following policies and procedures:[18]

- Use the system monitoring/auditing tools that are available.
- Some access control methods have alarm mechanisms

that send a message to the audit log when attempts are made to access a protected resource. Alarms are also sometimes available that alert operators, allowing them to log an intruder off.

- Acquaint users with normal operating behavior of the system so that they can help watch for anomalous behavior.

- Purchase or build system sweep programs to checksum files at night and then report differences from previous runs. Password checkers can be acquired that monitor whether passwords are being used effectively.

- Regularize security reviews that, among other things, include inspection of logged security problems. Such problems should always be logged and reported, even if they appear to be trivial.

- Enforce some form of sanction against users who consistently violate or attempt to violate security policies and procedures.

Network Issues

Network connections pose inherent risks of unauthorized access, whether wide area or local area networks. Yet, on a network of any significant size, it is not very practical to monitor all traffic and to differentiate between authorized and unauthorized access. The costs would be too great. Moreover, not only are workstations attached to networks, there may also be several or a large number of multi-user systems of significant size attached. The problem confronting a network manager, therefore, is one of providing connectivity to those who need it, without losing sight of the fact that it is necessary to minimize security threats in general and threats from malicious software in particular. Some possible actions that might be taken, include requiring separate passwords for network and computer access, severely restricting what can be done on "guest" accounts, and, to the extent possible, monitor network activity for anomalous behavior.

Contingency Planning

Any well-run network or computing facility should have some contingency plan in place that covers the policies and procedures to be followed in the event that disaster strikes or if there is clear evidence of a security threat. Whatever other contingency planning takes place, probably the most important concerning *any* security issue, but including threats from viruses and related problems, is a coherent backup procedure. A secure system depends on regular and frequent backups of all critical data and programs. Most multi-user systems have some backup policy and procedure in place. Typically, even with a relatively small LAN, a procedure will be in place to back up the primary file server. However, most users (this author included) do a relatively poor job of backup for individual workstations. Even without the threat of viruses, therefore, good backups are an important part of system management. Nothing can substitute for a good set of backups, which can save many days or months of work when a program or a data file is lost. The potential harm caused by computer viruses only increases the need for backups.

Backups, however, can be a two-edged sword. They are necessary for recovery, but backups can also present a place for a virus to hide. It is this characteristic that makes backup procedures for virus protection somewhat different than for other security threats. Great care must be taken, therefore, not to reintroduce the virus into the system in the process. One contingency procedure that should be in place, therefore, is one that includes inspection of backups, to ensure that the virus is not present before the backup is used to restore lost data or programs. Regular backups are, however, an important part of software and data management. When a virus attack has been experienced, it is probably best to restore software from the original vendor's distribution disks or tapes, rather than from recent backups, since the backups may have been infected. Only data should be restored from backups.

In addition to appropriate backup procedures, a contingency plan for virus control may also include accurate records of each system's configuration (location, software, network connections, and the name of the system manager or other responsible person, etc.); a skilled group of users to deal with virus incidents and a means for contacting these people; a prioritized list of people to contact (with telephone numbers) should a problem arise; and the ability to quickly disconnect systems from the network.

A part of the contingency plan should be a way of detecting viruses. Procedures to detect viral infections are very important, but by themselves are of relatively little use. More importantly, as White, Chess, and Kuo have noted, the "individual who makes the first detection must have a procedure to follow to verify the problem and to make sure that appropriate action occurs."[19] It should be apparent that if information concerning a virus attack is allowed to "fall through the cracks," then detection is of only limited value. In addition to the contingency planning already noted, it may be well to have virus-removing programs in place.

For microcomputers there have been developed a number of programs to check for the existence of viruses, and some of the concepts used in those programs can be applied to large multi-user systems as well. It would be possible, for example, to run a checksum or cyclical redundancy check (CRC) on each program in a program library as baseline (before any virus attack), and then to periodically rerun the program and compare the results to the base data. This is not foolproof, since a virus could be written that would not change the results of a checksum or CRC, but this is a good first step. Once an attack has occurred and the virus has been studied, programs can be written or obtained to help remove that particular virus. In addition to a checking program such as that just described, it would also be possible to attempt the restoration of the object to its uninfected form. Removal programs are less useful than checking programs, since the original software should be backed up in a secure fashion and restored from the backups, unless there is reason to believe that no secure copy exists.

The suggestions given above provide only the barest guidelines. For specific organizations there may be extensions and modifications that should be put in place. The point is that everyone involved should know what to do if an attack occurs so that "clean" service can be promptly restored.

Summary and Conclusions

This final section will be given almost in the form of a checklist that should provide some direction in protecting a network from incursions by malicious software.

- Viruses and other malicious software represent a relatively recent and somewhat different kind of security threat than other security problems.
- Malicious software is any software, such as a virus, worm, logic bomb, bacterium, rabbit, rogue, time bomb, Trojan Horse, or something else that has the *unauthorized* capacity to modify or erase data or software and/or to reproduce itself in an *unauthorized* manner.
- Viruses and other malicious software can spread rapidly and cause widespread damage.
- Viruses can enter a computing environment either through malicious intent or inadvertence.
- No system can be made completely immune from viral attacks, although some steps can be taken:
  - Use good general security practices, as described throughout this book, including at least the following:
    - Maintain an appropriate backup procedure.
    - Have periodic security reviews to determine weaknesses.
    - Maintain and use access control facilities.
    - Make certain that users are trained in security procedures.
  - Designate a malicious software response team (which may be part of or the same as a general security threat response team).

— Have a plan to deal with malicious software in place
before a problem occurs.

— Test the response plan periodically, but *do not* use a
real virus in the test.

• The risks from malicious software can be minimized with
appropriate action.

When reading over a list of issues such as that just given, it is easy
to become paranoid, which we must avoid. Most systems are not
attacked by viruses. On the other hand, some are, and the magni-
tude of the attacks, particularly in large networked environments,
can be immense. In the end, good judgment will dictate the levels
of security that should be used in a particular installation. There
must be some balance between protection to the point that
people's productivity is affected, and not protecting the system at
all.

Notes

1. Dave Powell, "Fighting Network Inffection," *Networking
   Management*, Vol. 7, No. 9, Sept. 1989, p. 38(8).

2. There have been numerous attempts to clearly distinguish
   among various "infecting" techniques, none of which have
   been particularly successful. See, for example, the discussion
   by Deborah Russell and G. T. Gangemi, Sr., *Computer Security Basics* (Sebastopol, CA: O'Reilly & Associates, Inc.,
   1991), pp. 79–88, but particularly p. 80, where they note that
   viruses and worms are often confused.

3. Steve R. White, David M. Chess, IBM Thomas J. Watson
   Research Center, Yorktown Heights, NY, and Chengi Jimmy
   Kuo, IBM Los Angeles Scientific Center, Los Angeles, CA,
   "Coping with Computer Viruses and Related Problems," Re-
   search Report (RC 14405), January 30, 1989. IBM Thomas J.
   Watson Research Center, Distribution Services F-11 Stormy-
   town, Post Office Box 218, Yorktown Heights, NY 10598
   (This report was available from this address up to Jan. 1990,

although it is available in machine readable form on the Byte Information Service fBIXg as VIRUSD.ARC). The report is provided without distribution restrictions. It should be noted that this report does not reflect the opinions, policies, or recommendations of IBM or any other organization. Two other easily available sources were used extensively and are highly recommended as well: John P. Wack and Lisa J. Carnahan, *Viruses and Related Threats: A Management Guide*, National Institute of Standards and Technology (NIST) Special Publication 500-166 (also reprinted in *Datapro Reports on Information Security* fDelran, NJ: McGraw-Hill, 1990g), document IS09-330, and a report written specifically for *Datapro* by Reed Phillips, Jr., "Computer Viruses: A Threat for the 1990s," *Datapro Reports on Information Security* (Delran, NJ: McGraw-Hill, 1990), document IS09-250.

4. Wack and Carnahan, *Datapro*, pp. IS09-330-105, 106. Italics for emphasis have been added.

5. Quoted from White, Chess, and Kuo, p. 4. Please note that this is a good illustrative list, but not necessarily exhaustive.

6. White, Chess, and Kuo do not discuss this issue, but it was the approach used by the Robert Morris Internet Worm in November 1988.

7. John Markoff, "A 'Virus' Gives Business a Chill: 'Bug' in Software Can Destroy Data," *The New York Times*, Vol. 137, No. 47,447, March 17, 1988, p. 27(2).

8. Eugene H. Spafford, "The Intemet Worm Incident," Purdue University Technical Report CSD-TR-933, 1989 (West Lafayette, IN: Purdue University, 1989), © 1989 by Eugene H. Spafford. This has been reprinted several times. See, for example, *Datapro Reports on Information Security* (Delran, NJ: McGraw-Hill, 1990), p. IS09-41-111.

9. White, Chess, and Kuo, p. 6.

10. Ibid., p. 5. The issue here is one of change and dispersal. Dr. Fred Cohen, who has done much of the original research on computer viruses, defines a virus as: "a program that can 'infect' other programs by modifying them to include a pos-

sibly evolved copy of itself" See Fred Cohn, "Computer Viruses: Theory and Experiment," *Computers & Security*, Vol. 6, 1987, pp. 22–35. Spafford, by the way, credits science fiction author David Gerrold with being the first to use the term "virus" as a computer attacker in his stories of the G.O.D. machine. These stories were combined into a book, *When Harlie Was One* (New York: Ballantine Books, 1972), although in later editions of the book the virus plot was removed. Ken Thompson, in "Reflections on Trusting Trust," *Communications of the ACM*, Vol. 27, No. 8, August 1984, described what may have be the first computer virus.

11. Wack and Carnahan, *Datapro*, p. IS09-330-106.

12. White, Chess and Kuo, p. 6.

13. Wack and Carnahan, *Datapro*, p. IS09-330-106.

14. This list is a combination of suggestions made by Wack and Carnahan for multi-user systems and networks, *Datapro*, pp. IS09-330-112, 113 and IS09-330-116, 117.

15. White, Chess, and Kuo, p. 11.

16. White, Chess, and Kuo, pp. 13–14.

17. Martin L. King, "Do we have a virus problem with MVS systems?," *Computer Security Journal*, Vol. 5, No. 2, Winter, 1990, p. 57(7).

18. Wack and Carnahan, *Datapro,* p. IS09-330-113.

19. White, Chess, and Kuo, p. 16.

CHAPTER **8**

Micros, Minis, and Mainframes

This chapter is probably misnamed, and that misnaming may mislead the unwary. The emphasis will, indeed, be directed toward the comparative problems of securing various kinds of computer systems that may be part of a network. Yet the problem is not so much with the size of the computers, or even their specific hardware architectures, as it is with the operating systems that are used on those platforms. The other facet of this issue is the distinction between single-user and multi-user systems, but this too is largely an issue of operating systems rather than of the hardware platform. Finally, it should be clearly understood that the once useful distinctions among micros, minis, and mainframes that designated computers of different sizes and power has lost its analytical clarity (if, indeed, there was ever any clarity in these distinctions at all). An illustration of this loss of clarity is the way in which the literature cites Digital Equipment Corporation's (DEC) VAX computers. The same machines are variously described as minicomputers, super-minicomputers, and mainframes, even at the high end.

So why have I labeled the chapter in this manner? The reason is partly historical and partly linguistic. Historically, the industry has made the distinctions, and they continue linguistically to be used by many people. Also, these terms call attention to the fact that there are specific products that have been tailored to the typical operating systems available on or popular with the various platforms. It is also true that, at least for those systems that can clearly be identified as micros, minis, or mainframes, there are distinctive architectural differences even today. Although speed and memory capacity (two of the features that have been used to distinguished among the three "types" of computers) no longer provide specific differentiation, there persist some distinctive differences in the capacity to manage and control peripheral devices, particularly large amounts of disk storage.

In many respects, better distinctions can be made between computers used as *clients* and those as *servers*, or between those used as *hosts* and those used as *terminal devices*, or those used as *master* systems and those used as *slaves*. Given the current technology, however, it is often not clear how a specific functional relationship is operating in a given network, and, indeed, that functional relationship may change from application to application. Consequently, all systems in today's networks need security as both clients and servers, hosts and terminals, and masters and slaves. Thus, these distinctions are no more useful than those of micro, mini, and mainframe. Yet, intuitively, we still tend to feel that differences do exist, and when we go shopping for appropriate security hardware and software, we certainly find characteristically different products.

Although distinctions may be difficult to make, we must remember that information resides on some host somewhere. That host may be a micro, mini, or mainframe computer. Various classes of host machines provide different problems and opportunities for security arrangements. In addition, the operating systems that are typically used with these systems also affect the level of security that can be achieved. The point is that in this chapter the emphasis is on the computer rather than on the network. The distinction I am trying to arrive at is one of distinguishing between those computers that are used as network control devices (terminal servers, routers, bridges, etc.) and those that are used for end-user computing. Most of the rest of this book has dealt conceptually with both kinds of systems, but the emphasis has been on network issues. In this chapter we will take a little time to explore security issues related to end-user computing.

Micros

With the enthusiastic acceptance of microcomputers by organizations of all kinds, we saw during the first decade[1] of the omnipresence of the IBM-architected personal computer (PC) a microcomputer buying frenzy that seems to be continuing almost unabated. In 1982, before it was even clear that the IBM PC would gain the dominance it did, I wrote that through "the late 1980s microcomputers will become as common in large organizations as calculators and perhaps even as telephones."[2] It was clear at that time that the "big market for micros in the mid-1980s is with the giants fcorporations, institutionsg, although it is likely that growth in personal computing will occur as well."[3] Even close to the beginning of the microcomputer revolution it was clear that by the 1990s we would have moved from 8-bit processors to 32-bit machines, and from a paltry 64Kb of memory to well over 1Mb of memory.[4] It was also predictable that we would move from asynchronous communications using telephonic technologies to local area networks (LANs), and from micros used as glorified calculators to networks encompassing large masses of people. What was missing then, and is still missing to a large extent, was appropriate planning in the deployment of micros. Part of the planning should have been, and still should be, concern over security.

The onslaught of micros in business, industry, education, and government has fundamentally changed our approach to computing. When the first micros were hooked into a large multi-user computer system (mini or mainframe) to emulate a "dumb" terminal, it was soon discovered that distributed data processing could take place even when the central system managers were not planning for or executing the deployment of a distributed system. The result was almost an instant security problem, for it became clear that data integrity, and perhaps even hardware security, no longer meant the same thing as it had previously. It is clear, as Reed Phillips, Jr. has recently noted, that "even in organizations with security policies governing mainframes and midrange systems, microcomputer security is left up to the user, with no established policy governing security of the information processed."[5] This is true even though the information kept on micros is apt to be fundamental to the continued operation of the company.

By 1993 there may be as many as 60 million *additional* micro-computers sold and deployed, doubling the number in use in 1991. Some of these, of course, will replace older machines, but a substantial number will be additions to an organization's inventory. One of the suggestions for securing networked micros that is frequently heard is to use micros without local disk drives, thus prohibiting users from bringing data and programs into the system that might damage the network as a whole. In such an arrangement the diskless micros would boot off the server to which they are attached and all software and data would be held centrally. While this may appeal to security managers, this approach very nearly obviates the utility of micros as personal productivity enhancement tools, turning the micro back into something more akin to the dumb terminal of yore. Moreover, the sociological impact of such a decision on those workers using micros would almost certainly be negative. In my opinion, therefore, the use of diskless micros as a security mechanism, while certainly available, is an approach to be avoided at almost all costs. As we look at the security threats stemming from micros, and at the solutions for such threats, it is important to keep in mind the reason why people wanted micros in the first place: to help them work better.

The typical variables that concern security officers of large systems—program change control, data security, system documentation, backup and recovery procedures, and others—are often nonexistent in the microcomputer environment. Because micros are controlled largely by the end user, these and similar security controls are difficult or impossible to enforce. In a very large organization, in fact, central system managers may not have much of an idea who their users may be, nor do they often have reliable systems to ensure that only properly authorized users are actually accessing the corporate database. Before networking, if someone wanted an inappropriate change in the corporate database it was usually necessary to suborn an employee of the computing center. In today's networking environment many users may have the knowledge and technology available to compromise that database.

Vulnerabilities

With the introduction of microcomputers, an additional set of vulnerabilities was introduced into computing. Before micros, system managers generally did some standard things to maintain system security. They backed up the software and data periodically, they used User IDs and passwords to limit access, and in the early 1970s they started putting computer rooms in less public and less accessible places than previously in order to improve physical security. Moving the computer room, however, was made possible because of improving networking and data communications. By the early 1980s even the central programming staff rarely saw the physical computer, accessing it by a terminal. By the mid-1980s it was becoming clear that institutional networks were rapidly being integrated into larger national and international networks (which is only accelerating in the 1990s). And with the widespread use of LANs in the late 1980s, and their consequent integration into larger networks, even very remote systems often have extensive access to corporate and public computing resources.

We can list some of the security vulnerabilities we confront with the use of microcomputers, although it should be recognized that no list can be comprehensive, since new threats will continue to arise:

- Lack of management awareness of the fact that micros, just as surely as mainframes, make an organization vulnerable to security threats.
- Related to the foregoing point is the lack of commitment on the part of management to provide security controls for micros—it is not easy and may be relatively expensive.
- Expanding access to networked computers in all kinds of organizations, including customer access to corporate files, franchisees to access operational information, end-user funds transfers, and the like.
- "Hackers" both inside and outside an organization, testing the limits of what they can do, or specifically engaging in harmful behavior.
- "Improved" opportunities for industrial espionage.
- Threats to data integrity as a by-product of the ability to upload and download information between a corporate database and a microcomputer—This, in fact, was one of the earliest concerns of system managers relating to the deployment of micros. Most people dealing with security issues have recognized the potential threat to the integrity of corporate data as a result of the ability to upload information from the micro. Less well recognized is the fact that, when data are downloaded to the micro and massaged for reports at a local level, the integrity of the data as presented may be either purposely or inadvertently compromised, since there is little or no external validation of what is done to the data at the local level. Yet the corporation may depend on the integrity of the process. Moreover, the ability to upload may also mean that there is the capacity to upload programs that may contain a virus or other malicious software.
- Because of the nature of microcomputers as personal productivity tools, they are usually physically accessible.

Thus, while multi-user systems have become increasingly inaccessible, they have become more electronically accessible through networking and through the use of micros at the remote end.

Before micros, but during the period when networks of dumb terminals were available, workers—as a memory aid—commonly pasted notes to their terminals that had their User IDs and passwords noted. With the use of micros the notes may have gone away, but that is due to the use of automatic "scripts" that allow a user (or anyone else with access to the micro) to automatically log on to the host system simply by executing a program. This problem is exacerbated with the use of dial-access from home or hotel. In fact, it is possible and quite inexpensive for a user to set up a remote link themselves without recourse to the central computing administration. A micro linked to a LAN, which in turn is connected to a corporate network, may be equipped with a modem and a piece of software that allows someone to dial in and have complete remote control over the micro, including access to the corporate system. As long as a phone is available, this could be done with commercial software (plus a modem) for $200 or less. By using public domain software and a used modem, that cost might decrease to $50 or less. The host site managers would not even know this is happening.

- Viruses and other malicious software (see Chapter 7) are more common on micros than on other machines.
- Software piracy (the unauthorized duplication of copyrighted software) is rampant in many business, government, and educational institutions, notwithstanding policies against it.
- Even when we can preclude other problems, from a corporate point of view the fact that sensitive data may reside on a micro's hard disk that is almost publicly available may present a security problem.

Many organizations routinely shred sensitive documents (this may range from memoranda to program listings to unused checks) in order to preclude them falling into the wrong hands. Yet the data from which those documents were generated resides on some computer system. If that computer system is only a marginally secure micro, then shredding the paper may be only a minor impediment to someone who really wants to find out the secrets of the organization. Nor does someone have to simply sit down at a desk to benefit from this phenomenon. Micros are easy to steal, and the theft of micros happens every day.

- Lack of appropriate procedures, such as regular backups, of microcomputer disk drives, to aid in securing micros—One of the sad things about the increasing deployment of networks, particularly LANs, is that while they may increase security problems on the one hand, they can also be used to improve security on the other hand. For networked micros, for example, it would be possible to establish a procedure that would allow the system manager to back up user micros onto a server disk at regular intervals and to have the server disk(s) backed up with appropriate procedures. The same is true for the use of mini and mainframe computers for the same purpose. Software has been available for several years on DEC VAX superminis and IBM mainframes that, if purchased and used, would allow micros to be backed up to the central system. Although I have not done a survey to determine how frequently such facilities are used, my observation is that *very few* institutions have implemented such resources.

- Virtually all organizations lack any semblance of disaster recovery or contingency planning for micros. In businesses, for example, it is not at all unusual for a finance officer to maintain financial analyses critical to the running of the business on his or her micro. What happens when that micro fails and there is no recent backup, not to mention a plan to get a new micro into the office?

Serious vulnerabilities exist more with some micros in an organization than in others. For example, a micro that is used as a data
entry device by an end user, that obtains information from a host
system, that is used in the control of organizational assets, that is
used to prepare critical reports on which important business
decisions are made, that updates files on a host system, and/or
that stores information sensitive to the organization poses some
very real security problems and vulnerabilities. On the other
hand, a micro that is not used for these or equally sensitive
purposes may not be as much of a security problem, even though
its absence would have a negative impact on an individual's
productivity. The assessment of vulnerabilities must take place
almost on a machine-by-machine basis or at least be based on
narrow classes of machines and their use.

Security for Microcomputers

Now that we have glimpsed the problem, what do we do about it?
The first thing that must be done, whether we are thinking about
our own computer at home or our small business or our giant
multi-national corporation or government, is to devise a policy
that will govern microcomputer security in the organization. This
issue of security policies, or the lack thereof, has been reiterated
in virtually every chapter of this book. We cannot solve security
problems unless we think about them. The time to think about
them is before a security threat occurs. It is not enough to close
the barn doors *after* the horse is stolen. Further, we do not want
our policies and procedures to limit personnel productivity just
out of fear of a security problem. There are, after all, many more
instances of the need for improved productivity than there are of
security threats. While I do not propose to give a solution for each
of the vulnerabilities noted above, be advised that there are some
things that can be done about each of those points. The first two
(lack of management awareness of and commitment to micro
security), in fact, will be addressed by the process of writing a
microcomputer security policy.

A microcomputer security policy shares most of the requirements that we have already discussed elsewhere, with some differences to account for the different uses of the machines. It should contain reference to and recognition of at least the following points:

- *Access control*—Access control is a little different from access control of network devices or multi-user systems in that the most significant element of access control consists of securing physical access. Physical access security is also important with other systems, but that issue has been addressed extensively for decades for centralized computers and even for (though less so) distributed network devices. Simply the gross number of micros in many organizations provide problems with physical security, and, as noted above, most have experienced the theft of such devices. It may be desirable to physically lock a micro to the table or desk on which it resides. It may also be useful to make use of the physical keys that lock the keyboard of most IBM AT–type machines. It is also possible to provide software that requires password access before the boot process is complete, although this can be completely negated by the ability to boot from a diskette. If the ability to boot from a diskette is circumvented, another kind of security problem may occur, in that it could at least become difficult to repair the machine should a problem occur. At minumum, proper inventory control techniques should be used to ensure that a micro is where it is supposed to be and that it is not arbitrarily moved without some managerial supervision. Some kinds of work activity might be restricted to a specially secured pool of micros, although this is difficult to set up and enforce.
- *Data security*—Data security may be enhanced through the use of encryption, as with other systems. This would help preclude the reading of sensitive files by an attacker. If a micro is equipped with software that demands a password, it is also possible to expand that concept to include the logging of who accesses the machine, includ-

ing efforts to bypass the password or repeated attempts with various passwords. The need for backup procedures has already been noted. This may mean equipping micros with tape drives, providing a means of backing up to the server or multi-user system, backup software, and explicit education concerning the need for such procedures. By reading the memory of the micro it would be possible for an attacker to glean some information on recently run data and programs. For very sensitive data, a procedure for turning the machine off and then on again to wipe out residual information in memory might be mandated for selected software and data.

- *Software security*—There are two elements of software security that should be addressed: limiting the software that comes in from the outside (note the issues discussed relating to viruses in Chapter 7), and the removal of company software (piracy) to a personal machine at home or elsewhere. The first can be addressed by having a procedure that allows users to bring in software from the outside, providing it is checked for malicious software before it is installed. The second is more difficult, since copy protection software is often only a minor inconvenience rather than a real protection. It is possible, however, to buy such software and to "copy protect" existing programs. This will, however, make the overall management of software more difficult and is not likely to be widely used. On the other hand, there should at least be a consistent policy applied throughout the organization. If it is desirable for an employee to work at home, and to use company designated software, then the company should provide legitimate copies of that software. Such a policy would, more than anything else, diminish the illegal copying of software.

- *Disaster recovery*—Something akin to the disaster recovery mechanisms sometimes in place for large systems should also be part of a microcomputer security policy. Can data on a failed disk be recovered (or need it be)? Is there a spare machine available that a worker can use so that productivity will not be lost? Is there a technical staff in place that can deal with such issues as data recovery? Can machines be fixed quickly and economically when they fail?

The basic purpose of a microcomputer security policy in an organization or for an individual is to preclude the loss of critical data, to prevent the disclosure of sensitive data, and to limit the loss of data integrity due to the lack of quality control mechanisms.[6] If your policies and the procedures that ensue from them do these things satisfactorily, then for your organization microcomputer security has been achieved.

Multi-user Host Systems

By *multi-user host systems,* for the purpose of this chapter, I mean mini (mid-range) and mainframe computers using operating systems specifically designed to support multiple users concurrently. Granted that smaller multi-user systems, such as an 80386 or 80486 micro system running UNIX or even a multi-user MS/DOS look-alike, shares many or all of the security problems of mid-range and mainframe systems. It is frequently possible, however, to use software and hardware security products designed for microcomputers to be used with the small multi-user computers, while systems that service large numbers of users, having drastically different architectures, require unique software and hardware solutions. Bear in mind, however, that virtually all of the comments made in this section, with the exception of references to specific products, apply to *all* multi-user systems. Because the mid-range and mainframe systems have more in common (with respect to security) than they have differences, I have not tried to persist with the micro/mini/mainframe trichotomy.

The first computer systems—those sold and used from the 1940s through the late 1960s (or early 1970s) were primarily single-user systems. Multi-user operating systems and the hardware to support them did not come along until the 1960s. Those early computers were single-user in the sense that only one user at a time could run a program, since the operating system could only control one program at a time, much like MS/DOS for IBM-type microcomputers today. Once hardware and operating systems became available for a multi-user environment,[7] however, it quickly became apparent that there would have to be a means for multiple users to have access to the systems. At this point networks were born. Those early networks were star topologies. That is, when a terminal accessed the central system it did so by a more or less direct wire to that system, as did all other terminals.[8] Because modern networks and multi-user systems have their origin in the 1960s, there has been a quarter century or more of development of security procedures. This is to be contrasted to the much shorter history of microcomputers and LANs.

Vulnerabilities

As with microcomputers, multi-user computing environments have a set of peculiarities that are specific to them, although it will become apparent that some vulnerabilities are shared by all types of computer systems. One of the distinctive differences between relatively large multi-user environments and that of the microcomputers are the resources traditionally available. Before proceeding to a list of multi-user vulnerabilities, it may be well to review those resources. Typical multi-user systems have:

- At least some significant upper management support.
- Funding for specialized technical support personnel that can pay attention to issues like security (although this, too, is sometimes a problem).
- At least a quarter century of experience with access control and other security issues.
- Mature security software to deal with access control and encryption.
- A staff that has almost certainly had the experience of having some security incursion problems.
- In place procedures for backup.

- Some sense of what to do in case of a disaster, although disaster recovery is one of the most widely ignored security measures in large systems.
- Sufficient resources for some redundancy in peripherals such as disk drives and for the acquisition of uninterruptible power supplies (UPS) that will carry the system long enough for an orderly shut down.
- Personnel that specialize in the operation of the system, often on a 24-hour-a-day basis.

Virtually all of these, or analogous resources, are missing from the microcomputer environment and, often, from the small multi-user systems.

In addition to the fact that those who manage large computer systems have more resources that can be used for security, there has been considerably more work done on how to secure those systems and how to measure the adequacy of that security. Part of this has arisen because one of the major consumers of large systems has been, in the United States and elsewhere, defense establishments. In the United States the need to quantify security and to measure trust was the development of the U.S. Department of Defense's *Trusted Computer System Evaluation Criteria*, or *Orange Book*.[9] Because no system, as we have already seen, can be made totally secure the Department of Defense adopted the concept of *Trusted Computer Systems*.

The *Orange Book* defines a trusted computer system as a system that can process simultaneously a spectrum of sensitive or classified information, because it employs sufficient hardware and software security measures. Central to the idea of a trusted system is the *trusted computing base* (TCB), which refers to the hardware, firmware, and software protection mechanisms within a computer system that are responsible for enforcing a security policy. The way in which a person at a terminal can communicate directly with the trusted computing base is called a *trusted path*. Only the person or the TCB can activate this mechanism; it cannot be imitated by untrusted software. *Trusted software* is a trusted computing base's software segment.

One organization that now evaluates products for use by the U.S. government is the National Computer Security Center (NCSC). Its responsibilities are to encourage the development and use of trusted computer systems and products by developing and promulgating standards for computer security, as well as conducting and sponsoring research in computer and network security technology, security analysis, and testing methods and tools. NCSC's counterpart in the Department of Commerce is the National Institute of Standards and Technology (NIST), discussed earlier in this book. The result of NCSC evaluations is to classify software and hardware in levels of trust (as noted in both Chapters 2 and 3). Each level of security involves security models of varying formality.[10]

The rules by which trusted systems are assigned to these categories is based on a set of criteria that can be turned into explicit, often quantitative evaluations:

- The explicitness of the rules for granting or denying access.
- The extent to which the protected resources are defined.
- The precision with which users are identified.
- The detail of the record of occurrence of security-related events and user activity.
- The assurance the user has that the systems perform their stated functions.
- The quality of the documentation of trusted system functions, features, and operations.

All of this is based on certain assumptions concerning vulnerability that revolve around security policy, accountability, and authentication. In other words, lack of a reasonable security policy, lack of accountability, and deficiencies in authentication cast doubt on products that are supposed to secure a system. This includes characteristics of the operating system and add-on products that work specifically with a given operating system to further secure the system from unauthorized access and problems of data integrity. From all this we can adduce at least some of the vulnerabilities that may face medium and large-scale computer systems:

- Lack of management belief that the organization is actually vulnerable to security threats.
- Related to the foregoing point is the lack of commitment on the part of management to provide funding for appropriate security controls.
- Also, as a management issue, the failure to establish a clear security policy for the organization.
- The shortage of personnel to adequately review reports that monitor system activity or the failure to process the data in order to provide security-relevant reports.
- The tendency to opt for what is cheap rather than what is appropriate in order to achieve security.
- A large number of users with whom the computing facility has little relationship. This is particularly problematic when we recall that users can be an important part of the effort to secure a system.
- Failure to use the tools that may be available in order to secure data, even when the user is allowed access to the system.
- Insufficient management oversight of central system personnel needing to have access to the security systems—In a large installation this is one of the more ticklish problems. A large IBM mainframe shop, for example, will have a staff of several system programmers and several operators, all of whom will likely be enabled to work around the security barriers and to deal with files over which there is usually little security (such as electronic mail messages). It is not at all uncommon to have such people browse through mail messages or pass through security barriers for one reason or another. Sometimes the activity is justi-

fied, but often it is not. Even in a small LAN the system administrator will have the capacity to do such things, but when there are anywhere from 5 to 30 people so empowered in a large installation, it can get out of control.

Security for Large Multi-User Systems

As was mentioned earlier, in a multi-user environment security is more affected by the operating system (OS) than by the hardware on which the OS runs. In this section, therefore, we will take a brief look at three OS's: IBM's MVS; DEC's VMS; and UNIX. The first two are proprietary, while UNIX runs on everything from a microcomputer through the largest mainframes. This approach, hopefully, will give some sense of the options available. Actual products will be briefly described in Chapter 9, although you should be forewarned that Chapter 9 *is not* a buyer's guide. In general, with the larger systems, security is primarily a function of access control at two levels: access to the machine itself and access to data. In the IBM environment, there is typically an intermediate level: access to applications.

The term "application" has a special meaning in IBM parlance, in that it refers not to user applications but to system software that allows access to user programs. Teleprocessing monitors (TP) are an example and include IBM's CICS as well as third-party TP monitors. Thus, in order to access a database under IBM's MVS operating system it is necessary to log on initially using a User ID and password, then get into a TP monitor, also with at least another password, and then to execute the database system, which may require yet another password. DEC's VMS and UNIX may not require as many levels of password access control, although add-on security products may.

International Business Machines (IBM): MVS

IBM currently markets three operating systems for large mainframes: MVS, VM, and VSE. MVS and VSE are essentially batch-oriented operating systems to which transaction processing capabilities have been added. VM was developed to provide IBM mainframes with an alternative interactive operating system. MVS is IBM's strategic operating system for the 3090 series of computers and later models. It is currently sold in three versions: MVS/SP, MVS/XA, and MVS/ESA. Each version is progressively more powerful than the previous one, although they each require additional hardware to operate effectively. By itself MVS is not designed to be a secure operating system. For that to happen it is necessary to add a security software system. The major systems are RACF from IBM and Computer Associate International's CA-ACF2 and CA-Top Secret. These three security packages have been assigned C2 ratings by NCSC.

Although MVS is not itself a secure OS, it has embedded within it a System Authorization Facility (SAF) that allows the installation of security software. Centralized control over system security processing is provided through interfaces to SAF. Security control is passed by SAF to products such as RACF, CA-ACF2, or CA-Top Secret. Thus, MVS provides the base on which access control is based, although it does not itself provide such facilities. Optional MVS licensed products are available for additional file security, although the products mentioned also furnish data protection.

Security software can be oriented toward resource protection or toward restriction of user access. A *resource* is anything used or consumed while performing a function. Categories of resources include time, information, objects (information containers), or processors (the ability to use information). CA-ACF2, for example, is resource oriented. That is, it is designed to look at security through a specification of what resources need protection, and then to identify the users who should have access to the resource in question. The basic data on which access is based is organized by resource rather than by groups of users. On the other hand, CA-Top Secret starts with controls over a user or group of users by maintaining user information in "accessorid" collections. Thus, access control information is organized first by user group rather than by resource. RACF (IBM) combines the two approaches by maintaining both kinds of access control information. Control over resources can be maintained down to such detail as the physical address on a disk drive of a specified resource. MVS facilities provide the information for the audit trail required by a security system.

Within the NCSC scheme, all of these products have only modest ratings. All this means, of course, is that they have problems in being accepted for use in the most security conscious areas of the U.S. government. With multiple layers of access control, however, these products provide substantial access control for business environments. IBM has been struggling to achieve a higher NCSC rating for RACF, and with future enhancements from both CA and IBM their products are likely to climb the rating ladder.

Digital Equipment Corporation (DEC): VMS

DEC has standardized on VMS as the general-purpose operating system for all classes of VAX computers, including VAX microsystems, superminicomputers, and VAXclusters. The same security subsystems are available for all hardware platforms at any given release level of VMS. VMS Version 4.3 was evaluated C2 in July 1986, by NCSC. VMS provides access control to the operating system and to resources. Access control is maintained through the use of passwords, which may be user selected, system manager selected, or generated automatically. A dual password scheme (primary and secondary) is available for high-security applications and login time is limited to discourage guessing. Users may be restricted to specific terminals in the network. Restrictions can also be established based on the type of user (local, dial-up, network), type of processing (interactive, batch, network) and working times (time of day and length of session).

In order to mediate access attempts, secure the authorization database, and provide an audit trail, VMS uses the *reference monitor concept*. The reference monitor concept is an information systems access control concept that refers to an abstract machine that mediates all accesses to objects by subjects. The point of this is that files (objects) are protected through the User Identification Code (UIC) mechanism and Access Control Lists (ACLs). The UIC controls access through the user classification of *system, owner, group*, and *world*. Each category of user may be allowed or denied read, write, execute, or delete privileges. A UIC-based protection code is associated with each file on the system. When medium to high security is required, or for complex patterns of file sharing, ACLs can be used in conjunction with UICs. For each object, the ACL matches the specific access being either denied or granted with specific users. The ACL is dependent on the use of a "rights database" maintained by the system's security manager. DEC also offers a *Security Enhancement Service* (SES) for installations needing a higher level of security that meets NCSC's B1 criteria (although at this writing it had not been approved). Both an audit trail mechanism and a security alarm feature may be implemented.

AT&T UNIX System V

UNIX comes in many flavors, and security arrangements vary enormously by which subset of UNIX is being used. It is also difficult to classify UNIX as to class of machine, since it is available in one form or another from micros to mainframes. It is, however, most often thought of as a minicomputer or mid-range operating system. The importance of UNIX is that it has become a generic operating system, since it is available on such a wide variety of platforms. All UNIX systems stem from AT&T and are licensed for use by AT&T, although some have been modified extensively. The most current UNIX product from AT&T is UNIX System V. XENIX, for example, is a single-user variation of UNIX used on many small systems. The other significant sublicensed versions of UNIX are the Sun OS (from Sun Microsystems), Berkeley 4.3BSD (from the University of California, Berkeley), and now System V. In November 1989, AT&T released System V, Version 4.0, which incorporated XENIX, Sun OS, Berkeley 4.3BSD, and System V into a single standard. A variation of System V, System V/MLS, has been produced by

AT&T for high-security applications (particularly by the U.S. government). System V/MLS has achieved an NCSC rating of B1. System V itself is expected to gain a C2 rating. UNIX System V is a general-purpose, multiprogramming, multitasking, interactive operating system.

UNIX consists of a *kernel,* a *shell,* and the *file system.* The kernel is the fundamental part of a program, such as an operating system, that resides in memory at all times. A shell is an outer layer of a program that provides the user interface, or way of commanding the computer. Shells are typically add-on programs created for command-driven operating systems, such as UNIX and DOS. The shell may provide a menu-driven or graphical icon-oriented interface to the system in order to make it easier to use. The file system consists of a hierarchical directory method for organizing files on a disk storage device. Like VMS, System V uses password protection that may be selected by the user, the system administrator, or automatically. The password itself is stored in an encrypted form. There are provisions for managing password aging and for secondary passwords. It is also possible to limit a user's access to specified file areas as well as limiting the commands available through the shell. At login time a user profile is executed that may specify where the user resides, to what group the user belongs, and what processes the user may perform.

Each file is assigned an entry record stored in a system table that includes an identification number of the owner of the file and seven bits that determine the security level of the file. The file security level functions through protection modes that allow all combinations of read, write, delete, and execute access. UNIX System V/MLS has enhanced password protection, limits on numbers of tries for log-in, and higher levels of protection for the password files. System V/MLS, in conformance with NCSC standards, provides mandatory access control that limits the distribution of information to specifically authorized users. These and other features provide a more secure version of System V.

Conclusions

In some sense all contemporary multi-user systems are both computer and network controlled. It is difficult, therefore, to imagine a multi-user system without a network, even if the "network" consists only of directly connected terminals. It is no longer possible to have a system consisting only of a single card reader, for example, through which all access takes place. In an environment where a multi-user system exists, it exists for the purpose of servicing several users. It may not have an elaborate network that connects those users, but they must be connected in some manner. Networking itself grew out of this phenomenon and is now at a point where the network is an independent entity (or entities) that can exist apart from any specific processor. Even the most primitive "stand-alone" multi-user system, however, has most of the characteristics of a network, although a network may have specialized systems available to perform security or other control functions. The three multi-user operating systems described above are probably the most important of those now in use. They clearly offer many of the same security advantages, as would be expected since they all meet or exceed the same NCSC levels of trust.

The *Orange Book* model has been criticized because it addresses only computer systems (although computer systems are the focus of this chapter).[11] It has also been suggested that the *Orange Book* model is appropriate only to a government classified environment; that only the issue of secrecy is addressed; that the emphasis on *unauthorized access* misses the point that most security threats arise from inside an organization; and that the limited range of security ratings miss features that would not fit into the system. It should be noted, however, that the *Orange Book* was devised for the U.S. government, not for commercial enterprises. It should also be noted that the primary concerns of commercial computing is data integrity, accuracy, availability, and authenticity, rather than secrecy. The point being that, because government and industry have different security concerns, the emphases are likely to be different. When all this is said and done, however, the

NCSC trusted computing base model does provide some guidance for comparative evaluations of the extent to which manufacturers take security issues seriously.

Because of the extent to which microcomputers have been and are being deployed, even within a network environment there are specific security concerns that must be taken seriously. Some security practices are appropriate even for stand-alone micros: proper backup procedures, for example. Others are germane for micros attached to an LAN or a WAN. It should not be overlooked, however, that networks of micros may provide opportunities for security lacking in a stand-alone situation. There are overlapping security concerns between micros and multi-user systems, but there are also some unique issues that crop up.

Notes

1. The IBM PC was introduced in 1981. Microcomputers were actually available from the mid-1970s, using a variety of operating systems, but with Digital Research's CP/M being the most widely deployed. What IBM was able to do, however, was to give great impetus to the creation of a huge business and consumer market that was only slowly building prior to 1981. Prior to 1981 there were many manufacturers of micros based on the Z80, 8080, and other CPU architectures. Both Radio Shack (Tandy) and Apple Computers had, during the late 1970s introduced consumer microcomputers, using proprietary operating systems. Neither Apple nor Tandy had the presence in the computer marketplace of IBM, however. IBM was able not only to force standardization on an operating system (MS/PC-DOS), but also on a hardware architecture (Intel's 8086 family). Today the primary alternative to this "standard" in the mass marketplace is Apple's MacIntosh, which still uses a proprietary operating system and is based on Motorola's 68xxx chip.

2. Thomas Wm. Madron, *Microcomputers in Large Organizations* (Englewood Cliffs, NJ: Prentice-Hall, Inc., 1983), p. 1.

3. Ibid.

4. See Ibid. Table 1, "Hardware Trends," p. 148.

5. Reed Phillips, Jr., "Planning for Microcomputer Security," *Datapro Reports on Information Security* (Delran, NJ: McGraw-Hill, 1991), Vol. 1, p. IS30-100-101.

6. Note the discussion by Hal Tipton, "Developing Microcomputer Awareness," *Datapro Reports on Information Security,* Vol. 1 (Delran, NJ: McGraw-Hill, 1990), p. IS30-150-104ff.

7. For IBM and similar mainframes, a large multi-tasking operating environment actually came before a multi-user system. The early IBM 360 architecture and OS allowed a number of jobs to be run concurrently, but most jobs were typically submitted through only one or two card readers, since jobs were submitted on punched cards.

8. Be advised that this brief history is vastly over-simplified.

9. *Department of Defense Trusted Computer System Evaluation Criteria* (DOD 5200.28-STD, December 1985). The designation as the "Orange Book" came about because of the color of the publication's cover.

10. National Computer Security Center, *Trusted Computer Systems Evaluation Criteria* (*Orange Book*), DOD Standard 5200.28.

11. Note, however, that the NCSC has also published the so-called *Red Book: Trusted Network Interpretation of the Trusted Computer System Evaluation Criteria* (NCSC-TG-005), Library Number S228,526, Version 1, National Computer Security Center, Gaithersburg, MD, 1987. This publication asserts that "the specific security features, the assurance requirements, and the rating structure of the TCSEC are extended to networks of computers ranging from isolated local area networks to wide-area internetwork systems."

CHAPTER 9

A Survey of Security Products

The purpose of this chapter is to make a quick survey of the security products available and the systems on which they work. It is not a consumer's guide to such products, but it does point the way to where such products can be acquired, and where possible, the cost of such products. Because new products are constantly arriving on the market, when an installation is ready to implement new or expanded security arrangements, a search should be conducted to determine what products are available. Security products for networks are growing in popularity as theft, human error, and virus attacks become more threatening. A wide variety of manufacturers are offering an impressive variety of access-control, data encryption, and other devices. Smart cards, fingerprint readers, and retina scanners provide encoded buffers between users and computers at the high end of the security device spectrum. The fundamental approach to protection, however, is encryption—particularly hardware-based encryption devices. The Data Encryption Standard (DES) algorithm is the most widely used, although, as we have already noted, RSA Data Security, Inc. offers a competing encryption system that it claims is faster and more secure. DES is primarily a private key encryption system, while the RSA product is based on public key encryption methods.

Over the past few years the demand for security products has been growing at a relatively steady rate. Many of the products specific to networks have focused on the issue of access control. Within that context occur the use of encryption software and hardware. Even when privacy issues have been paramount, however, the primary security technique is encryption. A parallel development, not surprisingly, has also taken place with multi-user computer systems. At the LAN and microcomputer level, the concern over malicious software has been dominant, and that is reflected in many of the products available. There has been something of a movement in recent years toward the use of hand-held password generators as well as other hardware devices for authenticating the user. The dominant security mechanism, however, is some form of password control, perhaps several layers deep. It has also become apparent, however, that such devices as call-back modems or other call-back schemes do not offer the level of security as was once thought.

It should be noted that simply a mention of a product in this book is not an endorsement for that product.

Access Control Products

Not all access control software (or hardware) needs to be purchased in the market place. In fact, it may be desirable to improve login access control, for example, in such a way that it would be a local programming task. An example might be to add a questionnaire to the login procedure in addition to the normal User ID and password. Although there are probably commercial products on the market that will provide this service, I am not certain what they may be. There are several strategies that might be used in such a situation, however. Either a host OS or a network NOS may provide "hooks" that would allow modification of the login procedure. In this case the modification would be straightforward: some code that would generate the questionnaire and receive the answers coupled with a simple lookup procedure to verify the information. The file of user-supplied answers to an initial questionnaire logon should probably be encrypted.

Another strategy might be used when the login command is itself a stand-alone program for which the source code is unavailable. This is the situation, for example, with Novell's NetWare 386 (and perhaps other versions). LOGIN is simply an MS/DOS program. It may be possible to rename LOGIN.EXE to something else, say LOGIN!.EXE. Then we could write another program that we would call LOGIN.EXE or LOGIN.COM. Our program, when executed, would first (or perhaps last) generate the questionnaire and receive the user's responses, comparing those responses to a database containing the user's profile. If the profile matches, then our new program could itself execute (by SHELLing to DOS) LOGIN!.EXE where NetWare would ask for the User ID and password, which would be the official login. These and probably other strategies could be used to devise a questionnaire procedure to improve access control if that was deemed appropriate. The point is that adding a questionnaire to the login procedure is not necessarily an arduous or expensive approach.

Domestic and International WAN Access Control

With commercial products the availability of a device or software is largely a function of the historical marketplace. Access to domestic WANs, and here we are talking primarily about corporate networks, has often been through the standard dial-up telephone system. Early on it became desirable to improve access control under those conditions, and the result was a fairly large array of products that create some sort of a dial-back process. We have discussed the deficiencies of dial-back elsewhere, so suffice it to say at this point that today's dial-back techniques are often coupled with other forms of access control, such as an additional layer of passwords. Some products for either dial-access or direct connect supply a variety of techniques for access control. Such methods in addition to call-back, where appropriate, may include hand-held password generators (HPG), direct connect, or other token devices. They may also require log-ons (User IDs and passwords). There are variations on the theme as well. In a dial-access environment the device may answer a call with a synthesized voice asking for an access code. If the code is supplied, then a modem takes over; otherwise the call is terminated.

Because such devices are designed for WANs, by definition they interface to public communications networks, such as the telephone system, even when access is through a dedicated line rather than dial-access. The device, therefore, must be configured somewhere on the network. That "somewhere" may be either on the analog side of the communication link (that is, directly connected to the telephone line) or to the digital side of the link (between the modem and the other network devices or computers). This implies that the device may need to know something about data transmission rates. Typically, those rates are relatively slow, usually not more than 19.2 Kb/s, although there are at least two products that allow data rates up to 38.4 Kb/s (Radius Computer Services Ltd. *Datasafe 2000* and *Datasafe 3000*). Cylink Corp. offers *CIDEC-HS*, which will operate over networks running from 56 Kb/s to about 7 M/bs, and at DS-1 speeds of 1.544 M/bs, using either DES or RSA algorithms. Some products also interface to LANs (Digital Pathways (U.K.) Ltd. *ICAN*, for example). More often than not the manufacturers of devices outside the United States provide interfaces based on international standards, while U.S. firms tend to be more concerned with U.S. standards.

Other features of access control devices include the number of incoming and outgoing lines controlled by the device; support for facilities such as PBX extensions; designated time slots; prioritized queuing of incoming calls; variations in the number of concurrent calls allowed; encryption capabilities; diagnostics; and logging devices to create an audit trail. The number of lines controlled by a single device can range from one to several thousand. If dial-back is a feature of the device, the number of outgoing lines for dial-back purposes may be different (usually fewer) than the number of incoming lines. A smart device may be able to be programmed to allow specific users in only during specified periods of time and may be able to queue incoming calls in order to manage the lines available to the host system.

Both the pricing and the capabilities of products vary greatly. One recent list of 23 U.S. WAN access products[1] seemed to suggest that the price per port secured ranged (in 1992) from $15.83 to $2,787.50. The problem with these numbers is that various vendors obviously reported somewhat differently from one another on the one hand and the actual level of protection provided ranged from almost nothing to extensive, roughly correlated (although not always) with the average price per port. Although the actual numbers are suspect, the fact remains that wide variations in pricing and protection do exist among the products available. Similar variations occur in the international market, as well. Most of the devices surveyed provide one or more of the following access control mechanisms:

- Hand-held password generator;
- Token systems other than HPGs;
- Passwords;
- Encryption;
- Simple call-back;
- Programmed call-back;
- Calling and called address checking; and
- Multiple-call call-backs.

In addition to these relatively "standard" approaches to access control, some biometric devices, more commonly used for physical access control, may also be appropriate for high-end access to network systems.

Mini and Mainframe Access Control

As was noted in Chapter 8, multi-user (mini and mainframe) access control tends to be a combination of operating system features and stand-alone products that work in conjunction with specific operating systems. These systems are software rather than hardware, and ordinarily run on the host machine being protected. Some products may also be CPU dependent, regardless of the operating system. Moreover, some of the software systems may require additional hardware in order to operate. These additional requirements may include disk storage, specialized terminals, or, in the case of large IBM systems, particular TP monitors such as CICS. In virtually every product the basic technique is some form of password protection. As with other security products, prices vary according to several variables, but these systems are generally expensive to buy and maintain. Pricing is often geared to the size of system or processor group.

Typical products for IBM mainframes have already been discussed to some extent in Chapter 8, but some reiteration may be useful. Computer Associates International, Inc., has several products, including CA-ACF2 MVS (1992 pricing: $21,800 to $54,450 plus a maintenance fee of 15% of the purchase price per year), CA-ACF2 VM (1992 pricing: $12,500 to $31,500 plus 15%/year), for MVS and VM operating systems. CAI also sells CA-ACF2 VS1 for the VS1 operating system. As a result of corporate acquisitions, CAI also manufactures and sells another series of products for the IBM mainframe market: CA-Top Secret MVS (1992 pricing: $21,730 to $54,450 plus 15%/year); CA-Top Secret VM (1992 pricing: $12,600 to $31,500 plus 15%/year); and CA-Top Secret VS1 (1992 pricing: $12,600 to $31,500 plus 15%/year). Each of these versions has approximately the same capabilities but, with many of the IBM mainframe products, the pricing is market driven rather than cost-of-production driven. Thus the price differentials.

IBM itself is the major competitor to CA with RACF (Resource Access Control Facility). It offers RACF/MVS (1992 pricing:

$27,800 to $69,440 plus $751 to $1,120 per month) and RACF/VM (1992 pricing: $6,890 to $54,930 plus $665 to $886 per month). Other products of the same general sort include Goal Systems International, Inc., *Alert/CICS* (1992 pricing: $9,000 for VSE, $15,000 for MVS plus 15%/year), *Alert/VM* (1992 pricing: $16,000 plus 15%/year), *Alert/VSE* (pricing: $9,000 plus 15%/year); and Systems Center, Inc., *VMSecure* (1992 pricing: $14,000 plus a maintenance fee after the first year). Similar products exist for other mainframe systems, such as Unisys Corp.'s *InfoGuard* for Unisys B5900, B6900, and B7900 mainframe computers (1992 pricing: $8,450 to $34,300 plus $250 to $700/month). Various financing schemes exist, but the pricing quoted is about what would be paid by a mainframe owner as an initial fee plus additional yearly (or monthly) costs. Sometimes the monthly/yearly fees are call maintenance and sometimes license fees. From the standpoint of a mainframe owner, however, these are the amounts that would have to be budgeted regardless of what the vendor calls the money they charge.

Somewhat parallel systems exist for most of the major super-mini and mini computer systems. Satcom, for example, sells *Interface/3000* for the Hewlett-Packard 3000 (1992 pricing: $3,000 plus maintenance fee) and Unitech Software, Inc. provides *USecure* for various UNIX platforms (1992 pricing: $400 to $3,000 plus maintenance). More closely locked into their respective operating systems are the security systems for Data General's *AOS/VS* and Digital Equipment Corporation's (DEC) *VAX/VMS*. The latter two are not strictly comparable in pricing because much of the security system is intrinsic to the operating environments. On the other hand, DEC, for example, does offer additional add-on security features and services (as noted in Chapter 8). The same is true of UNIX V/MLS from AT&T.

If one is in the mainframe business and needs to secure access to the system, it will not be cheap. Pricing is largely a function of how many machines (or operating systems) are sold per year, rather than differentials in the cost of producing and supporting the products. Generally, the higher the machine/operating system price, the higher the security system price. Typically, too, the higher these prices, the fewer the number of machines/operating systems sold per year.

LAN/Micro Access Control

I have stressed elsewhere[2] that LANs are not just for microcomputers. It is true, however, that when LANs link a wide variety of computer systems the total configuration is likely to be quite large, with at least some of the products already discussed in use on specific host systems or on WANs that link LANs together. It is in the area of micro-based LANs that there are new concerns being raised. Quite sophisticated microcomputer LANs are now being installed in organizations that previously had little or no in-house computing at all, or to replace mid-range to large-scale computing systems. In the case of a microcomputer LAN being an organization's first computing facility, no matter how small, it is soon discovered that the problems with security (and other operational details) are parallel to those of shops that have had larger-scale computing for many years.

With microcomputer LANs it is possible that we will ultimately find the problem of security somewhat more complicated than with multi-user host systems. First, there is the issue of the NOS. If the NOS is server-based (such as Novell or Banyan systems), then the problem of securing the server is similar in concept (if not entirely in execution) to the problem of securing multi-user systems. In fact, through User IDs and passwords, and through varying levels of user security, access to the servers can be restricted or denied. If the NOS is a peer-oriented LAN (such as Artisoft's *LANTastic*), not requiring a server, then security may have to be pushed back to each individual machine on the system. Even with a server-based LAN, however, it should be understood that access to files on the server may also be a problem. With such a LAN the server does not usually act as a multi-user computer system. Rather, it acts as a database repository, since the processing continues to take place on each individual workstation attached to the server.

Typical access security software for the microcomputer LAN environment tends to include such techniques as additional (beyond the NOS and certainly beyond DOS) password protection, some ID other than passwords (an encoded diskette, for example), controlled access to DOS as well as the NOS, protection for individual files or groupings of files, security over the directory file structure, and perhaps other access control characteristics. The security software may also include automatic scanning for malicious software. Some products provide only access control, while others provide encryption mechanisms. The use of encryption does not directly address the problem of access control, although, as applied to data, this may augment other techniques considerably. As with other systems, if encryption is applied to secure files of passwords, or in some other fashion used to directly support access controls, then it must be considered as part of the access control mechanism. In early 1991 *Datapro Reports on Information Security*[3] listed nearly 60 products for LAN/microcomputer access control. Pricing was generally consistent with other LAN/micro products, with both single-user and LAN rates.

Physical Access Control

Unlike some books on computer security, physical security has been discussed only in passing in previous pages. Physical security consists of the measures necessary to protect the computer and related equipment and their contents from damage by intruders, fire, accident, and environmental hazards. It is based on physical access control—the procedures used to authorize and validate requests for physical access to computer, communication, or network physical facilities, to help ensure the physical integrity of those systems and facilities. One of the reasons why we have paid scant attention to physical access control is that with modern networks there may be no "central site." On the other hand, even with modern networks there are always points at which critical equipment exists. In a broadband system it is the headend. In other networks it may be important switching locations or even more traditional computer rooms.

There are a variety of physical access control systems available in the market place, stemming from a simple door lock to state-of-the-art biometric control systems. The purpose of physical security is to control access to the physical environment, to control access to stored data, to monitor traffic and system usage at an installation, and perhaps to take employee time and attendance. The most typical systems in addition to standard physical locks are mechanical or electronic locks keyed with the use of an access code given by the entrant. A step up is a lock keyed by a credit card–type device and read by a reader. At the top are biometric devices. There are five biometric technologies currently in use: fingerprint patterns, hand geometry, retinal scanning, voice verification, and signature dynamics. The first three are physical characteristics, while the latter two are essentially behavioral traits. Biometric devices provide a virtually foolproof method of verification of the identity of the person requesting access. The cost of biometric access systems range (in 1992) from about $1,200 (for a signature reader) to approximately $7,000 (for a retinal scanner) for minimum configurations.

From what has already been suggested it should be easy to infer that there are three types of physical access control systems: stand-alone, on-line, and distributed. A stand-alone device is one that requires no attachment to a central computer—it contains all the electronics necessary to provide access control. An on-line system is one that requires connection to a computer. With a distributed system each reader has intelligence, but it is also networked so that it can be programmed from a central site. Many people reading this book, even if they have never seen a computer room, will recognize these descriptions as fitting the electronic locks now becoming common in hotels. Most access systems use one of three techniques: combination lock, portable key, or biometrics. The combination lock may be mechanical, electronic (triggered by a keypad), or the use of key questions. Portable keys include common mechanical keys and locks, plastic magnetic- or punched-coded cards and/or tokens, or proximity devices. Proximity devices are those, like garage-door openers, that use infrared or radio waves to unlock or open doors. We have already discussed the common biometric techniques: face recognition, fingerprint, signature, hand geometry, voice, and retinal scanners.

Data Encryption

There is, apparently, some difference in the approach to algorithms used for encryption on large systems and those used with micro-based networks. Although the products listed by *Datapro* involve vendor self-selection (thus we do not know the representativeness of the sample), of the total of 71 encryption algorithms for LAN/micro systems mentioned in the article cited above, 38 implemented the Data Encryption Standard (DES), 30 implemented proprietary schemes (and usually a product had both), while only 3 used some other system, including 2 with RSA. On the higher-end host side, however, of the 21 encryption algorithms used by the products listed, not one implemented RSA, 4 used proprietary algorithms, 15 employed DES, and 2 used something else. Clearly, DES is the most popular encryption algorithm, both for LAN/micro systems and for larger-scale multi-user computing environments. This breaks down to 71% of the algorithms employed by mainframe products being DES, while 54% of the algorithms built into the LAN/micro products were DES. When we realize that virtually all LAN/micro products that used a proprietary algorithm also used DES, however, the percentage for DES works out to about 93% for LAN/micro products. Virtually all these products are used to encrypt data files to protect the privacy of those files as they reside on disk or are transmitted over communication lines in a network.

Like other software, there is a substantial difference in price between micro-based products and multi-user-based programs. For IBM mainframe operating systems the prices range (in 1992) from about $1,750 to $23,500. The micro software typically runs (in 1992) from about $100 (single-user) to about $600 (LAN-based). A major difference between the two types of software is that most of the mainframe products include subroutines that can be called from application programs in

COBOL, FORTRAN, or other mainframe languages, as well as coming with a version able to run as a stand-alone program. The micro-based software is universally encapsulated in stand-alone programs. With micros, of course, there are other ways for an application program to make use of a secondary program—namely, the ability to shell to DOS to run such software. An equivalent facility is not usually available, or not available in a convenient form, on large systems.

Disaster Recovery

If it is difficult to get management to fund adequate security arrangements for networks and computers, it is well nigh impossible to get adequate funding for disaster recovery in most organizations. The requirement for disaster recovery comes from two sources: auditors who question whether an organization can stay in business if a disaster to its computer systems occur, and various legal requirements for disaster recovery that may exist by virtue of contractual, legislative, or regulatory obligations. *Disaster,* in this sense, means a condition in which an organization is deemed unable to function as a result of some natural or human-created occurrence. Disasters can occur in networks to host systems, to LAN servers, and/or to critical subsets of the network itself (nodes, routers, bridges, or even the wiring plant). In order to have a disaster recovery operation—the act of recovering from the effects of disruption to a computer facility and restoring, in a preplanned manner, the capabilities of the facility—there must exist a disaster recovery plan. A disaster recovery plan consists of the preplanned steps to be taken that make possible the recovery of an organization's computer facility and/or the applications processed there. Such a plan is sometimes called a contingency plan or business resumption plan. Unfortunately, all these things are easier to say than to do, even when money is not at issue.

When disasters are discussed it is often in the context of some "Act of God" happening, such as an earthquake, a hurricane, or a war. While these disasters can be real enough, disasters, like security threats in general, are more apt to be lower key and stem from internal sources rather than from major cataclysm. It is this issue that is not well understood. One or two examples will suffice. The outage of an AT&T switching computer in early 1991 eliminated long distance calling for a large number of people. It turned out that the problem was a staff failure to respond to alarms given off when power for the system shifted to its uninterruptible power supply (UPS). A UPS is typically configured to allow an orderly shutdown—not to power a system for a long period of time. In this case the batteries were allowed to run down, thus creating the outage. A second example is also UPS related. At a fairly large computer operation I once managed we also had a significantly sized UPS. There was a large battery room filled with storage batteries. Storage batteries of a certain type give off hydrogen gas, which is inflammable. In such an environment, if a connection on a battery is loose, so that it occasionally sparks, then the room may catch fire or explode. That is what happened to us. That would not, ordinarily, have been a disaster in the ordinary sense, but the ash from the burning batteries was sucked into the air conditioning system that serviced the computer room as well as the battery room.

This was a case where, even though we had contingency plans, they were not good enough. The use of a UPS is part of disaster protection, certainly. And a separate air conditioning system apart from that which services the building generally is also part of an effort to avoid difficulties. Unfortunately, those people designated with the responsibility to check the batteries (not on the computer center staff) had not done their jobs well enough. Although the ash from the battery fire did not irreparably damage the computer equipment, it was all over the place. We had to shut down for 24 hours to clean up the mess before we could reliably restart the equipment. In this particular case our network (a CATV-based broadband system) continued to function throughout the period servicing systems not in the central computer room, but the mainframe systems were out of action. It was fortunate that the problem occurred on a Friday evening and service was restored by Sunday. In both these instances there was no natural disaster; the problems were oversights by employees or contractors of the organizations in question. If it had taken a week to restore service to my own organization, rather than 24 hours, we would have had a disaster of classic proportions.

Apart from a contingency plan that specifies disaster avoidance, what can we plan for in order to ensure that recovery from a disaster is fast and certain. First, there needs to be a *real* disaster recovery plan. Second, there needs to be testing of the plan on a regular and periodic basis. Some of the relatively simple things that can be done are part of good operating procedures: off-site backup storage, fault-tolerant architectures for critical systems, and a realistic set of agreements allowing the operation of the business from an alternative site. Off-site backup storage ensures that we will have the data and programs to recover if a disaster strikes, no matter how we proceed with the recovery. Particularly with LAN servers, fault-tolerant or mirroring architectures are becoming increasingly feasible economically because of the falling price of hardware, the availability of software to support such an activity, and the networking available to join systems together. With large mainframe systems, however, the two-computer or n-computer solution may be out of the question financially. The alternative is to contract with a vendor of disaster recovery services for a hot or cold site backup facility. Such facilities are shared by multiple clients on the gamble that major disasters will not affect all clients (or even more than one) concurrently.

This concept of a hot or cold site backup was much more appropriate in the days when computers were fed from cards rather than from extensive networks. Part of the failure of backup sites is often the lack of communications support. It does not help to have an alternative computer system if we cannot get the data to it. Nevertheless, vendors of disaster recovery services do provide facilities for both hot and cold site support. A *hot site* is a backup facility that is fully operational and compatible with the site's hardware and software. It provides security, fire protection, and telecommunications capabilities. In contrast, a *cold site* is a DP hardware-ready room, or series of rooms, which is ready to receive hardware for disaster recovery. Finally, a *warm site* is similar to a cold site, but with telecommunications facilities. Of these three, a cold site is the most economical but the most difficult to get operational, and may involve contracts with hardware vendors for right of first shipment in case of a disaster. The hot site is the most expensive, but should be able to provide operational uptime in a matter of a few hours. A warm site is somewhere between these two extremes.

There are a number of companies that furnish cold, warm, and hot site disaster recovery services for varying amounts of money. While these services originated for large mainframe shops, as the popularity of minis and super-minis has increased there has been a growing demand for similar services. Once the province of independent vendors, manufacturers of computer equipment, such as DEC and IBM, now have disaster recovery services. Among the largest vendors of disaster recovery services are Comdisco Disaster Recovery Services, Inc. and SunGard Data Systems, Inc. There are several other fairly major disaster recovery vendors and a host of smaller ones around the United States. Several of these vendors also provide consulting services to assist in disaster recovery planning. For hot site contracts, part of the service includes mandatory test procedures that test the plan on a periodic basis. For a business dependent on a mainframe or large mini this kind of service may be the most appropriate approach to disaster recovery. Perhaps the most difficult part of a true hot site is the provision of appropriate networking services.

For server-based LANs it may be more feasible for an organization to set up its own alternative hot site. First, most LANs can support more than one file server. It is feasible, therefore, to have a backup server either stored away for potential future use, or on-line as a mirroring or fault-tolerant device on the LAN, but in another part of the building or in another building. If the network in question is essentially an extended LAN—a network of LANs—a secondary file server, perhaps mirroring the primary server, could even be placed on the other side of a campus or even in another state.

Physical Security

As we have noted elsewhere, physical security consists of the measures necessary to protect the computer and related equipment and their contents from damage by intruders, fire, accident, and environmental hazards. Physical security is not so much a matter of products as of prudence in planning. For physical security we certainly want appropriate physical access controls in place. Perhaps more important than physical access controls, however, are provisions for properly monitoring physical facilities, for dealing with fires, and for maintaining the integrity of the facility. For a computer room, for example, the latter issue means precluding operators or others from excessive leaving and entering, as well as maintaining good environmental controls.

In a network, physical security may also mean securing the cabling plant and ensuring that network devices are environmentally safe as well as safe from intruders. Physical protection, which has become a kind of hallmark of mainframe computer rooms, should also be considered for other kinds of sensitive information processing facilities. If a business is dependent on the continued operation of its network and computer system(s), then no matter how small the system, it needs protection. There seems to be a growing feeling that simply because computers are becoming smaller, and organizations are able to downsize their computer facilities yet continue to do the same level of computing, the computers and network nodes no longer need a secure environment. We must remember, however, that what we are protecting, first and foremost is not the hardware per se, but the information the hardware contains.

When an organization does decide that it needs physical access control for its information systems, it often implements such devices to control access to the physical environment, to control access to stored data, to monitor traffic and system use, and to take employee time and attendance. Not everyone in an organization needs access to all parts of a facility at all times. A mail clerk, for example, may not be authorized to walk around the computer room, although an executive vice president may be so empowered. Data that supports the ongoing operation of any organization should be considered sensitive, since in the absence of that information the organization may stop functioning. The monitoring of traffic flow on a network or through a computer system may be used both for further security analyses as well as for budgeting purposes. Finally, some physical access control systems can log the time and date of the entrance and exit of employees, thus providing an audit trail of who had access, should a problem occur. Even in these days of powerful small systems and local area networks, some physical access controls should be in place in order to prevent either intentional or accidental loss of stored information.

Conclusions

In this chapter I have attempted a brief overview of some of the many security products available today. When an organization actually goes shopping for security devices and products, it should be preceded by some research and use of standard reference works. A very useful, continuously updated product is the *Datapro Reports on Information Security,* cited elsewhere in this chapter, among other available publications. Some of the U.S. government publications cited in this book can also be useful guides to products. New products are coming to market with some frequency, so the intent of this chapter has been simply to give a glimpse of the classes of products available. It should be kept in mind that the acquisition of security products should be made in the context of a well thought out security policy for a specific organization. Otherwise, too little or too much protection may be acquired. Network security, after all, is a compromise between the level of protection needed or desired and the ability to pay for that protection.

Notes

1. Anon., "Network Access Control Systems," *Datapro Reports on Information Security* (Delran, NJ: McGraw-Hill, 1991), pp. IS36-001-153 to 159.

2. Thomas Wm. Madron, *Local Area Networks: The Next Generation* (New York: John Wiley & Sons, 1990); and *Enterprise Wide Computing* (New York: John Wiley & Sons, 1991).

3. *Datapro Reports on Information Security* (1991), pp. IS31-001-153ff.

C H A P T E R **10**

How Much Protection Is Enough?

This book could not be, nor have I attempted to make it, an encyclopedia of network and information security. The primary objective in writing the book was to provide a technical/managerial audience with the materials necessary to understand the issues and the vulnerabilities involved in the operations of networks and their associated peripheral devices, including all shapes and sizes of computers. Too often books on this subject have been written for an audience—often auditors or technicians—that give short shrift to the practical problems involved in managing a network. As a tool for use during the reading of this book and for future use I have also provided a glossary that covers at least the most important security, network, and computing terms. In short, this should be a book capable of providing the reader with the information necessary to begin planning for network security.

A major subtheme, reiterated throughout, is the necessity for security planning. Network and other security does not happen magically. Moreover, because of the cost of securing a network, adequate planning will help focus on the real security needs of the organization, rather than on assumed, presumed, or fictional needs. Thus, in Chapters 1–3 we saw that, first, there was a need to be concerned about security, and second that, security threats are real, but that there is a cost, both monetary and procedural (and hence, behavioral from the end users standpoint). Second, we looked at how we might think about security needs by building an informal management model of network security. After all, if we cannot think clearly about security, it is very difficult to do anything about it. Emphasis at that point was placed on the development of a security policy for an organization that would realistically meet that organization's needs. As an aid to thinking about network security issues, and because "open systems" is of unique importance in the 1990s, the third chapter described the OSI Security Architecture. A result of reading Chapter 3 should have been a deeper understanding of how the various components of a complete security system may fit together, even under circumstances where our network is not built on formal OSI models. During this discussion we saw the relationship between security services and security mechanisms. The latter are the actual methods that can be used for securing a network in order to provide the needed services.

The planning theme was extended in Chapter 4 to a review of the methods available for understanding and recognizing our own security risks. These techniques include security audits and risk analysis (both qualitative and quantitative). Just to assert, with no justification, that there is a security "problem" is probably too apocalyptic. After all, we don't want to be in the situation of Chicken Little running around screaming that the "sky is falling" when it is not. To do so is to use up our supply of credibility. On the other hand, managers of technical environments are the first salespersons of security to their own organizations. For the most part, nothing good ever happens accidentally. We also do not want to be caught with a significant security threat, never having given thought to what we might do about it. Risk analysis is a way to define the problem specifically in the context of a particular organization. In other words, reading this book is a first step, not the end point of considering security issues.

Early in the book it became clear that the *primary* method for protecting the data transport on a network was encryption. In Chapter 5, therefore, we took a longer look at what encryption is all about, how it works, and where it should take place on a network. If encryption is the primary technique for maintaining privacy, the primary *problem* is access control to the network and its peripherals. The issues surrounding access to a network and the ways in which access can be controlled were discussed in some depth in Chapter 6. Not all networks, of course, need the same level of access control, but where the need is great, we saw that there are methods for tightening up that control. A particular contemporary security problem, malicious software (worms, viruses, etc.), was discussed in Chapter 7, largely because it is an important contemporary threat and we must be prepared to deal with the problem. We saw in that discussion, however, that many of the general ways of dealing with security threats also apply to the control of viruses.

While this book focuses on network security as opposed to computer security, the two are closely related. For that reason Chapter 8 focused on the varying demands of micros and multi-user (minis and mainframes) computer systems and their peculiar security needs. Finally, in Chapter 9, there was a review of various classes of security products that can aid an installation in protecting its network. Particularly important in that discussion were access control products. We also introduced a few issues, as a by-product of discussing hardware and software, that had not been previously mentioned in any depth. I might add that there are some network security issues that have not been discussed, including the specific topic of micro-to-mainframe security. Part of the reason is that this issue has been noted at various places throughout the book and is tied directly into the discussions in Chapter 8. Suffice it to say at this point that several link vendors are selling systems to control user access to micro-to-mainframe applications. When purchasing a micro-mainframe software package, users should be aware of the available security options. According to D. Boyd, an adequate package will provide security at both the database level and the terminal or microcomputer level.[1] Common security facilities include the support of a security log and user-changeable passwords.

The Impact of Security Measures

Enterprise-wide computing provides significant potential for improving the operations of an organization. For a business, it also becomes a strategic issue, for it should also provide a competitive advantage for that business. Unfortunately, enterprise-wide computing also can create possibilities for confidential data to be illegally appropriated by downloading it to personal computer diskettes from mainframe resident files, according to H. Landgarten.[2] With the proliferation of microcomputers and the potential for remote access, as well as various federal directives and right to privacy laws, data security became a matter of concern. We have noted throughout this book that all the features of modern computing and networking present both problems and opportunities. Yet it is important to understand that there is no way to provide 100-percent, total security. Security awareness is the key to providing a useful security policy, and that policy is the key to building a security program.

There are other unresolved problems with increased protection, however. We have briefly touched on the problem of the impact of security measures on system performance elsewhere. It is appropriate at this point, however, to review this issue. First, virtually any security measure will have a detrimental impact on the performance of the system being secured. Second, almost without fail users will object to security measures, since those measures make the network more difficult to use. It was the security procedures traditionally used on large mainframe systems that bothered many users to the point where they insisted on moving first to microcomputers and then to a departmental LAN environment. It is difficult to imagine user-friendly security, since security features are designed primarily to keep people out—not make it easier to get in. Yet, as local networks become linked in regional, national, and international networks, it behooves corporations and governments to pay attention to security.

It is difficult to overemphasize the negative side of security systems, since they, in turn, will affect productivity, morale, and even budgetary considerations. Moreover, the ultimate success of security systems requires the cooperation of those using the systems. If they don't take security seriously, then it will be even more difficult to apply successful security measures. The importance of personnel in the security process was underscored in an analysis of the distribution of security budgets when in mid-1990 *ComputerWorld* reported that "to prevent damaging accidents as well as calculated offenses, most of a company's security budget is spent on educating its personnel."[3] Specifically, *Computer-World's* data suggested that on the average 68 percent of a company's security budget is spent on personnel. Although the *ComputerWorld* report is somewhat difficult to interpret, since they did not define the meaning of "personnel" or other categories, it nevertheless clearly demonstrates the point made above regarding the need for employee compliance in the security process. I have already suggested that an important part of a security plan will be the provision for ongoing security education and training of the users of the network. Such training must include not only how to deal responsibly with the security measures, but also with the need for and desirability of having those measures in the first place. After all, if people do not believe that security is an issue, they will not take it seriously.

In general then, we can list several areas where the implementation of security measures will impact an organization:

- Personnel and their behavior.
- Throughput across the network.

In this context we need to be aware that both end-to-end and link encryption will slow throughput down, since every time a file is encrypted and then decrypted will use up time. The actual amount of time will vary, depending on whether the entity being encrypted is a password or a very large file or something in between those two extremes. If a transaction normally takes, on a terminal connected directly to a computer system, two seconds to complete, then the following items will add additional (hypothetical in this case) time to that transaction:

1. The network—Less than one second to five or more seconds, depending on the nature of the network.
2. Security measures—Less than one second to several seconds, depending on how much encryption is taking place along the way and the size of the "files" being encrypted (these may be blocks of data that constitute screen displays).
3. Security and network layering (see the discussion of OSI)—If security measures are initiated at only one layer of a network protocol stack, the situation may be as indicated in (2) above. If, however, multiple layers of security are used at the three network layers most likely to be affected, then the times could be tripled.

Thus, without regard for anything else, a two second transactional response time may end up as say, a ten second response. The cumulative effect of ten second vs. two second response times can considerably influence the productivity levels of at least some personnel. These estimates may, in fact, be low. In a test of a software implementation of the DES algorithm, for example, it took 48.39 seconds to encrypt a 27Kb file. A file of significant size, therefore, might take a while. Actual timings are, of course, a function not only of the algorithm used, but also of the skill of the programmer in implementing the algorithm in code. The timing might also be improved by firmware implementations. Other factors affect speed as well. Other algorithms/programs, I might add, were able to encrypt the same file in a second or less. The point is, however, that encryption may well slow down a file transfer and increase throughput significantly.

- Processing time and response characteristics of the hosts on which the transactions reside.

Because of these problems it is unlikely that even in a security conscious environment everything would be encrypted. It is also true, however, that for very important and sensitive documents, the throughput issues are less important than is security of the material being transmitted.

Closing the Barn Door

Closely related to the issues of the data integrity and security in a large organization are "backup" and other operational problems. If your data are important to you and your organization, then they should be protected from inadvertent loss or damage, as well as from theft or inappropriate change. In a central data processing facility these issues are confronted by regular daily, weekly, monthly, quarterly, and yearly backups, storage of the backup tapes in secure locations, and storage in multiple locations. This means that in a well-run system the absolute loss of data is a rare occurrence. Any micro user knows, however, even if he or she understands all the admonitions about the need for backup, that backup rarely occurs in the single-user environment. If the mainframe is used as an archival machine for micro-based data, then proper backup and recovery are possible through normal mainframe channels.

The proper time to be concerned about security, however, is before a problem occurs—not after. It is easier and generally cheaper to prevent a problem than to recover from it. Of course, if an unexpected security problem does occur, it will impress upon management the need for a security policy and procedures. It is always appropriate to put a security plan in place if one does not now exist. Doing it after the fact just makes less sense than doing it before anything happens. A kind of security problem that could exist in many organizations may provide an example of a security threat. Many organizations have had the experience of having paper checks stolen and then having attempts made to cash a bogus check. Typically, check stock is placed under some kind of lock and key to minimize the possibility of theft. If those checks are written on a local printer, it is easier to secure them than on a remote printer. In some situations, however, it is necessary to print checks at remote locations, so that is where the check stock is stored. Still, if the checks are locked up, then they may have as good security as if they were back at the host site.

Often, such checks are printed on a remote printer connected via a leased telephone line to the host. The organization must maintain that line in order to do printing. Now we want to cut our communication costs. What are the alternatives? One alternative is to have the host site produce a print-image file for the checks and then download that file to a computer at a remote site for printing. Unfortunately, if the print file is not encrypted it might be possible for someone at the remote site to alter an amount or payee or even add an extraneous check to the print run. Even with the printer connected to the host via the leased line, however, it would be possible to intercept checks coming from the host by substituting a microcomputer for the printer and capturing the print output to disk. The print file is not, in other words, secure in any event, and we are paying a premium price for communicating with the printer. One solution may be to go to dial access and have the host site download the print file in an encrypted format. At the remote site, a specialized printing program for the checks might be written that would decrypt and print the print file, and then erase the print file (with a security erasure), following the completion of the print job. It is true that the print file would exist for a short time in unencrypted form, but the process is at least more secure.

We could further ensure the integrity of the data by requiring a password in order to start the printing process and to write the temporary file to a read-only class of files. There are other procedures that might be put in place that would further protect the check data. By the time we were finished, however, the security on the checks would be at least better than simply running the checks on the remote printer from the host site. We should give some thought to the security problem, however, before a problem occurs. In this case, before bogus checks are processed.

A Security Review Procedure

Clearly, an organization is responsible for its own protection. In Chapter 4 we discussed security audits and risk analysis. These steps are only part of an ongoing effort to secure a network. If no active planning has taken place, the first step might be to use an existing checklist, just to gain an overview on what the security requirements for a given organization might be. The use of a checklist is an appropriate first step, since it is a low-cost qualitative approach to getting a handle on potential problems. However, the process may not stop until a full-blown (though expensive) quantitative risk analysis has been undertaken. The checklist discussed in this chapter is taken from Charles Cresson Wood, *et al.*, *Computer Security: A Comprehensive Controls Checklist* [4], and is only part of a much larger checklist for an entire computing environment. The checklist used here may be found at the end of this chapter.

The checklist has been used *almost* verbatim from Wood. It has been updated in two ways. First, occasional changes in wording have been substituted or added to reflect recent advances in networking. Second, several new items have been added. In both cases the changes and additions have been printed in *italics*. One other caveat seems appropriate. The term *telecommunications* is often taken to mean a process that takes place over a telephone line. Here, as in this entire book, that term has a more general meaning: the transfer of data from one place to another over communications lines or channels; the communication of all forms of information, including voice and video. Telephone line technology is no longer a defining characteristic of telecommunications. To reiterate terms that have already been defined: a *communications network* is the total network of devices and transmission media (radio, cables, etc.) necessary to transmit and receive intelligence; a *network* itself is 1) A system of interconnected computer systems and terminals; or 2) a series of points connected by communications channels.

As you read over or use the checklist you will note that each item is a question that can be answered "yes," "no," or "not applicable." It will also become apparent that not every item is as important as every other item. For scoring purposes, subjective "weights" were given to each item by the checklist authors (and the added items by me). Those weights are implied at the end of each item, where a code has been inserted in parentheses, such as "VH" or "H." Those codes have the meanings and rough numeric values found in Table 10.1.

A "yes" answer to an item means that the control exists; a "no" means that the control does not exist (but probably should); and "not applicable" means that the control is not appropriate for a particular organization. A control is applicable when both the asset to be protected and a security threat exist. It is easy to confuse "no" and "not applicable," and, in using the checklist, those being interviewed should be made clearly aware of the difference. What a checklist can do is to sensitize management to

TABLE 10.1. Checklist Item Weighing

Code	Meaning—Level of Importance	Weight
VH	Very High importance	0.9
H	High importance	0.7
M	Medium importance	0.5
L	Low importance	0.3
VL	Very Low importance	0.1

system weaknesses. It can also provide an organized and well-documented catalogue of controls and weaknesses useful in subsequent, more detailed, analysis. The reader should be aware that there are weaknesses in the use of any checklist. First, no checklist, no matter how well prepared, will be so comprehensive that nothing is omitted. Second, the user should not be reticent about adding items to the checklist, providing that they have the same format and response capability as the originals. Remember, however, that in order to score the checklist it will be necessary to assign a subjective weight to any new items. In order to do so, someone can arbitrarily pick the weight. If a more systematic method is deemed necessary, it would be possible to use a modified form of the Delphi Method (see Chapter 4) with a group of "experts" to choose the weight.

To use the checklist, it is probably most appropriate to have a knowledgeable person who deals with computing and/or data communications discuss it with one or more persons familiar with the way in which your organization handles networking. The objective is not to obtain numerous opinions, but to determine as precisely as possible what controls are in place and what are not. It is probably not a good idea just to hand out copies and ask people to fill them in as a paper and pencil test. In fact, the checklist could also be filled in as a result of a group or departmental meeting. The form found in Figure 10.1 can then be used to summarize the results.[5] Although a simple count of the number of "yes" responses, converted to a percentage of the total number of "yes" and "no" responses, is probably not very useful (since the items have differential weights), a qualitative report can certainly be drafted from the summary sheet. It is also useful, however, to actually score the checklist numerically.

In order to assign a numeric score to the results of the checklist, it is necessary to remember that two factors affect that scoring: the differential weight of the items and the applicability of the items. If all the items were weighted equally, an "applicability index" (AI) could be calculated that was the reciprocal of the proportion of the items in the checklist that are relevant. If 50% of the items

Item No.	Comment of reviewer	Applicability			Rank	Initial Status	Remedial Action	To be corrected by:	Action completed
		Y	N	N/A					

230

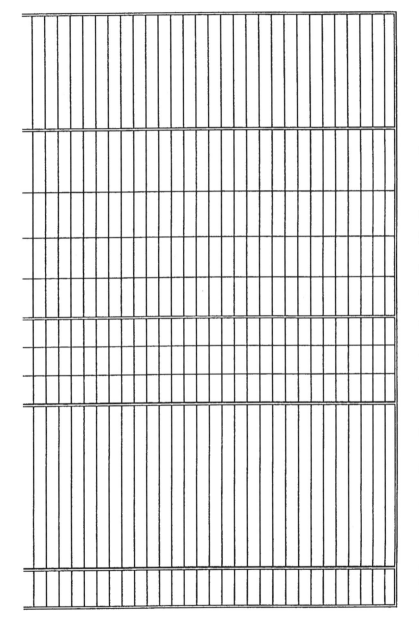

Figure 10.1 Networking/Data Communications Security Checklist Summary Form.

were applicable, for example, then AI 5 1/.5 (5 2). Because the items are given different weights, however, a *weighted fraction* must be developed. Let FW 5 weighted fraction; NR(i) 5 the *number* of checklist items assigned weight i that are *relevant* (those that are not checked "not applicable"); and N(i) 5 the *number of checklist items assigned* weight i. The codes within the parentheses are those symbolizing the weighted values. Then the following formula applies:[6]

$$FW\ 5\ \frac{(NR(VH)}{N(VH)}*0.36\ 1\ \frac{NR(H)}{N(H)}*0.28\ 1\ \frac{NR(M)}{N(M)}*0.2\ 1$$
$$\frac{NR(L)}{N(L)}*0.12\ 1\ \frac{NR(VL)}{N(VL)}*0.04$$

The AI is then calculated as the reciprocal of FW: *AI* 5 1/*FW*. The number of checklist items in each weighing category may be seen in Table 10.2. What this formula provides is the capacity to compare different systems with one another using *the same* checklist, but adjusting for item relevance.

In order to actually score a completed checklist, use the following procedure:

1. Count the number of items checked "yes," the number of items checked "no," and the number checked "N/A" (there should be none left blank). The total number of items should equal (No. of Yes) 1 (No. of No) 1 (No. of N/A).
2. Count the number of "yes" answers in each importance weight category (VH; V; M; L; VL), and then multiply all the "yes" answers by the appropriate importance weights (VH 5 .9; V 5 .7; M 5 .5; L 5 .3; VL 5 .1).

TABLE 10.2. Numbers of Checklist Items by Importance Weight Categories

No. of Items:	N(VH)	N(H)	N(M)	N(L)	N(VL)	Max Scr
Original 120	12	23	52	25	8	61.20
Plus 3 New	13	25	52	25	8	63.50

3. Sum the products obtained in 2. to get a total weighted "yes" score 5 SUM(yes).

4. For each weight category, calculate the fraction of items in each weight category that are relevant to the system being addressed; then calculate FW.

5. Take the reciprocal of FW to obtain the index of applicability: *AI* 5 1/*FW*.

6. Multiply the index of applicability by the item-importance "yes" score obtained in Step 3 to obtain a final adjusted score: Adj_Score 5 SUM(yes) * AI.

By itself, the Adj_Score is not easily interpretable. It can, however, be expressed as a fraction of the maximum possible score (MPS), called the "control comprehensiveness indicator" (CCI). The MPS is given by the weighted sum:

$$MPS\ 5\ N(VH) * 0.9\ 1\ N(H) * 0.7\ 1\ N(M) * 0.5\ 1\ N(L) \\ * 0.3\ 1\ N(VL) * 0.1$$

The MPS for the checklist under discussion has already been calculated and may be seen in Table 10.2. The CCI is easily calculated by:

$$CCI = \frac{Adj\_Score}{MPS}$$

This results in a score in the range of 0.0 to 1.0. Clearly, the closer to 1.0 we obtain, the better the security arrangements. A CCI of less than .5 should prompt an installation to establish additional controls, although high values of CCI do not necessarily mean that a network is adequately protected.

An additional level of detail can be derived from the checklist by "partitioning" the items into subcategories, and then calculating the CCI for each subcategory. One possible method of partition is given in Garcia, et al., using the analytical categories of the authors. They specify, for example, nine security *threat types* and seven *system assets* of particular relevance to telecommunications, and then, using the *threat types* as the columns of a matrix and *system assets* as the rows of the matrix (resulting in 63 cells), they classify each item by the cell into which it falls. Out of the original 120 items, therefore, the cell at the intersection of *threat type* "Unauthorized Access" and *systems asset* "People" contains a subset of 23 items. It is possible, therefore, to calculate all the indices for this total of 23 and for each of the other 62 cells. Such an analysis would provide at least a rough means for pinpointing potential problem areas. Some cells, of course, are empty, so there would not be a full 63 scores.[7] Other possible classification matrices might be Tables 3.2 and 3.3 (or modifications thereof), found in Chapter 3. There are, in other words, a variety of ways in which the results of a checklist might be used to assess a specific system or to make comparisons across systems (comparing results for several LANs, for example, in a large company).

There are many other factors that may not be accounted for in a checklist, such as threat occurrence probabilities, direct and indirect value of system assets to the user or the user's organization, and so forth. A more complete and justifiable security assessment must also take into account situation-specific factors, such as the type of users, information, and equipment used, as well as the physical environment in which the network operates and the risks involved in not having adequate security. It is well to remember that "no methodology provides a replacement for competence and good judgment."[8] It should also be kept in mind that checklists, while very useful, should be thought of springboards that will launch the user in the direction of the correct issues and solutions. Consequently, when the checklist is being completed, there should be time made available to discuss, in an open-ended fashion, security concerns and observations made by those participating in the analysis.

Conclusions

Security is important, and problems of security should be heeded. On the other hand, an excessive concern for security will ensure a certain amount of paranoia on the part of network managers. Some security problems exist because some data may be essential to national security, or to the economic well-being of a corporation. Other security issues exist because there are "hackers" (computer enthusiasts given to tinkering) and vandals all around us. Better laws that protect data, as legislation has traditionally protected other property, might be one better way to deal with computer network security, although such laws are likely to be only marginally effective. In the end, the use of *technology* is probably the only way we can secure information. The investment in information that individuals and organizations have made, are making, and will make in the future is enormous, however, and security systems aid us in protecting that investment.

Notes

1. D. Boyd, "Micro-Mainframe Links Pose Array of Security Risks," *ComputerWorld*, Vol. 18, No. 51, Dec. 17, 1984, pp. 41, 48.

2. H. Landgarten, "Beware of Security Risks when Implementing Micro-Mainframe Links," *Data Management*, Vol. 23, No. 4, April 1985, pp. 16–18.

3. "Trends," *ComputerWorld*, August 5, 1990, p. 114.

4. Charles Cresson Wood, William W. Banks, Sergio B. Guarro, Abel A. Garcia, Viktore E. Hampel, and Henry P. Sartorio, *Computer Security: A Comprehensive Controls Checklist* (New York: John Wiley & Sons, 1987), pp. 97–109, used by permission of the publisher.

5. Wood, p. 207.

6. Wood, pp. 12–13, illustrates in detail this calculation and the derivation of the formula.

7. See Wood, p. 189, for the "Telecommunications Control Matrix" discussed in this paragraph.

8. Wood, p. 8.

	YES	NO	N/A

Network Security Checklist*

1. Is a log-in procedure that includes a unique individual password (or some other identification technology, such as biometrics) required whenever a user employing telecommunications submits input or obtains output? (This applies to local area networks, in-house coaxial calling networks, and other on-site networks, as well as those that use public switching systems and other off-site facility.) (VH)

   a. Is each actual user provided a unique UserID/Password? (VH)

2. Must remote users linked by telecommunications positively identify themselves via fingerprint, eye blood vessel print, voice print, or some other biometric technique in addition to passwords? (H)

3. Is the provision of "help" information, system status, and other information in every instance restricted to logged-in users? (M)

4. If not constantly connected, do users employing telecommunications channels receive a last session log-in time/date whenever they log in again? (This may indicate unauthorized use of a User ID/account.) (L)

5. Are input and output transaction identification (or sequence) numbers used on all transmissions between a central computer and remote equipment, such as terminals and remote job entry (RJE) stations, supported by data communications? (M)

---

*Adopted from Abel A. Garcia (ed.), *Computer Security: A Comprehensive Controls Checklist* (New York: John Wiley & Sons, 1987). Used by permission of the publisher. All rights reserved.

6. Are exception reports produced if there is | YES | NO | N/A
a disruption in either input or output transaction identification numbers, or in other
controls over the flow of traffic on communication channels? (M)

7. If users/processes are not constantly logged
in, are sessions that use remote telecommunications gear supported with session identification numbers? (Such session identification numbers can be used to control access
(e.g., different password for each session) and
to assist in the logging of activity.) (M)

8. Are users of telecommunications gear informed of possible duplicate messages
(PDMs) and possible duplicate entries
(PDEs)? (Without such indicators, parties/
computers on either end of a telecommunications channel may erroneously process a
message/transaction twice.) (M)

9. Are actions taken (identified by transaction
type, command type, or some other
method) controlled on a station/terminal
basis, such that privileged actions are reserved for certain stations/terminals? (M)

10. Are user-transparent, protocol-related error
detection and recovery procedures in effect
(e.g., cyclic redundancy checks, vertical
redundancy checks, longitudinal redundancy checks, echo checks, forward error
correction routines, and parity checks)?
(Without such checks, parties/computers
on either end of a telecommunications
channel run the risk of processing erroneous data as though it was correct.) (VH)

11. If errors and consequential retransmissions
on the network exceed certain thresholds,

	YES	NO	N/A

is the network management center alerted to this fact via automatic alarms? (M)

12. Is encryption used to protect data in motion on telecommunications channels? (VH)

13. Is encryption used to protect data at rest in buffers, in main memory, on disk, and so on (particularly at intermediate nodes and other unattended locations and/or unsecured locations within a network)? (H)

14. If telecommunications channel encryption is used, is an automated key management system used to distribute the secret keys? (M)

15. If telecommunications channel encryption is used, are the channels kept busy with exchanges of random data whenever no genuine data or network management data are being exchanged? (This thwarts traffic analysis in which a wiretapper deduces information from the flows of messages on the network, rather than from the disclosure of the actual data.) (L)

16. If encryption is used, are the keys used to control the process changed whenever a compromise is suspected? (VH)

17. If encryption is used, is it implemented in hardware or firmware, as opposed to software? (L)

18. If data have not already been encrypted, are Message Authentication Code (MAC) checks performed on all sensitive data sent via telecommunications (going in both directions)? (Encryption can be used to provide the same data integrity checks that MACs can provide.) (VH)

	YES	NO	N/A

19. To ensure that a user is not establishing a connection with an active wiretapper, does the host system authenticate itself to the user (for example, by providing an answer-back code), prior to beginning a session? (H)

20. Are special controls (such as Message Authentication Codes) used to authenticate host log-off confirmation messages so that line grabbing is prevented? (Line grabbing entails an active wiretap where the wiretapper traps the sign-off message from a remote terminal, thus preventing this message from reaching the host; the wiretapper then sends a fictitious log-off confirmation to the terminal, and proceeds to use the privileges granted to the user at that terminal. (L)

21. If microcomputers or other computers are connected to a host computer, does the network control the down line loading of sensitive data, such that down line loading is not permitted unless the microcomputer or other computer has appropriate controls to handle the data? (The network might maintain tables reflecting the connected computer's controls (such as encryption) and the highest level of sensitive information that such computers are authorized to receive.) (H)

22. Are all user commands/messages sent via telecommunications acknowledged by the connected host machine, and likewise does the user equipment acknowledge all commands/messages sent from the host? (M)

23. Can users designate priorities (reflecting importance or urgency) for their messages/commands? (VL)

	YES	NO	N/A

24. Does the receiving computer check to see what type of transaction has been sent to it, and based on this decide what controls (e.g., Message Authentication Code checks) are to be applied? (VL)

25. Are messages sent via telecommunications handled with different controls if they have different sensitivity classifications (confidential, secret, etc.)? (M)

26. Are transactions/messages that have been in the communications system for a certain period of time, but not delivered, automatically aborted, and is a message to this effect sent to the initiating user/process? (L)

27. Is a log of all sensitive or important messages kept for a certain period of time, such that these messages are reconstructible in full? (M)

28. Are trace and snapshot facilities available to log suspect user activity in real time? (M)

29. Are message handling history logs kept such that users can find out when a message was delivered, when a transaction was processed, and so on? (M)

30. Are logging facilities in place that can automatically trace back to the originator the path taken by a particular transaction or message? (H)

31. Under normal operating conditions, are there at least two active functioning paths between any two nodes in the network? (H)

32. Is the telecommunications system designed such that data communications operations will automatically continue in spite of the

	YES	NO	N/A
fact that certain parts of the network are down/unavailable (e.g., using automatic traffic rerouting)? (VH)			
33. Are duplicate pieces of critical networking equipment provided for important network terminals/stations, nodes, and host computers? (H)			
34. If a critical piece of networking equipment fails, do network nodes, and perhaps host computers, have the ability to automatically switch from the failed equipment to hot standby equipment? (VH)			
35. If an important piece of networking equipment fails, is an automatic alarm sent to other parts of the network, so that maintenance actions can be immediately begun? (L)			
36. Are pathing tables in use such that the network can be dynamically reconfigured in response to different traffic patterns? (M)			
37. For critical information received via telecommunications, is recording on two separate computer-readable media performed (e.g., incoming transactions may be simultaneously recorded on two mirrored disks)? (VH)			
38. To prevent data loss while traveling through the network, are all critical or important messages sorted in at least two physical locations (as opposed to two devices at the same location)? (M)			
39. Are transmissions broken into packets, sent over one or more available channels, and resequenced at the destination? (The chances of the eventual arrival of a message at its destination may thereby be increased.) (H)			

	YES	NO	N/A

40. If dial-up or leased lines are used, are fall-back circuits readily available in case these lines become either unavailable or too noisy (i.e., have too many errors)? (VH)

41. Are terminals and other end-user data communications gear attended by staff on a 24-hour-a-day basis? (M)

42. If a network node or other remote equipment is unattended for part of the day or night, is it protected with electronic tampering alarms that will send an alarm to other parts of the network? (L)

43. If terminals/stations or other remote equipment is unattended for part of the day or night, is such equipment protected with special locking covers, cages, or the like, to prevent unauthorized persons from using or tampering with it? (M)

44. Is access to remote stations/terminals or other remote equipment controlled with physical keys, magnetic cards, *tokens,* or some similar mechanism? (M)

45. Are terminal *and/or workstation* keyboards locked via command from the connected host or other computer, to restrict access to certain periods of the day or for other access control purposes? (L)

46. If network node or other equipment requires certain environmental conditions (temperature, humidity, etc.), is there an environmental monitoring system in operation at each site that has the ability to trigger alarms, should there be a malfunction or some other problem? (M)

47. If certain sections of a network are deemed

	YES	NO	N/A

untrustworthy, can they be segregated from the remaining trusted parts of the network, and will messages between these two domains be held pending a validation of the trustworthiness of the combined network? (Alternately, under such circumstances, certain messages may be permitted to pass in one but not in both directions.) (H)

48. Does the network control center have the ability to forbid the use of any particular node, link, or station/terminal in the network in spite of the fact that such node, link, or terminal may be in good operating order? (H)

49. Does the system automatically disable a User ID/account, a line, or a port if it has evidence that an attack is underway (perhaps evidenced through repeated attempts to guess a password)? (VH)

50. Does the network control center have the ability to automatically log out a particular User ID/account on request? (H)

51. Does the network control center have the ability to automatically reduce the privileges of a particular User ID/account or class of User IDs/accounts on request? (H)

52. Are all network processes re-allocatable to other nodes/computers, (i.e., are no processes permanently associated with any one node or host computer)? (M)

53. Are test network messages clearly differentiated from production network messages? (M)

54. Must a user stay in one dedicated application after login; should the user wish to run

	YES	NO	N/A

another application, is another log-on or authentication process required? (VL)

55. Are user identities re-authenticated during the course of interactive sessions (perhaps by typing style/timing templates, reentering a password or the like)? (M)

56. Are pseudo-random number generators used to create user passwords that change each time a user logs in? (M)

57. To thwart passive wiretapping, are tables of passwords used so that different passwords will be used for different sessions? (M)

58. Are sensitive security parameters (passwords, encryption keys, encryption initialization vectors, etc.) protected with encryption when they are sent over telecommunications lines? (VH)

59. Are sensitive security parameters, such as encryption keys, protected via security modules (also known as "tamper proof" modules) when these parameters are in storage within notes, stations/terminals, and the like? (A security module provides, among other things, volatile memory that will erase security parameters stored therein if it is tampered with.) (VH)

60. Are fiber-optic lines, shielded lines, or lines through physically protected areas used as mechanisms to reduce the likelihood of wiretapping? (L) Note: As technology costs have dropped, and as technology has improved, fiber-optic and other lines are no longer as difficult nor as expensive to tap as they once were, although it is still some-

	YES	NO	N/A

what more difficult than with simple twisted pair.

61. Are unusual protocols or multiplexing used to, among other things, make wiretapping more difficult? (VL)

62. Are all interrupted telecommunications sessions automatically and promptly logged out such that another user coming in over the same line or port is not given carte blanche access to the work of the interrupted user? (H)

63. If there has been no activity for a certain period of time (say three minutes), will remote station/terminals connected via telecommunications be automatically logged out? (M)

64. Can a user signing out specify (optionally) that the system not allow a log-on with that user's particular User ID/account number or station/terminal until a certain time and date? (M)

65. Are station/terminal identification codes used to assure that only authorized devices are making connection with the network? (H)

66. Can stations/terminals be defined as active or inactive regarding certain applications, and will access to certain applications be refused when attempted from inactive stations/terminals? (M)

67. To avoid disclosure to unauthorized parties, are particularly sensitive data not permitted to be directed to printers that are remote to the user? (M)

68. Are the network and connected-computer log-in banners (e.g., "Welcome to XXX sys-

	YES	NO	N/A

tem running UNIX™ Version VII") kept to an absolute minimum, such that they do not divulge the organization maintaining the system, the operating system in use, the format for log-in statements, or any other information that may assist unauthorized individuals in an attack of the system? (M)

69. To thwart unauthorized access by dial-up users, are point-to-point, multi-drop, local area network, or other telecommunications arrangements that require users to be at certain physical locations in effect? (A point to-point link connects only two terminals/stations/nodes; a multi-drop or local area network has one or more discrete intermediate terminals/stations/nodes along the path between two such points.) (H)

70. If dial-up lines are employed, does the installation use automatic call-back devices, whereby a user wishing to initiate a session calls a host system's number, provides a password, hangs up, and is called back at a predesignated number? (H) *However, remember that there are problems with dial-back systems—with current technology they must be regarded as providing only a relatively low level of protection.*

71. If dial-up lines are employed, when the user initially reaches a front-end or the host computer, is a tone other than the carrier provided, such that individuals calling randomly to identify numbers with computers attached will not be alerted to the fact that a computer is connected to that line? (M)

72. Are network protocols other than the American Standard Code for Information Inter-

	YES	NO	N/A

change (ASCII) asynchronous transmission used, such that unauthorized user-controlled microcomputers and dumb terminals that use this protocol by default may not gain access to the network? (L)

73. If dial-up lines are employed, are high-speed modems used to thwart persons using the more commonly found 300, 1200, and 2400 baud modems? (VL)

74. If modems are used, do they have manual or remote actuated loopback switches for fault isolation to insure prompt identification of malfunctioning equipment? (VL)

75. If modems are used with leased lines, is an automatic or semiautomatic dial backup capability provided, in case the leased lines fail? (L)

76. If modems are used, do they have advanced facilities such as automatic equalization, to allow them to automatically adjust to characteristics of the line? (VL)

77. Is a telecommunications front-end used to control access to larger computer systems so that the host(s) need not be concerned with log-in, privilege checking, and similar security activities? (This approach creates several fences between attackers and targets and provides particularly valuable isolation.) (H)

78. Are signed malfunction reports submitted to management upon the completion of each corrective maintenance call, whether or not this call was performed by an outside firm? (L)

79. Is a toll-free number in service 24 hours a day, 7 days a week, for the reporting of

	YES	NO	N/A
network failures, operational problems, and security violations? (M)			

80. Are protocol converters and access method converters provided with front-end computers to support the dynamic change of network configuration in the event of problems? (M)

81. Is physical access to the network control center restricted to authorized personnel via locked doors, guards, badges, and the like? (M)

82. Are all persons in the network control center required to wear a badge indicating their status (visitor, employee, vendor) and the areas to which they have access permission? (M)

83. Are maintenance personnel and visitors accompanied whenever they are in the network control center? (L)

84. Are programmers and others who are not involved in network operations denied access to the network control center? (M)

85. Are at least two persons on duty at the network control center at all times? (L)

86. Is the network control center physically separated with access control mechanisms from the data processing operations areas? (L)

87. Has responsibility for network security been specifically assigned to a staff member? (M)

88. Are all gateways or bridges between networks equipped with sufficient controls, such that the security of neither network is unduly compromised by the connection? (H)

	YES	NO	N/A

89. If the network connects several organizations, networks, or computer systems, is a policy both in place and enforced that requires all connecting organizations, networks, and computer systems to provide security measures at least as stringent as those of the network? (H)

90. Are formal change controls in place for both network software changes and network hardware changes? (H)

91. Are the telephone numbers used for dial-up connections not published in a public directory, or otherwise available to persons without a need to know? (M)

92. Are the telephone numbers used for dial-up connections changed both periodically and whenever a compromise using these numbers has taken place? (M)

93. Are echo-off, overstrike faculties, or similar mechanisms used to prevent the display of passwords on terminals, printers, and similar devices? (M)

94. Are modems at the user's site preprogrammed with the telephone number of the targeted dial-up port, such that the user does not know and does not need to know the telephone number? (L)

95. Are passwords always entered by the individual user, as opposed to being programmed into an automatic log-in routine (perhaps stored on a *local disk drive*)?

96. Does the network have the ability to trace the telephone numbers of users coming in over dial-up lines or via value-added data networks? (H) *In many places it is now*

	YES	NO	N/A

possible to subscribe to Caller ID services from the local telephone operator and to read and store, along with the normal log-in accounting data, that number.

97. Is the system capable of switching messages directed to a down terminal/station to an alternate authorized terminal/station? (M)

98. Has the vendor of all networking computer software provided some statement, such as a guarantee, about the integrity of the code? (Some vendors state that they have taken care of all major operating system security vulnerabilities and that, if a user discovers a vulnerability, the vendor will make a modification to rectify the situation at no charge to the user.) (H)

99. If satellite, microwave, or other broadcast technologies for telecommunications are used, are the frequencies, channels, or transponders (as applicable) used by the organization kept a strict secret? (M)

100. If satellites are used for telecommunications, have backup systems been arranged for those occasions when the effects of solar radiation overwhelm the satellite's signal? (L)

101. If land lines are buried underground near the data processing center, are the locations of these line marked by signs so that construction crews and others will not mistakenly dig up the lines and cause network outages? (L)

102. Is access to all documentation describing telecommunications systems design, oper-

	YES	NO	N/A

ations, and security restricted to persons with a need to know? (L)

103. At all locations that use *wiring closets, such as phone lines, 10BASET 802.3 LANS, and so forth,* for data communications, are all *wiring* closets locked, except when being used by authorized personnel or contractors? (M)

104. Do telecommunications specialists periodically inspect wiring closets and lines, to check for wiretaps? (L)

    a. Are data communications devices checked on a regular and periodic basis for loose connectors? (In a broadband system, for example, where most connectors are screw-type F-Connectors, each connector should be tightened on a regularly established schedule, perhaps as frequently as once a week, to prevent network degradation.) (H)

105. Do telecommunications specialists periodically install special devices or go through special procedures (such as special limited terminal polling) to detect the presence of wiretaps? (L)

106. Are date/time stamps used to serially identify traffic traveling on the network? (L)

107. If particularly sensitive or critical transactions are sent via telecommunications, rather than having such transactions directly update organizational databases, are such transactions sorted in a special memo post file, buffer area, or other system location, so that the transactions may be reviewed prior to being used as database update transactions? (L)

108. If a sensitive or a critical database is updated via telecommunications transactions, are separate computers used to accumulate (and perhaps also validate) these transactions, and later submit such transactions to the database computer in batches that can be better controlled? (L)

YES	NO	N/A

109. Does the network have special monitoring programs that detect unusual traffic patterns and bring this to the attention of network operators? (If a dial-up telephone number were to be placed on a system's hacker electronic bulletin board, the volume of, duration of, and origin of calls accessing the system would probably change markedly, and thus draw attention to the problem.) (M)

110. Have special software routines been written that provide for the "graceful degradation" of service to telecommunications-assisted system users, such that users are notified, recovery is facilitated, files and databases do not have partially updated records, and so on? (M)

111. Are sensitive transactions/messages that are sent over non-encrypted telecommunications channels disguised with special codes or abbreviations? (VL)

112. If Message Authentication Codes are not used, are other tests of the integrity of the messages sent/received used (such as "wire test keys")? (M)

113. If Message Authentication Codes or other message test procedures are used, are the secret parameters used in these processes

	YES	NO	N/A

kept strictly confidential and accessible only to those who have a need to know? (M)

114. If Message Authentication Codes, encryption, or other techniques that rely on secret parameters are used, are such secret parameters changed on a regular and reasonably frequent basis? (M)

115. If network transactions are initiated by persons who call computer operators, who then actually enter the transaction in the system, are the identities of the transaction initiators always validated via unique individual passwords or some similar method? (H)

    a. *Is a log kept by the operator of transactions initiated by telephoned request and executed by the operator? (H)*

116. Are all network participants involved with processing/handling of sensitive or critical transactions in some way held both responsible and accountable for the security of these transactions? (H)

117. Are production and testing/development computers disconnected such that transactions originating on a testing/development computer cannot easily be submitted to the production system via telecommunications? (Movement of software from the testing/development computer to the production computer can be done by tape or other hand-carried magnetic media.) (M)

118. Are critical and/or sensitive network software routines protected via hash totals, file authentication codes, or other methods that can detect modification of such routines? (M)

	YES	NO	N/A
119. Does the invocation of very sensitive network commands require that two authorized persons be present (as enforced perhaps with two individually unique passwords)? (M)			
120. Are mechanisms whereby vendors can perform maintenance on network software, without properly logging in, strictly prohibited, and is this policy enforced? (L)			

Glossary

acceptable risk—in *risk analysis,* an assessment that an activity or system meets minimum requirements of security directives.

access—1) in data processing, interaction between a subject and an object that allows information to flow from one to the other; 2) in physical security, the ability to enter a secured building area.

access authorization—grating permission to an object (i.e., person, terminal, program) to execute a set of operations in the system. Generally, a profile matrix grants access privileges to users, terminals, programs, data elements, type of access (e.g., read, write), and time period.

access control—in a network or its components, the tasks performed by hardware, software, and administrative controls to monitor a system operation, ensure data integrity, perform user identification, record system access and changes, and grant access to users.

active threats—unauthorized use of a device attached to a communications facility to alter transmitting data or control signals; or to generate spurious data or control signals.

amplifier—in a broadband system, a device for strengthening the radio frequency signal to a level needed by other devices on the system.

answer modem—see *modem*.

ASCII—American (National) Standard Code for Information Interchange, X3.4-1968. A seven-bit-plus parity code established by the American National Standards Institute to achieve compatibility among data services and consisting of 96 displayed upper- and lowercase characters and 32 non-displayed control codes.

asymmetric encryption—see *public key cryptosystem*.

asynchronous transmission—a mode of data communications transmission in which time intervals between transmitted characters may be of unequal length. The transmission is controlled by start and stop elements at the beginning and end of each character; hence, it is also called start-stop transmission.

attachment unit interface (AUI)—the cable, connectors, and transmission circuitry used to interconnect the physical signaling (PLS) sublayer and MAU.

audit of computer security—as defined by NBS (now NIST) Special Publication 500-57, an independent evaluation of the controls employed to ensure:

1. The appropriate protection of the organization's information assets (including hardware, software, firmware, and data) from all significant anticipated threats or hazards;

2. The accuracy and reliability of the data maintained on or generated by an automated data processing system; and

3. The operational reliability and performance assurance for accuracy and timeliness of all components of the automated data processing system.

An examination of data security procedures and measures for the purpose of evaluating their adequacy and compliance with established policy.

authentication—1) ensuring that a message is genuine, has arrived exactly as it was sent, and came from the stated source; 2) verifying the identity of an individual, such as a person at a remote terminal or the sender of a message. In OSI nomenclature, authentication refers to the certainty that the data received comes from the supposed origin; it is not extended to include the integrity of the data that are being transmitted. See also *data origin authentication* and *peer-entity authentication*. Protection against fraudulent transactions by establishing the validity of messages, stations, individuals, or originators.

availability—that aspect of security that deals with the timely delivery of information and services to the user. An attack on availability would seek to sever network connections, tie up accounts or systems.

back door—a feature built into a program by its designer, that allows the designer special privileges that are denied to the normal users of the program. A back door in a log-on program, for instance, could enable the designer to log on to a system, even though he or she did not have an authorized account on that system.

bacterium (informal)—a program that, when executed, spreads to other users and systems by sending copies of itself; since it *infects* other programs, it may be thought of as a *system virus*, as opposed to a *program virus*. It differs from a *rabbit* in that it is not necessarily designed to exhaust system resources.

bandwidth—the range of frequencies assigned to a channel or system. The difference expressed in hertz between the highest and lowest frequencies of a band.

baseband (signaling)—transmission of a signal at its original frequencies (i.e., unmodulated).

batch—a group of records or programs that is considered a single unit for processing on a computer.

batch processing—a technique in which a number of data transactions are collected over a period of time and aggregated for sequential processing.

baud—a unit of transmission speed equal to the number of discrete conditions or signal events per second. Baud is the same as "bits per second" only if each signal event represents exactly one bit, although the two terms are often incorrectly used interchangeably.

bisynchronous transmission—binary synchronous (bisync) transmission. Data transmission in which synchronization of characters is controlled by timing signals generated at the sending and receiving stations in contrast to asynchronous transmission.

bit-mapped graphics—a method of representing data in a computer for display in which each dot on the screen is mapped to a unit of data in memory.

bit rate—the data throughput on the trunk coaxial medium expressed in hertz.

block—a group of digits, characters, or words that are held in one section of an input/output medium and handled as a unit, such as the data recorded between to interblock gaps on a magnetic tape or a data unit being transmitted over a data communications system; a block may or may not contain control information. A group of N-ary digits, transmitted as unit. An encoding procedure is generally applied to the group of bits or N-ary digits for error-control purposes.

BNC-connector—a bayonet type coaxial cable connector of the kind commonly found on RF equipment.

branch cable—the AUI cable interconnecting the data terminal equipment (DTE) and MAU system components.

bridge—the hardware and software necessary for two networks using the same or similar technology to communicate; more specifically the hardware and software necessary to link segments of the same or similar networks at the Data Link Layer of the OSI Reference Model (i.e., a MAC Level Bridge); a router that connects two or more networks and forwards packets among them. Usually, bridges operate at the physical network level. Bridges differ from repeaters because bridges store and forward complete packets, while repeaters forward electrical signals.

broadband—a communications channel having a bandwidth characterized by high data transmission speeds (10,000 to 500,000 bits per second). Often used when describing communications systems based on cable television technology. In the 802 standards, a system whereby information is encoded, modulated onto a carrier, and band-pass filtered or otherwise constrained to occupy only a limited frequency spectrum on the coaxial transmission medium. Many information signals can be present on the medium at the same time without disruption, provided that they all occupy nonoverlapping frequency regions within the cable system's range of frequency transport.

b/s (bits per second)—see *baud.*

bug—an error in the design or implementation of a program that causes it to do something that neither the user nor the program author had intended to be done.

bus—the organization of electrical paths within a circuit. A specific bus, such as the S-100, provides a standard definition for specific paths.

carrier sense—the signal provided by the physical layer to the access sublayer to indicate that one or more stations are currently transmitting on the trunk cable.

CATV—Community Antenna Television. See *broadband.*

CCITT—Consultative Committee International Telegraph and Telephone. An organization established by the United Nations to develop worldwide standards for communications technology (e.g., *protocols* to be used by devices exchanging data).

central processing unit—see *CPU.*

centralized network—a computer network with a central processing node through which all data and communications flow.

Centronics—a manufacturer of computer printers. Centronics pioneered the use of a parallel interface between printers and computers, and that interface, using Centronic standards, is sometimes referred to as a Centronics parallel interface.

character user interface (CUI)—classical character-based system for computer/human communications.

checksum—a fixed-length block produced as a function of every bit in an encrypted message; a summation of a set of data items for error detection; a sum of digits or bits used to verify the integrity of data.

cipher—an algorithm for disguising information according to a logical principle by working within the elements of whatever alphabet is in use, such as by shift substitution of the letters of the alphabet by other letters a certain number of places toward the beginning or end of the alphabet. Not to be confused with a *code*.

ciphertext—encrypted text that cannot be read without decryption; data in its encrypted form that is cryptologically protected; the opposite of *plaintext* or *cleartext*.

client-server—the model of interaction in a distributed system in which a program at one site sends a request to a program at another site and awaits a response. The requesting program is called a client; the program satisfying the request is called the server. It is usually easier to build client software than server software.

code—a technique by which the basic elements of language, such as syllables, words, phrases, sentences, and paragraphs, are disguised through being replaced by other, usually shorter, arbitrarily selected language elements, requiring a codebook (table) for translation. A term not generally used in relation to encryption. Not to be confused with *cipher*.

cold site—DP hardware-ready room, or series of rooms, which is ready to receive hardware for disaster recovery. See also *hot site* and *warm site*.

collision—multiple concurrent transmission on the cable resulting in garbled data.

command languages—software in which commands are typed in, rather than selected from, a set displayed on the screen.

communications—see *data communications*. Transmission of intelligence between points of origin and reception, without alteration of sequence or structure of the information content.

communications network—the total network of devices and transmission media (radio, cables, etc.) necessary to transmit and receive intelligence.

communications security (COMSEC)—the protection resulting from the application of cryptosecurity, transmission security, and emission security measures to telecommunications and from the application of physical security measures to communications security information. These measures are taken to deny unauthorized persons information of value that might be derived from the possession and study of such telecommunications. COMSEC includes: cryptosecurity, transmission security, emission security, and physical security of communications security materials and information. 1) Cryptosecurity: the component of communications security that results from the provision of technically sound cryptosystems and their proper use; 2) Transmission security: the component of communications security that results from all measures designed to protect transmissions from interception and exploitation by means other than cryptanalysis; 3) Emission security: the component of communications security that results from all measures taken to deny unauthorized persons information of value that might be derived from intercept and analysis of compromising emanations from cryptoequipment and telecommunications systems; 4) Physical security: the component of communications security that results from all physical measures necessary to safeguard classified equipment, material, and documents from access thereto or observation thereof by unauthorized persons.

communications security equipment—equipment designed to provide security to telecommunications by converting information to a form unintelligible to an unauthorized interceptor and by reconverting such information to its original form for authorized recipients, as well as equipment designed specifically to aid in, or as an essential element of, the conversion process. COMSEC equipment is cryptoequipment, cryptoancillary equipment, cryptoproduction equipment, and authentication equipment.

computer conferencing—a process for holding group discussions through the use of a computer network.

computer network—one or more computers linked with users or each other via a communications network.

computer security—the technological safeguards and managerial procedures that can be applied to computer hardware, programs, data, and facilities to ensure the availability, integrity, and confidentiality of computer-based resources. It also can ensure that intended functions are performed as planned.

confidentiality—the property that information is not made available or disclosed to unauthorized individuals, entities, or processes; an attack on confidentiality would seek to view databases, print files, discover a password, etc., to which the attacker was not entitled.

connectionless applications—those applications that require routing services, but do not require connection-oriented services.

connectionless service—a class of service that does not establish a virtual or logical connection and does not guarantee that data units will be delivered or be delivered in the proper order. Connectionless services are flexible, robust, and provide connectionless application support.

connection-oriented services—services that establish a virtual connection that appears to the user as an actual end-to-end circuit. Sometimes called a virtual circuit or virtual connection. See also *virtual circuit.*

connectivity—in a local area network, the ability of any device attached to the distribution system to establish a session with any other device.

CP/M—Control Program for Microcomputers. Manufactured and marketed by Digital Research, Inc.

CPU—central processing unit. The "brain" of the general-purpose computer that controls the interpretation and execution of instructions. The CPU does not include interfaces, main memory, or peripherals.

cryptochannel—a complete system of cryptocommunications between two or more holders. The basic unit for naval cryptographic communication. It includes: 1) the cryptographic aids prescribed; 2) the holders thereof; 3) the indicators or other means of identification; 4) the area or areas in which effective; 5) the special purpose, if any, for which provided; and 6) pertinent notes as to distribution, usage, etc. A cryptochannel is analogous to a radio circuit.

cryptogram—the ciphertext.

cryptography—the branch of cryptology devoted to creating appropriate algorithms.

crypto-information—information that would make a significant contribution to the crypt-analytic solution of encrypted text or a cryptosystem.

cryptology—the science that deals with hidden, disguised, or encrypted communications. It embraces communications security and communications intelligence. The art of creating and breaking ciphers.

cryptomaterial—all material, including documents, devices, or equipment that contains crypto-information and is essential to the encryption, decryption, or authentication of telecommunications.

CSMA/CD—Carrier Sense Multiple Access with Collision Detection. A network access method for managing collisions of data packets.

CUI—see *character user interface.*

cursor—a position indicator frequently employed in video (CRT or VDT) output devices or terminals, to indicate a character to be corrected or a position in which data is to be entered.

cyclic redundancy check (CRC)—an algorithm designed to generate a check field used to guard against errors that may occur in data transmission; the check field is often generated by taking the remainder after dividing all the serialized bits in a block of data by a predetermined binary number.

database—a nonredundant collection of inter-related data items processable by one or more applications.

data communications—the transmission and reception of data, often including operations such as coding, decoding, and validation.

data encryption standard (DES)—an algorithm to be implemented in electronic hardware devices and used for the cryptographic protection of digital, binary-coded information. For the relevant publications see "Data Encryption Standard," *Federal Information Processing Standard (FIPS) Publication 46,* January 15, 1977, also published as *American National Standard Data Encryption Algorithm,* American National Standards Institute, Inc., December 30, 1980, and supplemented with "DES Modes of Operation," *Federal Information Processing Standard (FIPS) Publication 81,* December 2, 1980; "Telecommunications: Interoperability and Security Requirements for Use of the Data Encryption Standard in the Physical Layer of Data Communications," *Federal Standard of the General Services Administration,* August 3, 1983, FED-STD-1026; "Telecommunications: General Security Requirements for Equipment Using the Data Encryption Standard," *Federal Standard of the General Services Administration,* April 14, 1982, FED-STD-1027; and "Telecommunications: Interoperability and Security Requirements for Use of the Data Encryption Standard with CCITT Group 3 Facsimile Equipment," *Federal Standard of the General Services Administration,* April 4, 1985, FED-STD-1028.

data file—a collection of related data records organized in a specific manner. In large systems data files are gradually being replaced by databases, in order to limit redundancy and improve reliability and timeliness.

datagram—a finite-length packet with sufficient information to be independently routed from source to destination without reliance on previous transmissions; typically does not involve end-to-end session establishment and may or may not entail delivery confirmation acknowledgement.

datagram service—one that establishes a datagram-based connection between peer-entities. In OSI parlance this type of service is called a *connectionless service.* See also *connectionless service.*

data link—an assembly of two or more terminal installations and the interconnecting communications channel, operating according to a particular method that permits information to be exchanged.

data link layer—the conceptual layer of control or processing logic existing in the hierarchical structure of a station that is responsible for maintaining control of the data link.

data management system—a system that provides the necessary procedures and programs to collect, organize, and maintain data files or databases.

data origin authentication—the corroboration that the source of data received is as claimed. For an OSI network, this refers to authentication in the context of a connectionless service.

data security—procedures and actions designed to prevent the unauthorized disclosure, transfer, modification, or destruction, whether accidental or intentional, of data.

DB-25—a 25-pin connector commonly used in the United States as the connector of choice for the RS-232-C serial interface standard.

dialog box—a rectangle that appears onscreen, prompting the user to enter data or mutually exclusive selection.

digital signature—a number depending on all the bits of a message and also on a secret key. Its correctness can be verified by using a public key (unlike an authenticator, which needs a secret key for its verification).

disaster—a condition in which an organization is deemed unable to function as a result of some natural or human-created occurrence.

disaster recovery operation—the act of recovering from the effects of disruption to a computer facility and restoring, in a preplanned manner, the capabilities of the facility.

disaster recovery plan—the preplanned steps to be taken that make possible the recovery of an organization's computer facility and/or the applications processed there. Also called a *contingency plan* or *business resumption plan.*

disk storage (disc storage)—information recording on continuously rotating magnetic platters. Storage may be either sequential or random access.

distributed data processing (DDP)—an organization of information processing, such that both processing and data may be distributed over a number of different machines in one or more locations.

distributed network—a network configuration in which all node pairs are connected, either directly or through redundant paths through intermediate nodes.

DOS (disk operating system)—a general term for the operating system used on computers using disk drives. See also *operating system.*

download—the ability of a communications device (usually a microcomputer acting as an intelligent terminal) to load data from another device or computer to itself, saving the data on a local disk or tape.

EDI—see *electronic data interchange.*

electronic data interchange (EDI)—the intercompany, computer-to-computer exchange of business documents in standard formats.

electronic mail—a system to send messages between or among users of a computer network, and the programs necessary to support such message transfers.

emulator, terminal—see *terminal emulator.*

encryption—the translation of one character string into another by means of a cipher, translation table, or algorithm, in order to render the information contained therein meaningless to anyone who does not possess the decoding mechanism. It is the reverse of *de*cryption.

encryption algorithm—a group of mathematically expressed rules that render information unintelligible by producing a series of changes through the use of variable elements controlled by the application of a key to the normal representation of the information.

end-to-end encryption—the encryption of data in a communications network at the point of origin, with decryption occurring at the final destination point.

envelope—a group of binary digits formed by a byte augmented by a number of additional bits that are required for the operation of the data network; the boundary of a family of curves obtained by varying a parameter of a wave.

Ethernet—a local area network and its associated protocol developed by (but not limited to) Xerox. Ethernet is a baseband system.

FAX (facsimile)—device that consists of three basic components—an image scanner, a FAX modem, and a printer—often integrated in a single unit with each FAX file treated as a cohesive image (rather than character data).

F-connector—a 75-ohm F-series coaxial cable connector of the kind commonly found on consumer television and video equipment.

FEP (front end processor)—a communications device used for entry into a computer system. The FEP typically provides either or both asynchronous or synchronous ports for the system.

fiber optics—a technology for transmitting information via light waves through a fine filament. Signals are encoded by varying some characteristic of the light waves generated by a low-powered laser. Output is sent through a light-conducting fiber to a receiving device that decodes the signal.

floppy disks—magnetic, low cost, flexible data disks (or diskettes), usually either 5.25 inches or 3.5 inches in diameter.

flow control—a speed matching technique used in data communications to prevent receiving devices from overflow, thus losing data.

frame—in data transmission, the sequence of contiguous bits bracketed by and including beginning and ending flag sequences. A typical frame might consist of a specified number of bits between flags and contain an address field, a control field, and a frame check sequence. A frame may or may not include an information field. A transmission unit that carries a protocol data unit (PDU).

gateway—the hardware and software necessary to make two technologically different networks communicate with one another; a gateway provides protocol conversion from one network architecture to another and may, therefore, use all seven layers of the OSI Reference Model; a special-purpose, dedicated computer that attaches to two or more networks and routes packets from one to the other. The term is loosely applied to any machine that transfers information from one network to another, as in *mail gateway.*

graphical user interface (GUI)—a means for computer/human communications characterized by ease of use, interaction, and intuitive feel, providing visual, direct, and immediate feedback in a WYSIWYG environment.

GUI—see *graphical user interface.*

hand-held password generators (HPGs)—sometimes called tokens, are pocket-sized devices that generate a unique one-time password for each access attempt to a properly equipped host or network.

HDLC—Hierarchical Data Link Control. A highly structured set of standards governing the means by which unlike devices can communicate with each other on large data communications networks.

headend—in a broadband local area network or CATV system, the point at which a signal processor upconverts a signal from a low inbound channel to a high outbound channel.

Hertz—a unit of frequency equal to one cycle per second. Cycles are referred to as Hertz in honor of the experimenter Heinrich Hertz. Abbreviated as Hz.

highsplit—in a broadband system the organization of the spectrum that places the guard band at about 190 MHz. The midsplit system offers the greatest amount of spectrum for return path channels (14 channels).

hot site—a backup facility that is fully operational and compatible with the site's hardware and software. It provides security, fire protection, and telecommunications capabilities. See also *cold site* and *warm site.*

IBM—International Business Machines. One of the primary manufacturers of computer equipment (usually, though not exclusively, large-scale equipment).

icon—a small graphic image on a computer screen that represents a function or program.

IEEE—Institute of Electrical and Electronic Engineers.

impedance—in a circuit, the opposition that circuit elements present to the flow of alternating current. The impedance includes both resistance and reactance.

information security—the protection of information assets from accidental or intentional but unauthorized disclosure, modification, or destruction, or the inability to process that information.

integrity (of data)—the property that data have not been altered or destroyed in an unauthorized manner; an attack on integrity would seek to erase a file that should not be erased, alter an element of a database improperly, corrupt the audit trail for a series of events, propagate a virus, etc.

interactive processing—processing in which transactions are processed one at a time, often eliciting a response from a user before proceeding. An interactive system may be conversational, implying continuous dialogue between the user and the system. Contrast with *batch processing.*

interface—a shared boundary between system elements, defined by common physical interconnections, signals, and meanings of interchanged signals.

ISO/OSI—International Standards Organization Open Systems Interface. A seven-tiered network model.

kernel—the fundamental part of a program, such as an operating system, that resides in memory at all times.

key—a piece of digital information that interacts with cryption algorithms to control cryption of information, which, thus, must be protected from disclosure.

key distribution center (KDC)—the element in a system that generates and distributes cryptographic key variables.

key generator—an object for encrypting-key generation.

key hashing—the method in which a long key is converted to a native key for use in the encryption/decryption process. Each letter number of the long key helps to create each digital bit of the native key.

key management—control of key selection and key distribution in a cryptographic system.

key notarization—a method for encrypting information at a terminal site before transmission to a host computer, over communications media that might not be secure. It is necessary for the host and the terminal to maintain the same encryption key and algorithm. This is frequently accomplished by *downloading* (sending information) from the host to the terminal on key changes. The downloaded information must also be encrypted.

kilohertz—one thousand hertz. See *hertz.*

link encryption—application of online crypto-operations to a communications system link so that all information passing over the link is encrypted completely. The term also refers to end-to-end encryption within each link in a communications network.

line extender—in a broadband system, an amplifier used to boost signal strength, usually within a building.

LLC—see *logical link control.*

local area network—a computer and communications network that covers a limited geographical area, allows every node to communicate with every other node, and does not require a central node or processor.

logical link control (LLC)—that part of a data station that supports the logical link control functions of one or more logical links.

logical record—a collection of items independent of their physical environment. Portions of the same logical record may be located in different physical records.

logic bomb—a program routine that destroys data; for example, it may reformat the hard disk or randomly insert garbage into data files. A logic bomb may be brought into a personal computer by downloading a public-domain program that has been tampered with. Once executed, it does its damage right away, whereas a virus keeps on destroying. See also *virus* and *worm.*

MAC—see *medium access control* or *message authentication code.*

mainframe computer—a large-scale computing system.

malicious software—any software, such as a virus, worm, logic bomb, bacterium, rabbit, rogue, time bomb, Trojan Horse, or something else, that has the *unauthorized* capacity to modify or erase data or software and/or to reproduce itself in an *unauthorized* manner.

manager's workstation—a microcomputer containing an integrated package of software designed to improve the productivity of managers. A workstation will usually, though not exclusively, include a word processor, a spread sheet program, a communications program, and a data manager.

Manchester encoding—a means by which separate data and clock signals can be combined into a single, self-synchronizable data stream, suitable for transmission on a serial channel.

manipulation detection code—see *MDC.*

masquerading—the attempt to gain access to a system by posing as an authorized client or host.

master-slave computer system—a computer system consisting of a master computer connected to one or more slave computers; the master computer provides the scheduling function and jobs to the slave computers(s).

MDC—Manipulation (Modification) Detection Code. A redundancy check field included in the plaintext of a chain before encipherment, so that changes to the ciphertext (an active attack) will be detected.

medium access control (MAC)—the portion of the IEEE 802 data station that controls and mediates the access to the medium.

medium attachment unit (MAU)—the portion of the physical layer between the MDI and AUI that interconnects the trunk cable to the branch cable and contains the electronics that send, receive, and manage the encoded signals impressed on and recovered from the trunk cable.

medium dependent interface (MDI)—the mechanical and electrical interface between the trunk cable medium and the MAU.

menu—a multiple choice list of procedures or programs to be executed; a list of command options currently available to the computer user and displayed onscreen.

menu trees—successions of menu displays that become more detailed.

message authentication code (MAC)—a method by which cryptographic check digits are appended to the message. They pertain to the transaction type, transaction account number, destination, and point of origin in computer security. Specifically, by using MAC, messages without the additional check digits are rejected by the computer system, and valid transactions cannot be modified without detection.

MHS—1) (Message Handling Service) An electronic mail system developed by Action Technologies, Inc., and licensed by Novell for its NetWare operating systems. It allows for the transfer and routing of messages between users and provides store and forward capabilities. MHS also provides gateways into IBM's PROFS, Digital's All-in-1 office automation system, and X.400 message systems; 2) (Message Handling System) An electronic mail system. MHS often refers to mail systems that conform to the OSI (open systems interconnect) model, which are passed on CCITT's X.400 international message protocol.

microcomputer—a computer system of limited physical size and, in former times, limited in speed and address capacity. Usually, though not exclusively, a single-user computer.

microprocessor—the central processing unit of a microcomputer that contains the logical elements for manipulating data and performing arithmetic or logical operations on it.

midsplit—in a broadband system the organization of the spectrum that places the guard band at about 140 MHz. The midsplit system offers a substantial amount of spectrum for return path channels (14 channels).

minicomputer—a computer system, usually a timesharing system; sometimes faster than microcomputers, but not as fast as large mainframe computers.

modem—MODulator/DEModulator. A device that modulates and demodulates signals transmitted over communication facilities. A modem is sometimes called a data set.

modification detection code—see *MDC*.

multimedia—software that permits a mix of text, speech, and static and dynamic visual images.

multi-tasking—the ability of a computer to perform two or more functions (tasks) concurrently.

multi-user system—a system where two or more people, using different access systems (terminals), can access one computer concurrently or simultaneously. Such a system must have multitasking capabilities.

National Institute of Standards and Technology—see *NIST.*

native key—the internal key (string of bits) that is required by the cryption algorithm.

network—see also *communications network* and/or *computer network.* 1) A system of interconnected computer systems and terminals; 2) A series of points connected by communications channels; 3) The structure of relationships among a project's activities, tasks, and events.

Network security—the measures taken to protect a network from unauthorized access, accidental or willful interference with normal operations, or destruction, including protection of physical facilities, software, and personnel security.

NIST—National Institute of Standards and Technology. Formerly (prior to 1988) the National Bureau of Standards (NBS) of the U.S. government.

node—any station, terminal, computer, or other device in a computer network.

notarization—the verification (authentication) of a message by a trusted third party, similar in logic to classic notarization procedures; normally an automated procedure.

object—an entity (e.g., record, page, program, printer) that contains or receives information.

object protection—1) In computer system security, the mechanisms and rule used to restrict access to objects. 2) In physical security, a means to protect objects such as safes, files, or anything of value that could be removed from a protected area.

object reuse—reassigning some subject of a magnetic medium that contained one or more objects. To be securely reassigned, such media must contain no residual data from the previously contained object.

octet—a bit-oriented element that consists of eight contiguous binary bits.

off-the-shelf—production items that are available from current stock and need not be either newly purchased or immediately manufactured. Also relates to computer software or equipment that can be used with little or no adaptation by customers, thereby saving the time and expense of developing their own.

office automation—refers to efforts to provide automation for common office tasks, including word processing, filing, record keeping, and other office chores.

on-line processing—a general data processing term concerning access to computers, in which the input data enters the computer directly from the point of origin or in which output data is transmitted directly to where it is used.

operating system—a program that manages the hardware and software environment of a computing system.

originate-only modem—a modem that can originate data communications, but that cannot answer a call from another device.

outlet—access point, with an appropriate connector, to a communications medium.

packet—a block of data for data transmission. Each packet contains control information, such as routing and address and error control, as well as data; a group of data and control characters in a specified format, transferred as a whole; a group of binary digits, including data and call control signals, that is switched as a composite whole; the data, all control signals, and possibly error control information are arranged in a specific format.

packet switching—a discipline for controlling and moving messages in a large data communications network. Each message is handled as a complete unit containing the addresses of the recipient and the originator.

passive threats—monitoring and/or recording data while data are being transferred over a communications facility; with *release of message contents* an attacker can read user data in messages; with *traffic analysis* the attacker can read user packet headers to identify source and destination information as well as the length and frequency of messages. See also *threats, and active threats.*

passphrase—a phrase used instead of a password to control user access.

password—a unique word or string of characters used to authenticate an identity. A program, computer operator, or user may be required to submit a password to meet security requirements before gaining access to data. The password is confidential, as opposed to the user identification.

PBX/PABX—Private branch exchange or private automated branch exchange. A switching network for voice or data.

Peer-entity authentication—the corroboration that a peer-entity in an association is the one claimed. This exists in an OSI context only when an association has been established between peer-entities.

peer protocol—the sequence of message exchanges between two entities in the same layer that utilize the services of the underlying layers to effect the successful transfer of data and/or control information from one location to another location.

peer systems—computer/communication systems capable of performing equal or comparable tasks within defined limits or parameters.

peripheral—computer equipment external to the CPU, performing a wide variety of input and output functions.

personal computer—an alternative name for microcomputer, suggesting that the computer is to be used for personal and individual work production or entertainment.

personal identification number (PIN)—a sequence of decimal digits (usually four, five, or six) used to verify the identity of the holder of a bank card; a kind of password.

physical access control—the procedures used to authorize and validate requests for physical access to computer, communication, or network physical facilities, to help ensure the physical integrity of those systems and facilities.

physical record—a basic unit of data that is read or written by a single input/output command to the computer.

physical security—measures necessary to protect the computer and related equipment and their contents from damage by intruders, fire, accident, and environmental hazards.

plaintext—text that has not been encrypted (or has been decrypted) and can be easily read or acted upon.

private key cryptosystem (encryption)—a type of encrypting system that uses a single key to both encrypt and decrypt information. Also called *symmetric,* or single key, encryption.

program—a set of instructions in a programming language used to define an operation or set of operations to a computer.

protocol—a formal set of conventions governing the format and relative timing of message exchange in a communications network.

protocol data unit (PDU)—the sequence of contiguous octets delivered as a unit from or to the MAC sublayer. A valid LLC PDU is at least three octets in length, and contains two address fields and a control field. A PDU may or may not include an information field in addition.

public key—a cryptographic key used for encipherment, but not usable for decipherment. It is therefore possible to make this key public.

public key cryptosystem—an encryption methodology that depends on two keys: a public key—made available to anyone who wants to encrypt information—is used for the encryption process, and a private key—known only to the owner—is used for the decryption process. The two keys are mathematically related. Also termed *asymmetric encryption.*

pull-down menu—a menu that appears onscreen when accessed by a cursor placed on a box or bar at the top of the display.

questionnaire—a method of identity verification that makes use of information known to the authorized user, but unlikely to be known to others.

rabbit (informal)—a program designed to exhaust some resource of a system (CPU time, disk space, spool space, etc.) by replacing itself without limit; it differs from a *bacterium* in that a rabbit is specifically designed to exhaust resources; it differs from a *virus* in that it is a complete program in itself; it does not infect other programs.

RAM—random access memory. Semiconductor memory devices used in the construction of computers. The time required to obtain data is independent of the location.

reference monitor concept—an information systems access control concept that refers to an abstract machine that mediates all accesses to objects by subjects.

reliability—in data communications or computer equipment, the extent to which hardware or software operates in a repeatable manner, often characterized (for hardware) as a low mean-time-between-failures.

remote access—pertaining to communication with a computer by a terminal distant from the computer.

remote batch terminal (RBT)—a terminal used for entering jobs and data into a computer from a remote site for later batch processing.

remote job entry (RJE)—input of a batch job from a remote site and receipt of output via a line printer or other device at a remote site.

repeater—a device used to extend the length, topology, or interconnectivity of the physical medium beyond that imposed by a single segment, up to the maximum allowable end-to-end trunk transmission line length, by copying electrical signals from one network segment to another. Because repeaters transfer electrical impulses rather than data packets, they may also transfer noise.

repudiation—the denial by a message sender that the message was sent, or by a message recipient that the message was received.

resource—anything used or consumed while performing a function. Categories of resources include time, information, objects (information containers), or processors (the ability to use information).

risk analysis—a process of studying system assets and vulnerabilities to determine an expected loss from harmful events, based upon probabilities of occurrence of those harmful events. The object of risk analysis is to determine the degree of acceptability of each risk to system operation.

ROM—read-only-memory. A memory device used in computers that cannot be altered during normal computer use. Normally a semiconductor device.

router—The hardware and software necessary to link two subnetworks of the same network together; the hardware and software necessary to link two subnetworks at the Network Layer of the OSI Reference Model; any machine responsible for making decisions about which of several paths network traffic will follow. At the lowest level, a physical network bridge is a router because it chooses whether to pass packets from one physical wire to another. Within a long haul network, each individual packet switch is a router because it chooses routes for individual packets. In the Internet, each IP gateway is a router because it uses IP destination addresses to choose routes.

security—see also *data security* and *communications security.* 1) The state of certainty that computerized data and program files cannot be accessed, obtained, or modified by unauthorized personnel or the computer or its programs. Security is implemented by restricting the physical area around the computer system to authorized personnel, using special software and the security built into the operating procedure of the computer; 2) When applied to computer systems and networks, denotes the authorized, correct, and timely performance of computing tasks. It encompasses the areas of confidentiality, integrity, and availability.

security audit—see *audit of computer security.*

security mechanisms—operating procedures, hardware and software features, management procedures, and any combinations of these that are designed to detect and prevent either passive or active threats on any component of an information system.

security service—activity or provision of an activity that enhances the security of information systems and an organization's information transfer. In the OSI model the defined services consist of five groups: confidentiality, authentication, integrity, non-repudiation, and access control.

security threat—any action that compromises the security of information owned by an organization. See also *active threat* and *passive threat.*

server—a computer in a network that is shared by multiple users, such as a file server, print server, or communications server; a computer in a network designated to provide a specific service as distinct from a general-purpose, centralized, multiuser computer system.

session—active connection of one device to another over a communications system, during which interactions do or can occur.

shell—an outer layer of a program that provides the user interface, or way of commanding the computer. Shells are typically add-on programs created for command-driven operating systems, such as UNIX and DOS. The shell may provide a menu-driven or graphical icon-oriented interface to the system, in order to make it easier to use.

socket—the abstraction provided by Berkeley 4.3 BSD UNIX that allows a process to access the Internet. A process opens a socket, specifies the service desired (e.g., reliable stream delivery), binds the socket to a specific destination, and then sends or receives data. While the functional characteristics remain as defined, the concept has been generalized to include processes that access networks other than Internet.

software—a term used to contrast computer programs with the "iron" or hardware of a computer system.

spectrum—a range of wave lengths usually applied to radio frequencies.

spread sheet programs—computer programs that allow data to be entered as elements of a table or matrix with rows and columns, and that manipulate the data. Programs widely available on microcomputers are Lotus 1-2-3 and SUPERCALC.

start-stop transmission—see *asynchronous transmission.*

station—a physical device that may be attached to a shared medium local area network for the purpose of transmitting and receiving information on that shared medium.

subject—an active entity, such as a process, person, or device, that causes information to flow among objects or that changes the system's state.

subject security level—the security level of a subject that is the same as the security level of the objects to which it has both read and write access. The clearance of the user the subject is associated with always dominates the security level of the subject.

subsplit—in a broadband system the organization of the spectrum, which places the guard band at about 40 MHz. The subsplit system offers the least amount of spectrum for return path channels (4 channels).

symmetric encryption—see *private key cryptosystem.*

tap—a device that allows an exit from a main line of a communications system.

telecommunications—the transfer of data from one place to another over communications lines or channels; the communication of all forms of information, including voice and video.

teletex—one-way transmission of data via a television system.

terminal—a device that allows input and output of data to a computer. The term is most frequently used in conjunction with a device that has a keyboard for data entry and either a printer or a video tube for displaying data.

terminal emulator—a software or software/hardware system for microcomputers that allows the micro to behave like some specified terminal, such as a DEC VT100 or an IBM 3278/79.

text editor—a program that provides flexible editing facilities on a computer for the purpose of allowing data entry from a keyboard terminal, without regard for the eventual format or medium for publication. With a text editor, data (text, copy, or what have you) can be edited easily and quickly.

text formatter—a program for reading a data file created with a text editor and transforming the raw file into a neatly formatted listing.

threats—threats to an information system or its networks may be either *active* or *passive*. See also *active threats* and *passive threats.*

time bomb—a *logic bomb* activated at a certain time or date. See also *logic bomb.*

token—1) (LAN protocols) The symbol of authority that is passed between stations using a token access method to indicate which station is currently in control of the medium; 2) A hand-held password generator designed to provide a unique password for each access attempt to a LAN (or other network) or multi-user computer system (see *HPG*).

token passing—a collision avoidance technique in which each station is polled and must pass the poll along.

traffic—the information moved over a communications channel.

traffic analysis—when communication traffic is in cipher form and cannot be understood, it may still be possible to get useful information by detecting who is sending messages to whom and in what quantity. This is traffic analysis.

traffic flow confidentiality—concealment of the quantity of users' messages in a communication system and their sources or destinations, to prevent traffic analysis.

traffic flow security—the protection resulting from features, inherent in some cryptoequipment, that conceal the presence of valid messages on a communications circuit, normally achieved by causing the circuit to appear busy at all times.

traffic padding—a function that generates a continuous stream of random data or ciphertext, thus making it 1) very difficult for an attacker to distinguish between true data flow and noise; and 2) making it very difficult to deduce the amount of traffic.

transaction processing—a style of data processing in which files are updated and results generated immediately as a result of data entry.

trojan horse—any program designed to do things that the user of the program did not intend it to do. An example of this would be a program that simulates the log-on sequence for a computer and that, rather than logging the user on, simply records the user's User ID and password in a file for later collection. Rather than logging the user on, it steals the user's password so that the trojan horse's designer can log on as the user.

trunk cable—the trunk (usually coaxial) cable system.

trusted computer system—a system that can process simultaneously a spectrum of sensitive or classified information, because it employs sufficient hardware and software security measures.

trusted computing base (TCB)—refers to the hardware, firmware, and software protection mechanisms within a computer system that are responsible for enforcing a security policy.

trusted path—the way in which a person at a terminal can communicate directly with the trusted computing base. Only the person or the trusted computing base can activate this mechanism; it cannot be imitated by untrusted software.

trusted software—a trusted computing base's software segment.

turn-key system—a system in which the manufacturer or distributor takes full responsibility for complete system design and installation, and supplies all necessary hardware, software, and documentation.

twisted pair—The two wires of a signaling circuit, twisted around each other to minimize the effects of inductance.

UNIX—a multi-tasking, multi-user operating system developed by Ken Thompson, Dennis Ritchie, and coworkers at Bell Laboratories (AT&T); a powerful operating system implemented on a wide variety of computers, from mainframes to microcomputers.

upload—refers to the ability to send data from an originating terminal (usually a microcomputer) to another computer or terminal.

videotex—a two-way method of communications, integrating video and a related communications system.

virtual circuit—a communication arrangement in which data from a source user may be passed to a destination user over various real circuit configurations during a single period of communication (i.e., during a single session). Also called a logical circuit. See also *connection-oriented service.*

virus—A program that is used to infect a computer. After virus code is written, it is buried within an existing program. Once that program is executed, the virus code is also activated and it attaches copies of itself to other programs in the system. Whenever an infected program is run, the virus copies itself to other programs. A virus cannot be attached to data. It must be attached to an executable program that is installed on a computer. The virus-attached program must be executed in order to activate the virus. See *logic bomb* and *worm.*

warm site—similar to a cold site, but with telecommunications facilities. See also *cold site* and *warm site.*

Winchester disks—hard magnetic disk storage media in sealed containers. Not all sealed disks are Winchester drives.

window—a rectangular onscreen image within which the user accesses particular features of a system. With operating environment software, windowing is often combined with multi-tasking capabilities.

word processing—the transformation of ideas and information into a human-readable form of communication through the management of procedures, equipment, and personnel. Generally refers to text editing and formatting on a computer.

worm—1) A destructive program that replicates itself throughout disk and memory, using up the computer's resources and eventually putting the system down (see *virus* and *logic bomb*); 2) A program that moves throughout a network and deposits information at each node for diagnostic purposes, or causes idle computers to share some of the processing workload; 3) WORM (Write Once Read Many): a storage device that uses an optical medium that can be recorded only once. Updating requires destroying the existing data (zeroes f0g made ones f1g), and writing the revised data to an unused part of the disk.

WYSIWYG—What You See Is What You Get.

Trademarks

The following products and company names, which are referenced in this work, may be protected by federal, state, or common law trademark laws.

Aldus Corp.

Alert/CICS, Alert/VM, and Alert/VSE are trademarks of Goal Systems International, Inc.

All-in-!, DEC, DECNet, Digital Network Architecture, and VAX/VMS are registered trademarks of Digital Equipment Corporation.

AOS/VS is a registered trademark of Data General.

AT&T, Unix, and Unix V/MLS are registered trademarks of American Telephone and Telegraph.

CA-ACF2 MVS, CA-ACF2 VM, CA-ACF2 VS1, CA-Top Secret MVS, CA-Top Secret VM, and CA-Top Secret VSS are registered trademarks of Computer Associates International, Inc.

CICS, IBM, PROFS, PS/2, RACF/MVS, RACF/VM, and PS/2 are registered trademarks of International Business Machines.

Comdisco Disaster Recovery Services, Inc.

CompuServe.

Datasafe 2000 and Datasafe 3000 are registered trademarks of Radius Computer Services.

Delta Data Systems Corp.

FiberCom, Incorporated.

ICAN is a registered trademark of Digital Pathways (U.K.) Ltd.

Ilex Systems, Inc.

InfoGuard is a registered trademark of Unisys Corp.

Interface/3000 is a registered trademark of Satcom.

LANTastic is a registered trademark of Artisoft.

Lotus 1-2-3 is a registered trademark of Lotus Development, Inc.

MHS is a registered trademark of Action Technologies, Inc.

MicroSecure Self Assessment is a registered trademark of Boden Associates.

Microsoft.

Mitek Systems, Inc.

NetWare is a registered trademark of Novell.

Ridge Reader is a registered trademark of Fingermatrix, Inc.

RiskWatch is a registered trademark of Expert System Software.

Sun OS is a registered trademark of Sun Microsystems.

SunGard Data Systems, Inc.

ThumbScanner is a registered trademark of ThumbScan, Inc.

Time & Space Processing, Inc.

USecure is a registered trademark of Unitech Software, Inc.

VINES is a registered trademark of Banyan.

VMSecure is a registered trademark of Systems Center, Inc.

Xerox.

Index

information security department, 43–44
manager's security model, 32–37
model of, 32–37
nature of, 6
network control devices, 39
network security checklist, 236–254
scope of, 28–31
security policy, 42–43
steps in, 38
types of:
  bio feedback systems, 41
  call back systems, 40
  encryption devices, 40
  host resident security software, 39–40
  token devices, 40–41
Network Security Center, 133
Non-repudiation, 71
Non-wire media, tapping of, 139
Notarization, 79
Novell LAN, 140, 141
Novell Netware, 142

Omniguard, 145
Open systems, 33
  meaning of, 48
Open Systems Interconnection Model,
  48–57
  cooperation of systems, meaning of,
    53–54
  environments, 52–54
  layers of, 34, 48–51
    Application Layer, 48, 49
    concept of layered architecture, 54–56
    Data Link Layer, 49, 50–51
    and entities, 54, 55
    Network Layer, 49, 50
    and peer-entities, 54
    Physical Layer, 49, 51
    Presentation Layer, 49
    Session Layer, 49, 50
    sublayers, 56
    Transport Layer, 49, 50
  networks, access control, 144–145
  network security model, 32–37
  overview of, 51–52
  Reference Model, 52
  security architecture, 57–58
  security mechanisms, 72–79
  security service, 4, 65–72
  security threats:
    active threats, 58, 62–65
    denial of message service, 63–64
    masquerading, 64
    message service modification, 64–65
    passive threats, 58–62
    release of message content, 59

traffic analysis attack, 60–62
Orange Book, 77, 190, 198
Organization
  impact of security measures on,
    222–225
  security review procedure, 227–234
Output Feedback, 112, 113
Overstrike facilities, 249

Packet radio, 114
  tapping of, 139
Parker, Donn B., 24, 100
Passphrase, 74
Password:
  access control, 133–134
  management problems and, 135
  nature of, 74–75
Password generators, 39, 130, 135–136,
  204
  asynchronous password generation,
    136
  functions of, 40
  and LAN, 143
  operation of, 135–136
  synchronous password generation,
    136
Peer-entities, 54
Personal identification number, 40, 78,
  136
Physical access, 63
  and biometric systems, 131
  control, products for, 209–210
Physical Layer, OSI, 49, 51
Physical security, 28
  definition of, 5, 28
  meaning of, 216
  products for, 216–217
Pirated software, and viruses, 163
Plaintext, 109
  definition of, 108
Policy:
  access policies, 148–149
  security policy, 42–43
  viral infection policy, 160–173
Possible duplicate messages, 237
Preparatory abuse, 27
Presentation Layer, OSI, 49
Preventive controls, 30
Privacy, and internal protection codes, 37
Private key cryptosystems:
  data encryption standard, 110–113
  definition of, 108
  future view of, 113–114
  uses of, 109
Private networks:
  and access control, 140–148